SAFETY SYMBOLS

SAFETY SYMBOLS	HAZARD	PRECAUTION	REMEDY
Disposal	Special disposal required	Dispose of wastes as directed by your teacher.	Ask your teacher how to dispose of laboratory materials.
Biological	Organisms that can harm humans	Avoid breathing in or skin contact with organisms. Wear dust mask or gloves. Wash hands thoroughly.	Notify your teacher if you suspect contact.
Extreme Temperature	Objects that can burn skin by being too cold or too hot	Use proper protection when handling.	Go to your teacher for first aid.
Sharp Object	Use of tools or glassware that can easily puncture or slice skin	Practice common sense behavior and follow guidelines for use of the tool.	Go to your teacher for first aid.
Fumes	Potential danger from smelling fumes	Must have good ventilation and never smell fumes directly.	Leave foul area and notify your teacher immediately.
Electrical	Possible danger from electrical shock or burn	Double-check setup with instructor. Check condition of wires and apparatus.	Do not attempt to fix electrical problems. Notify your teacher immediately.
Irritant	Substances that can irritate your skin or mucous membranes	Wear dust mask or gloves. Practice extra care when handling these materials.	Go to your teacher for first aid.
Chemical	Substances (acids and bases) that can react with and destroy tissue and other materials	Wear goggles and an apron.	Immediately flush with water and notify your teacher.
Toxic	Poisonous substance	Follow your teacher's instructions. Always wash hands thoroughly after use.	Go to your teacher for first aid.
Fire	Flammable and combustible materials may burn if exposed to an open flame or spark	Avoid flames and heat sources. Be aware of locations of fire safety equipment.	Notify your teacher immediately. Use fire safety equipment if necessary.

Eye Safety
This symbol appears when a danger to eyes exists.

Clothing Protection
This symbol appears when substances could stain or burn clothing.

Animal Safety
This symbol appears whenever live animals are studied and the safety of the animals and students must be ensured.

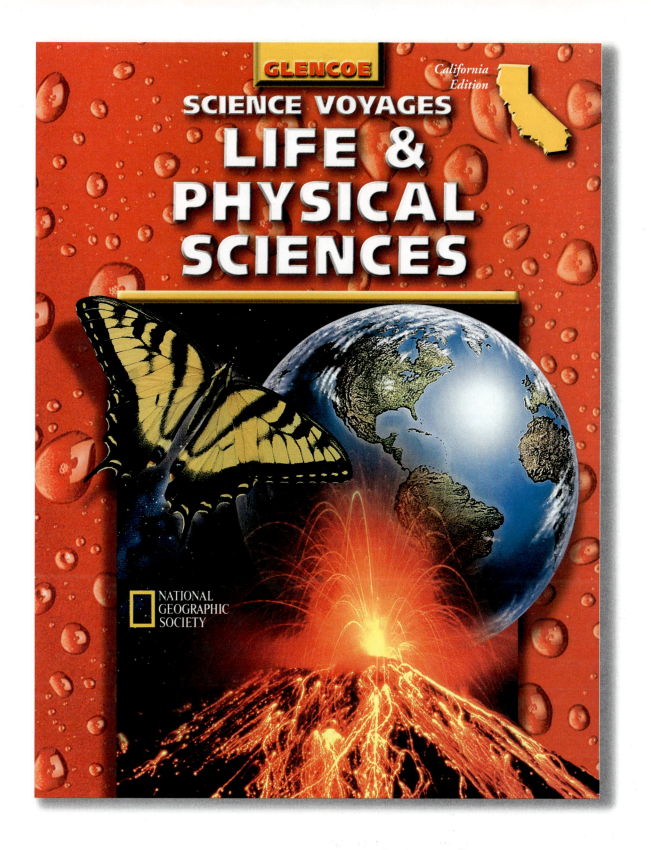

GLENCOE

California Edition

SCIENCE VOYAGES
LIFE &
PHYSICAL
SCIENCES

NATIONAL GEOGRAPHIC SOCIETY

Glencoe
McGraw-Hill

New York, New York   Columbus, Ohio   Woodland Hills, California   Peoria, Illinois

A Glencoe Program

California Edition

Glencoe Science Voyages

California Student Edition
California Teacher Wraparound Edition
Assessment
    Chapter Review
    California Science Content Standards Practice
      Questions
    Performance Assessment
    Assessment—Chapter and Unit Tests
    ExamView Test Bank Software
    Performance Assessment in the Science
      Classroom
    Alternate Assessment in the Science Classroom
Study Guide for Content Mastery, SE and TE
Chapter Overview Study Guide, SE and TE
Reinforcement
Enrichment
Critical Thinking/Problem Solving
Multicultural Connections

Activity Worksheets
Laboratory Manual, SE and TE
Science Inquiry Activities, SE and TE
California Home Involvement
Teaching Transparencies
Section Focus Transparencies
Science Integration Transparencies
Spanish Resources
California Lesson Plans
Lab and Safety Skills in the Science Classroom
Cooperative Learning in the Science Classroom
Exploring Environmental Issues
MindJogger Videoquizzes and Teacher Guide
English/Spanish Audiocassettes
Interactive Lesson Planner CD-ROM
Interactive CD-ROM
Internet Site
Using the Internet in the Science Classroom

THE PRINCETON REVIEW

The "Test-Taking Tip" and "Test Practice" features in this book were written by The Princeton Review, the nation's leader in test preparation. Through its association with McGraw-Hill, The Princeton Review offers the best way to help students excel on standardized assessments.

The Princeton Review is not affiliated with Princeton University or Educational Testing Service.

Glencoe/McGraw-Hill

A Division of The **McGraw·Hill** Companies

Send all inquiries to:
Glencoe/McGraw-Hill
8787 Orion Place
Columbus, OH 43240

ISBN 0-07-823980-X
Printed in the United States of America.
3 4 5 6 7 8 9 10 071/055 06 05 04 03 02 01

Series Authors

Alton Biggs
Biology Instructor
Allen High School
Allen, Texas

John Eric Burns
Science Teacher
Ramona Jr. High School
Chino, California

Lucy Daniel, Ph.D.
Teacher, Consultant
Rutherford County Schools
Rutherfordton, North Carolina

Cathy Ezrailson
Science Department Head
Oak Ridge High School
Conroe, Texas

Ralph Feather, Jr., Ph.D.
Science Department Chair
Derry Area School District
Derry, Pennsylvania

Patricia Horton
Math and Science Teacher
Summit Intermediate School
Etiwanda, California

Thomas McCarthy, Ph.D.
Science Department Chair
St. Edwards School
Vero Beach, Florida

Ed Ortleb
Science Consultant
St. Louis Public Schools
St. Louis, Missouri

Susan Leach Snyder
Science Department Chair
Jones Middle School
Upper Arlington, Ohio

Eric Werwa, Ph.D.
Department of Physics and Astronomy
Otterbein College
Westerville, Ohio

National Geographic Society
Educational Division
Washington D.C.

Contributing Authors

Al Janulaw
Science Teacher
Creekside Middle School
Rohnert Park, California

Penny Parsekian
Science Writer for
The National Geographic Society
New London, Connecticut

Gerry Madrazo, Ph.D.
Mathematics and Science Education
   Network
University of North Carolina, Chapel Hill
Chapel Hill, North Carolina

Series Consultants

Chemistry

Douglas Martin, Ph.D.
Chemistry Department
Sonoma State University
Rohnert Park, California

Cheryl Wistrom, Ph.D.
Associate Professor of Chemistry
Saint Joseph's College
Rensselaer, Indiana

Earth Science

Maureen Allen
Science Resource Specialist
Irvine Unified School District
Laguna Hills, California

Tomasz K. Baumiller, Ph.D.
Museum of Paleontology
University of Michigan
Ann Arbor, Michigan

Connie Sutton, Ph.D.
Department of Geoscience
Indiana University
Indiana, Pennsylvania

Physics

Thomas Barrett, Ph.D.
Department of Physics
The Ohio State University
Columbus, Ohio

David Haase, Ph.D.
Professor of Physics
North Carolina State University
Raleigh, North Carolina

Life Science

William Ausich, Ph.D.
Department of Geological Sciences
The Ohio State University
Columbus, Ohio

Dennis Stockdale
Asheville High School
Asheville, North Carolina

Daniel Zeigler, Ph.D.
Director
Bacillus Genetic Stock Center
The Ohio State University
Columbus, Ohio

Reading

Nancy Farnan, Ph.D.
School of Teacher Education
San Diego State University
San Diego, California

Gary Kroesch
Mount Carmel High School
San Diego, California

Safety

Mark Vinciguerra
Lab Safety Instructor
Department of Physics
The Ohio State University
Columbus, Ohio

Curriculum

Tom Custer, Ph.D.
Maryland State Department of
   Education
Challenge/Reconstructed Schools
Baltimore, Maryland

Series Reviewers

Jhina Alvarado
Potrero Hill Middle School
   for the Arts
San Francisco, California

Richard Cheeseman
Bert Lynn Middle School
Torrance, California

Linda Cook
Rider High School
Wichita Falls, Texas

John B. Davis
Niagara-Wheatfield
   Central School
Sanborn, New York

Shirley Ann DeFilippo
Timothy Edwards
   Middle School
South Windsor, Connecticut

Janet Doughty
H J McDonald Middle School
New Bern, North Carolina

Jason Druten
Jefferson Middle School
Torrance, California

Lin Harp
Magellan Middle School
Raleigh, North Carolina

Doris Holland
West Cary Middle School
Raleigh, North Carolina

Deborah Huffine
Noblesville Intermediate School
Noblesville, Indiana

Paul Osborne
DeValls Bluff High School
DeValls Bluff, Arkansas

Erik Resnick
Robert E. Peary Middle School
Gardena, California

Robert Sirbu
Lowell Junior High School
Oakland, California

Michael Tally
Wake County Public Schools
Raleigh, North Carolina

Cindy Williamson
Whiteville City Schools
Whiteville, North Carolina

Maurice Yaggi
Middlebrook School
Wilton, Connecticut

Donna York
Anchorage School District
Anchorage, Alaska

Activity Testers

Clayton Millage
Science Teacher
Lynden Middle School
Lynden, Washington

Science Kit and Boreal Laboratories
Tonawanda, New York

Contents in Brief

State of California Science Content Standards

GRADE SIX: FOCUS ON EARTH SCIENCE

What are science content standards and why does California have them? Standards are guidelines for schools, students, and parents that describe the essential science concepts and skills for understanding the world in which we live. In 1999, The California State Board of Education established science content standards, and these standards will be the basis for state assessments that measure student achievement in science.

ADDITIONAL CONTENT STANDARDS FOR GRADE 6

- California Science Standards and Case Studies, found at the back of the book
- California Science Content Standards Assessment Practice booklets
- Chapter Assessments at the end of each chapter
- Science Voyages Website at www.glencoe.com/sec/science/ca

Plate Tectonics and Earth's Structure

1. Plate tectonics explains important features of the Earth's surface and major geologic events. As the basis for understanding this concept, students know:

   a. the fit of the continents, location of earthquakes, volcanoes, and midocean ridges, and the distribution of fossils, rock types, and ancient climatic zones provide evidence
   Sections 9-1, 9-2, 9-3, 10-1, 11-1, pages 616-617

   b. the solid Earth is layered with cold, brittle lithosphere; hot convecting mantle; and dense, metallic core.
   Sections 9-2, 9-3, 10-2, pages 617, 633

   c. lithospheric plates that are the size of continents and oceans move at rates of centimeters per year in response to movements in the mantle.
   Sections 9-2, 9-3, 11-1, pages 617, 620

   d. earthquakes are sudden motions along breaks in the crust called faults, and volcanoes/fissures are locations where magma reaches the surface.
   Sections 5-1, 9-2, 9-3, 10-1, 10-2, 11-1, 11-2, 11-3, pages 627, 635

   e. major geologic events, such as earthquakes, volcanic eruptions, and mountain building result from plate motions.
   Sections 5-1, 9-3, 10-1, 11-1, 11-2, 11-3, pages 628, 620-621

   f. how to explain major features of California geology in terms of plate tectonics (including mountains, faults, volcanoes).
   Sections 9-3, 10-1, pages 618, 620-621, 635-636

   g. how to determine the epicenter of an earthquake and that the effects of an earthquake vary with its size, distance from the epicenter, local geology, and the type of construction involved.
   Sections 9-3, 10-2, 10-3, pages 618-619

Shaping the Earth's Surface

2. Topography is reshaped by weathering of rock and soil and by the transportation and deposition of sediment. As the basis for understanding this concept, students know:

   a. water running downhill is the dominant process in shaping the landscape, including California's landscape.
   Sections 6-2, 7-1, 7-2, 8-1, 8-2, pages 622-625

   b. rivers and streams are dynamic systems that erode and transport sediment, change course, and flood their banks in natural and recurring patterns.
   Sections 5-1, 7-1, 7-2, 8-1, 8-2, 24-3, page 623

   c. beaches are dynamic systems in which sand is supplied by rivers and moved along the coast by wave action.
   Sections 7-3, 8-1, 8-3, 9-3, 17-3, 24-3, pages 623-624

   d. earthquakes, volcanic eruptions, landslides, and floods change human and wildlife habitats.
   Sections 7-1, 8-1, 9-3, 10-1, 10-2, 10-3, 11-1, 11-2, 11-3, pages 623-626

Heat (Thermal Energy) (Physical Science)

3. Heat moves in a predictable flow from warmer objects to cooler objects until all objects are at the same temperature. As a basis for understanding this concept, students know:

   a. energy can be carried from one place to another by heat flow, or by waves including water waves, light and sound, or by moving objects.
   Sections 8-3, 14-1, 14-2, 17-3, 23-3, 26-1, 26-2, 26-3, pages 622-625

   b. when fuel is consumed, most of the energy released becomes heat energy.
   Sections 4-1, 4-2, 26-3, page 628

   c. heat flows in solids by conduction (which involves no flow of matter) and in fluids by conduction and also by convection (which involves flow of matter).
   Sections 9-3, 14-1, 14-2, 14-3, 26-2, pages 628-629

   d. heat energy is also transferred between objects by radiation; radiation can travel through space.
   Sections 14-1, 14-2, 16-3, 26-2, page 629

Energy in the Earth System

4. Many phenomena on the Earth's surface are affected by the transfer of energy hrough radiation and convection currents. As a basis for understanding this concept, students know:

   a. the sun is the major source of energy for phenomena on the Earth's surface, powering winds, ocean currents, and the water cycle.
   Sections 4-2, 14-1, 14-2, 14-3, 16-1, 16-3, 17-2, pages 632, 637

   b. solar energy reaches Earth through radiation, mostly in the form of visible light.
   Sections 14-1, 14-2, 16-1, 16-3, 26-2, 570-571, 602-603, pages 632-633

   c. heat from Earth's interior reaches the surface primarily through convection.
   Sections 9-3, 11-1, pages 630-631, 633, 635

   d. convection currents distribute heat in the atmosphere and oceans.
   Sections 14-2, 14-3, 16-3, 17-2, pages 633-634

   e. differences in pressure, heat, air movement, and humidity result in changes of weather.
   Sections 14-1, 14-3, 15-1, 15-2, 15-3, 16-1, 16-3, page 634

Ecology (Life Science)

5. Organisms in ecosystems exchange energy and nutrients among themselves and with the environment. As a basis for understanding this concept, students know:

   a. energy entering ecosystems as sunlight is transferred by producers into chemical energy through photosynthesis, and then from organism to organism in food webs.
   Sections 23-1, 23-3, 26-3, page 635

   b. over time, matter is transferred from one organism to others in the food web, and between organisms and the physical environment.
   Sections 23-3, 26-3, pages 637-638

   c. populations of organisms can be categorized by the functions they serve in an ecosystem.
   Sections 23-1, 23-2, 23-3, pages 638-639

   d. different kinds of organisms may play similar ecological roles in similar biomes.
   Sections 22-1, 23-2, 23-3, 24-2, 24-3, page 639

   e. the number and types of organisms an ecosystem can support depends on the resources available and abiotic factors, such as quantity of light and water, range of temperatures, and soil composition.
   Sections 22-3, 23-1, 23-2, 24-1, 24-2, 24-3, page 639

Resources

6. Sources of energy and materials differ in amounts, distribution, usefulness, and the time required for their formation. As a basis for understanding this concept, students know:

   a. the utility of energy sources is determined by factors that are involved in converting these sources to useful forms and the consequences of the conversion process.
   Sections 4-1, 4-2, 16-3, pages 630-633, 642-643, 645-646

   b. different natural energy and material resources, including air, soil, rocks, minerals, petroleum, fresh water, wildlife, and forests, and classify them as renewable or nonrenewable.
   Sections 4-1, 4-2, 4-3, 4-4, 6-2, 14-2, 23-1, page 643

   c. natural origin of the materials used to make common objects.
   Sections 4-1, 4-4, 6-2, pages 643-644

Investigation and Experimentation

7. Scientific progress is made by asking meaningful questions and conducting careful investigations. As a basis for understanding this concept, and to address the content the other three strands, students should develop their own questions and perform investigations. Students will:

   a. develop a hypothesis.
   Sections 1-1, 1-2, 9-3, 14-1, 14-2, 15-3, 16-1, 23-2, 25-3, 27-3, pages 623, 643-646, 674-675

   b. select and use appropriate tools and technology (including calculators, computers, balances, spring scales, microscopes, and binoculars) to perform tests, collect data, and display data.
   Sections 2-2, 2-3, 6-1, 6-2, 7-1, 8-3, 9-3, 10-1, 14-1, 16-1, 22-3, 23-1, 23-2, 24-2, 25-3, 26-2, 27-2, 27-3

   c. construct appropriate graphs from data and develop qualitative statements about the relationships between variables.
   Sections 1-2, 2-3, 6-1, 6-2, 8-1, 9-3, 10-2, 10-3, 14-1, 14-2, 15-1, 16-3, 17-1, 21-3, 25-2, 27-3, pages 631, 633, 641

   d. communicate the steps and results from an investigation in written reports and verbal presentations.
   Sections 1-2, 1-2, 4-1, 4-3, 6-1, 6-2, 14-2, 15-1, 16-3, 21-1, 21-2, 22-2, 25-1, 25-3, 27-3, pages 621, 626, 637, 644, 646

   e. recognize whether evidence is consistent with a proposed explanation.
   Sections 1-2, 6-1, 7-3, 8-1, 9-1, 9-2, 9-3, 10-2, 10-3, 17-3, 23-3, 25-3, 27-3, pages 622, 627, 632

   f. read a topographic map and a geologic map for evidence provided on the maps, and construct and interpret a simple scale map.
   Sections 1-1, 4-4, 5-1, 5-2, 5-3, 9-2, 9-3, 11-1, pages 618, 636, 638, 643, 698

   g. interpret events by sequence and time from natural phenomena (e.g., relative ages of rocks and intrusions).
   Sections 4-1, 5-1, 6-2, 8-1, 8-2, 9-2, 9-3, 10-1, 11-1, 11-2, 11-3, 14-2, 16-3, pages 622-624, 632

   h. identify changes in natural phenomena over time without manipulating the phenomena (e.g., a tree limb, a grove of trees, a stream, a hillslope).
   Sections 6-1, 6-2, 9-3, 15-3, 16-1, 16-3, 21-3, 23-1, 24-2, 24-3, pages 622-623, 632, 641

Contents

Contents

Contents

Science Connections

NATIONAL GEOGRAPHIC

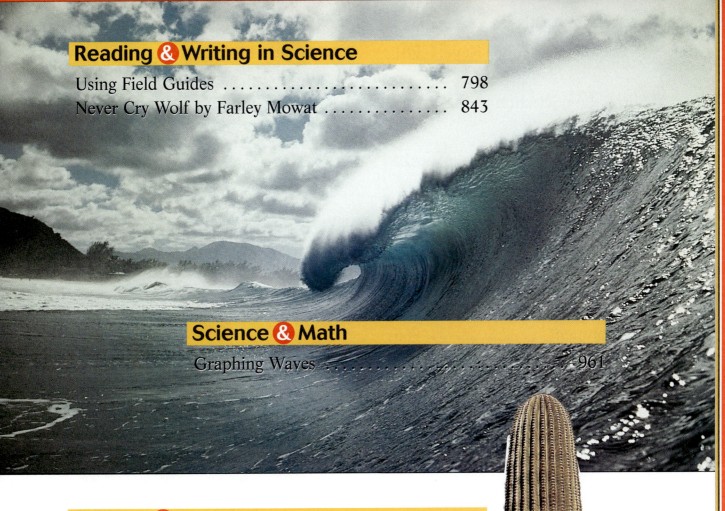

Reading & Writing in Science

Science & Math

Science & Society

Activities

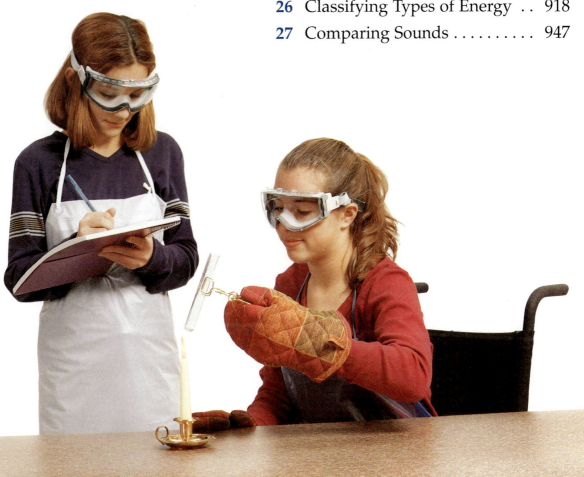

Explore Activities

Problem Solving

Skill Activities

Skill Builders

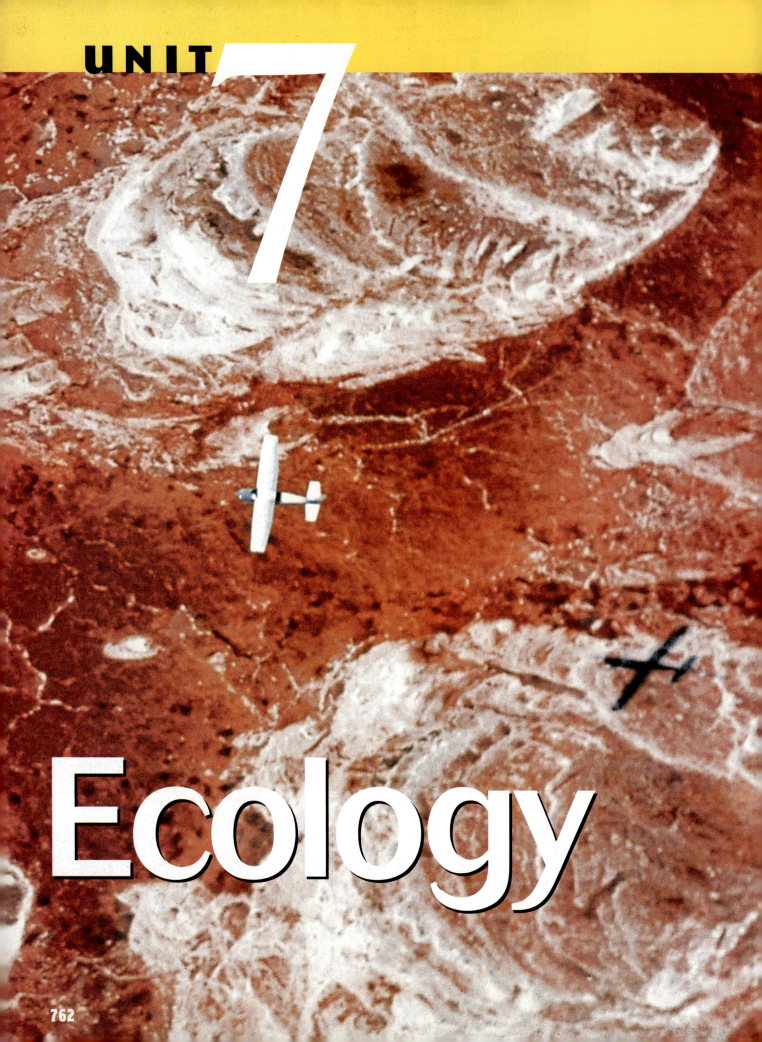

Ecology

What's Happening Here?

A small plane flies over one of the soda lakes of eastern Africa (left). Dotted with islands of foam, where liquid and gas bubble through its salt crust, Tanzania's Lake Natron appears to be a wasteland. Yet, notice the color. Pink algae bloom everywhere. After a rain, fresh water collects on the salt flats, and there the algae survive. The algae feed the flamingos (below) that flock to the lake by the millions to breed, and the birds' droppings feed the algae. The algae also give the birds' feathers their pink hue. Moreover, the harsh salt crust keeps many predators from crossing the treacherous flats—thereby providing a safe place for the flamingos to nest. Thus, living and non-living parts of the environment—the algae and the salt crust—work together to support life. In this unit, you will learn that complex webs connect living things and are key to supporting life, even in hostile environments.

interNET CONNECTION

Explore the Glencoe Science Web Site at **www.glencoe.com/sec/ science/ca** to find out more about topics found in this unit.

Classifying Living Things

Chapter Preview

Skills Preview

Skill Builders
- Observe and Infer
- Map Concepts

MiniLabs
- Classify
- Communicate

Activities
- Form a Hypothesis
- Use a Key

Reading Check ✔

As you read this chapter, use context clues to figure out unfamiliar terms. For example, what clues help you understand the term *evolution* in Section 21-2?

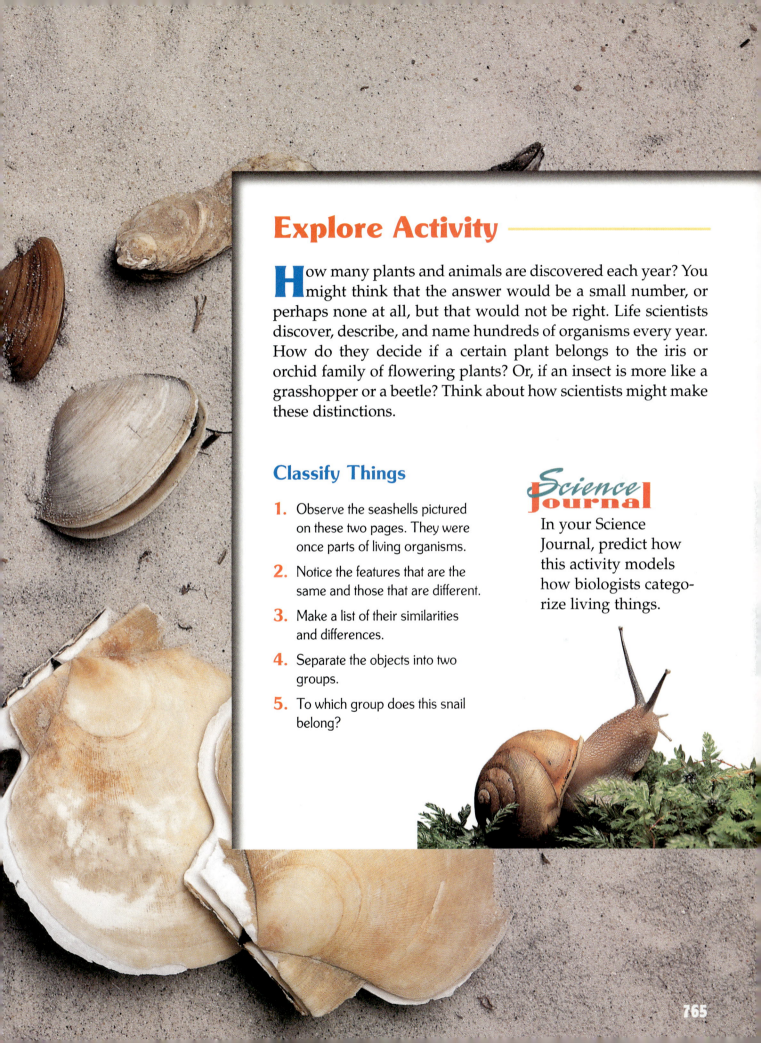

Explore Activity

How many plants and animals are discovered each year? You might think that the answer would be a small number, or perhaps none at all, but that would not be right. Life scientists discover, describe, and name hundreds of organisms every year. How do they decide if a certain plant belongs to the iris or orchid family of flowering plants? Or, if an insect is more like a grasshopper or a beetle? Think about how scientists might make these distinctions.

Classify Things

1. Observe the seashells pictured on these two pages. They were once parts of living organisms.

2. Notice the features that are the same and those that are different.

3. Make a list of their similarities and differences.

4. Separate the objects into two groups.

5. To which group does this snail belong?

Science Journal

In your Science Journal, predict how this activity models how biologists categorize living things.

What is classification?

What You'll Learn

▶ Why classification systems are needed
▶ Aristotle's system of classification
▶ Linnaeus's system of classification

Vocabulary
classify
taxonomy
kingdom
binomial nomenclature
genus
species

Why It's Important

▶ Classification helps you to find the connections among the differences in nature.

Classifying

When you go into a grocery store, do you go to one aisle to get milk, to another to get margarine, and to a third to get yogurt? Most grocery stores group similar items together. You would find the dairy products mentioned above in one area. When you place similar items together, you classify them. To **classify** means to group ideas, information, or objects based on their similarities. The science of classifying is called **taxonomy** (tak SAHN uh mee).

Classification is an important part of your life. Grocery stores, bookstores, and department stores group similar items together. In what other places is classification important?

Early History of Classification

More than 2000 years ago, Aristotle, a Greek philosopher, developed a system to classify living things. Aristotle thought that all living things on Earth could be placed in either the plant kingdom or the animal kingdom.

Figure 21-1 Aristotle's system of classification did not work for some organisms. For example, frogs can live in water and on land. **What other organisms don't fit into Aristotle's classification system? Why don't they fit?**

In taxonomy, a **kingdom** is the first and largest category. Aristotle began his classification of animals by grouping them according to their physical traits. Then, he used such things as where they lived, the presence or absence of blood, how they reproduced, and wing types to sort them into smaller groups.

Eventually, scientists began to criticize Aristotle's system because it had too many exceptions. Animals were classified according to where they lived, but what about frogs? Frogs spend part of their lives in water and part on land, as shown in **Figure 21-1.** His method of classifying included philosophical ideas that added to the confusion.

Scientific Naming

By the mid-eighteenth century, the classifications of Aristotle had changed and new systems had been developed. However, a lot of confusion remained. Sometimes, an organism had a different name in each country it lived in. Sometimes, it was known by different names in the same country.

Another problem was the length of names for organisms. By this time, many plants, animals, and other organisms had been identified and named. To avoid confusion, scientists gave organisms names that described them in great detail. The name often consisted of several words. For example, the

CHEMISTRY
INTEGRATION

Acid or base?
Classification of matter may include categories like solids, liquids, or gases; elements or compounds; and organic or inorganic. Another way to group matter is as an acid or a base. Using resources, find definitions for acids and bases. In your Science Journal, write a short definition for each, including something about pH.

Problem Solving

Classifying an Organism

Laquitia and her family were on vacation in southern Arizona. One evening, they were driving through a national park just as the sun was setting. Suddenly, a tawny, heavily marked cat with a long tail ran across the road and disappeared into the dense brush. The cat's spots included rings, speckles, slashes, and bars. Laquitia and her family were startled to see such a beautiful animal. No one in the car knew what it was.

Solve the Problem:

1. What important characteristics might be needed to identify an animal?

2. Would Laquitia need other information to be able to determine the animal's species?

Think Critically: How would you begin to figure out what cat Laquitia saw?

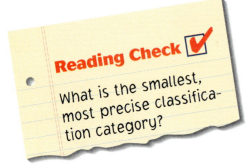
Figure 21-2 *Scabiosa caucasica* is also called the pincushion flower. During the fifteenth century, it was made into a medicine to treat scabies, a skin problem caused by mites. That's why the genus is named *Scabiosa.* The specific name means that the plant came from the Caucasus Mountains in Russia.

Reading Check ✔

What is the smallest, most precise classification category?

spearmint plant was named *Mentha floribus spicatis, foliis oblongis serratis.* This name means, more or less, "a member of the mint genus that has its flowers in a spike arrangement, and oblong, serrated leaves." These long names were difficult for scientists to work with. Can you imagine asking for "a member of the mint genus that has its flowers in a spike arrangement, and oblong, serrated leaves, chewing gum?" Carolus Linnaeus, a Swedish physician and naturalist, created a way to give each organism a simpler, unique name.

Binomial Nomenclature

Linnaeus's system, called **binomial nomenclature** (bi NOH mee ul•NOH mun klay chur), gives a two-word name to every organism. Binomial means "two names." The two-word name is commonly called the organism's scientific name. The first word of an organism's scientific name is the genus, and the second is the specific name. A **genus** (JEE nus) is a group of different organisms that have similar characteristics. Together, the genus name and the specific name make up the scientific name of a particular species, as shown in **Figure 21-2.** A **species** (SPEE sheez) is the smallest, most precise classification category. Organisms belonging to the same species can mate to produce fertile offspring. ✔

Mini Lab

Using Binomial Nomenclature

Procedure

1. Make a model of a fictitious organism.
2. Give your organism a scientific name.
3. Make sure that your name is Latinized and supplies information about the species.

Analysis

1. Present your organism to the class. Ask them to guess its name.
2. Why do scientists use Latin when they name organisms?

An example of a two-word name, or species, is *Canis familiaris*. This is a domesticated dog. Notice that the first word, the genus name, always begins with a capital letter. The second word, the specific name, begins with a lowercase letter. Both words in a scientific name are written in italics or underlined. Linnaeus's naming system uses Latin because when he developed it, Latin was the language used at European universities and understood by nearly all educated people. Today, it provides an international understanding of all scientific names. In Linnaeus's system, no two organisms have the same scientific name. Because of Linnaeus's system and the use of Latin, scientists around the world recognize the name *Canis familiaris* as a domesticated dog and not a gray wolf, *Canis lupus*. You can see the differences among a dog, a gray wolf, and a coyote in **Figure 21-3.**

Figure 21-3 The photo on the left shows a dog, *Canis familiaris*. Other members of the genus Canis are the coyote, *Canis latrans* (middle), and the gray wolf, *Canis lupus* (right). Notice that they are all different species. **Why are they placed in the same genus?**

Section Assessment

1. What is the purpose of classification?
2. What were the contributions of Aristotle and Linnaeus to taxonomy?
3. **Think Critically:** List two examples of things that are classified based on their similarities.
4. **Skill Builder**
   Observing and Inferring To learn how to classify organisms by observing them, do the **Chapter 21 Skill Activity** on page 1014.

Using Math

You have eight different members of the same genus to classify. What is the least number of characteristics required to separate them into eight species?

Species Diversity

Human Footprints

Are there any places on Earth untouched by humans? The old-growth forests of the northwestern United States as well as the rain forests of South America and Asia—previously untouched areas—are increasingly under pressure from human demands. Loggers and lumber companies want to harvest old-growth timber. Farmers want to clear the rain forest to grow crops.

What is species diversity?

Rain forests, coral reefs, and other environments provide homes to hundreds of thousands of organisms. In a hectare (about 10 sq km) of rain forest, for example, there may be 200 species of plants and more than 1000 species of animals. This great variety of plants, animals, and other organisms makes up species diversity. An ecosystem that has a high diversity of species is more stable than one with fewer species.

How is species diversity changed?

In the past, because humans have entered into undisturbed areas, particular species, such as the Carolina parakeet and the passenger pigeon, have become extinct. Extinction reduces species diversity and the stability of ecosystems. Even though extinction is a natural process, humans are contributing to extinction today at a far greater rate than has ever occurred before.

Every minute, more than 20 hectares of rain forest are cut for timber or are cleared for farming or mining. Some areas of old-growth forests in the United States are protected from cutting because the northern spotted owl (right), an endangered species, lives there. Protecting an entire forest because of one endangered species is one way to prevent a decrease in species diversity, but it is a controversial method. International organizations, communities, and individuals concerned about species diversity are working to figure out how best to protect and develop these areas.

interNET CONNECTION

The Smithsonian Institution created a biodiversity program in 1986 that focuses on problems associated with maintaining global forest diversity. Visit the Glencoe Science Web Site at **www.glencoe.com/sec/ science/ca** for more information on the Smithsonian Institution's program.

Modern Classification

Six-Kingdom System

How do the classification systems used today differ from those of the past? Aristotle and Linnaeus developed their systems of classification using only those characteristics of organisms that they could see. Today, scientists use those and other traits to classify organisms. For example, they may look at the chemical and genetic makeup of organisms. By studying fossils, they examine and compare ancestors to existing organisms. They may compare body structures or early stages of development. By studying all of these things and more, scientists can determine an organism's phylogeny. The **phylogeny** (fi LAH jon nee) of an organism is its evolutionary history or how it has changed over time. Phylogeny tells scientists who the ancestors of an organism were. Today, classification of organisms is based on phylogeny.

The classification system most commonly used today separates organisms into six kingdoms. These kingdoms are animal, plant, fungi, protists, eubacteria, and archaebacteria. Organisms are placed into a kingdom based on several characteristics. These characteristics include cell type, whether it is single celled or many celled, ability to make food, and others. The organisms in **Figure 21-4** all belong to the Kingdom Fungi.

What You'll Learn

- ► The names of the six kingdoms of living things
- ► How to identify characteristics and members of each kingdom
- ► The groups within each kingdom

Vocabulary

phylogeny	class
phylum	order
division	family

Why It's Important

- ► Modern classification helps you understand how living things are related.

Figure 21-4 Fungi have common characteristics. One characteristic is that they cannot make their own food.

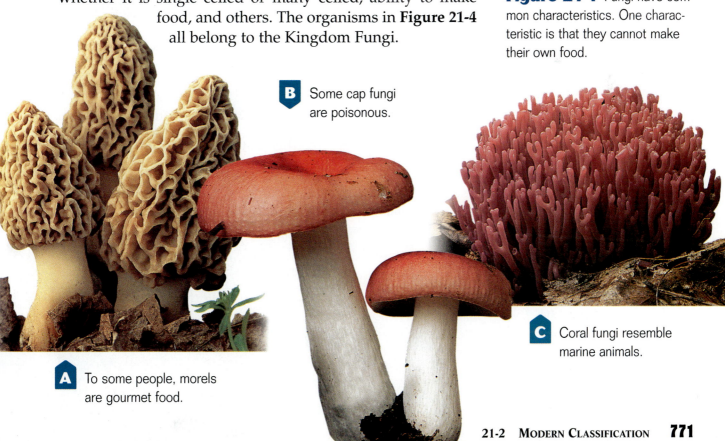

B Some cap fungi are poisonous.

C Coral fungi resemble marine animals.

A To some people, morels are gourmet food.

Figure 21-5 Classification systems change as new information is learned about organisms. One proposed system groups all organisms into three domains and then into kingdoms.

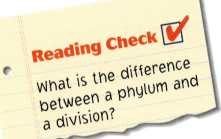

DOMAIN
Bacteria

KINGDOM
Eubacteria

DOMAIN
Eukarya

KINGDOMS
Animalia

Plantae

Fungi

Protista

DOMAIN
Archaea

KINGDOMS
Euryarchaeota

Crenarchaeota

Prokaryotes and Eukaryotes

Cell type separates two kingdoms from the other four kingdoms. The archaebacteria and eubacteria kingdoms contain organisms that are just one prokaryotic (proh kair ee AH tik) cell in size—a cell without a nucleus. Protists, fungi, plants, and animals have one or more eukaryotic (yew kair ee AH tik) cells—cells with a nucleus. **Table 21-1** lists information about each of the six kingdoms. Some scientists propose that before organisms are grouped into kingdoms, they should be placed in larger groups called domains. One proposed domain classification system is shown in **Figure 21-5**.

Groups Within Kingdoms

Suppose you go to a music store at the mall to buy a new CD. Will you look through all the CDs in the store until you find the one you're looking for? No, the CDs are separated into categories of similar types of music such as rock, soul, classical, country, and jazz. Within each category, the CDs are divided by artists, and then by specific titles. Because of this classification system, you can easily find the CD you want.

Scientists classify organisms into groups in the same way. Every organism is placed into a kingdom. Then, an organism is assigned to a **phylum** (FI lum), the next smallest group. In the plant kingdom, the word **division** is used in place of phylum. Each phylum or division is separated into **classes.** Classes are separated into **orders,** and orders are separated into **families.** A genus is a group within a family. A genus can have one or more species. ✔

Scientists use these categories to classify and name an organism, in the same way that you use categories to find a CD. To understand how an organism is classified, look at the classification of the bottlenose dolphin in **Figure 21-6**.

Reading Check

What is the difference between a phylum and a division?

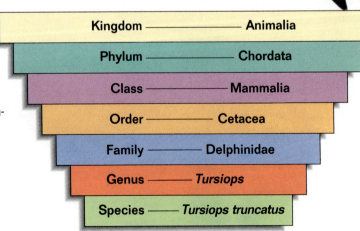

Kingdom	Animalia
Phylum	Chordata
Class	Mammalia
Order	Cetacea
Family	Delphinidae
Genus	*Tursiops*
Species	*Tursiops truncatus*

Figure 21-6 The classification of the bottlenose dolphin shows that it is in the order Cetacea. This order includes whales and porpoises.

Table 21-1

Life's Six Kingdoms					
Archaebacteria	**Eubacteria**	**Protista**	**Fungi**	**Plantae**	**Animalia**
Prokaryotic	Prokaryotic	Eukaryotic	Eukaryotic	Eukaryotic	Eukaryotic
One celled	One celled	One and many celled	One and many celled	Many celled	Many celled
Some members make their own food; others obtain it from other organisms. Some organisms live in extreme environments.	Some members make their own food; others obtain it from other organisms.	Some members make their own food; others obtain it from other organisms.	All members obtain food from other organisms.	Members make their own food.	Members eat plants, animals, or other organisms.

Section Assessment

1. Name and describe a member of each kingdom.
2. Why are there smaller groups within each kingdom?
3. **Think Critically:** Identify the kingdom a single-celled, eukaryotic organism that makes its own food belongs to.
4. **Skill Builder**
   Concept Mapping Use the following terms to make a network tree concept map: *cells, cell organelles, eukaryote, prokaryote, plants, animals, archaebacteria, eubacteria, no membrane-bound organelles, no nucleus, fungi, protists,* and *organized nucleus.* Provide linking words. If you need help, refer to Concept Mapping in the **Skill Handbook** on page 986.

Using Computers

Database Make a database that could be used to sort organisms based on any level of classification. Enter the classification information for humans, dogs, and cats. If you need help, refer to page 1005.

Design Your Own Experiment

Classifying Seeds

Possible Materials

- Packets of seeds (10 different kinds)
- Hand lens
- Metric ruler
- Sheets of paper (2)

Scientists have developed classification systems to show how organisms are related. How do they determine what features they will use to classify organisms? Can you learn to use the same methods?

Recognize the Problem

You are given several kinds of seeds and are asked to classify them into groups of similar seeds. How would you begin?

Form a Hypothesis

Make a hypothesis about the traits or physical features that may be used to help classify various kinds of seeds.

Goals

- **Observe** the seeds provided and notice their distinctive features.
- **Classify** seeds using your model.

Safety Precautions

Do not eat any seeds or put them in your mouth. Some may have been treated with chemicals.

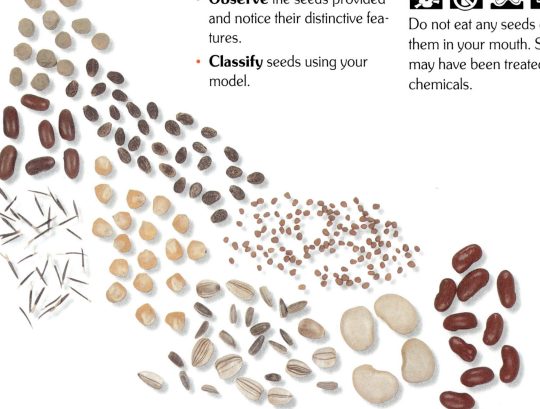

Test Your Hypothesis

Plan

1. As a group, list the steps that you need to take to classify seeds. Be specific, and describe exactly what you will do at each step. List your materials.

2. **Classify** your seeds by making a model.

3. Make a plan to identify your seeds.

4. Read over your entire experiment to make sure that all steps are in logical order.

Do

1. Make sure your teacher approves your model before you proceed.

2. Carry out the experiment as planned.

3. While you are working, write down any observations that you make that would cause you to change your model.

4. **Complete** the plan.

Analyze Your Data

1. **Compare** your key and model with those made by other groups.

2. Check your key by having another group use it.

Draw Conclusions

1. In what ways can groups of different types of seeds be classified?

2. Why is it an advantage for scientists to use a standardized system to classify organisms? What observations did you make to support your answer?

21•3 Identifying Organisms

What You'll Learn

▶ Why scientific names are more useful to scientists than common names

▶ The function of a dichotomous key

▶ How to use a dichotomous key

Vocabulary
dichotomous key

Why It's Important

▶ It is easy to identify organisms if you can use a dichotomous key.

Common Names and Scientific Names

Have you heard anyone call the bird in **Figure 21-7A** a *Turdus migratorius?* In much of the United States, this bird is commonly called a robin, or a robin redbreast. However, people who live in England call the bird in **Figure 21-7B** a robin. In much of Europe, the same bird is also called a redbreast. If you lived in Australia, you'd call the bird in **Figure 21-7C** a robin, or a yellow robin. Are these the same species of bird? No, these birds are obviously different from one another.

Figure 21-7 These three robins have the same common name but are three different species.

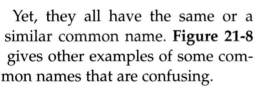

Figure 21-8 Common names can be misleading. Sea horses (A) are fish, but starfish (B) are not fish. Prairie dogs (C) are more closely related to squirrels than to dogs. **Do you know a misleading common name?**

Yet, they all have the same or a similar common name. **Figure 21-8** gives other examples of some common names that are confusing.

What would happen if life scientists used only common names when they communicated with others about organisms? There would be many misunderstandings. The system of binomial nomenclature developed by Linnaeus gives each bird a unique scientific name. The scientific names for the birds in **Figure 21-7** are: **A**, *Turdus migratorius*; **B**, *Erithacus rubecula*; and **C**, *Eopsaltria australis*.

Functions of Scientific Names

Scientific names serve four functions. First, they help scientists avoid errors in communication. A life scientist who studied the yellow robin, *Eopsaltria australis*, would not be confused by information he or she read about *Turdus migratorius*,

Try at Home
Mini Lab

Communicating Ideas

Procedure

1. Find a picture in a magazine of a piece of furniture that you could both sit or lie down on.
2. Show the picture to ten people and ask them to tell you what they call the piece of furniture.
3. Keep a record of the answers in your Science Journal.

Analysis

1. In your Science Journal, infer how using common names can be confusing when communicating with others.
2. How does using scientific names make communication between scientists easier?

Reading Check ✔

Where could you find the scientific name of an organism?

the American robin. Second, organisms with similar evolutionary histories are classified together. Because of this, you know that organisms with the same genus name are related. Third, scientific names give descriptive information about the species. What can you tell from the species name *Turdus migratorius*? It tells you that this bird migrates from place to place. Fourth, scientific names allow information about organisms to be organized and found easily and efficiently. Such information may be in a field guide, a book, or a pamphlet that lists related organisms and gives their scientific names.

Tools for Identifying Organisms

You've been asked to identify the organism in **Figure 21-9.** What do you do? The easiest thing would be to ask someone. You could contact a professor at a university, an exterminator, a county extension specialist, an expert at a natural history museum, or any knowledgeable person. However, no one knows or is expected to know all members of any taxonomic group. The person would probably tell you that the organism is a tick. He or she might look in a field guide to find its scientific name. If you were to use a field guide, you might be able to identify the organism. ✔

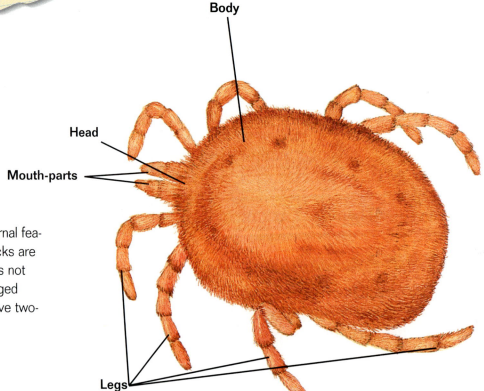

Figure 21-9 Two external features used for identifying ticks are eight legs and a body that is not in sections. Other eight-legged arthropods, like spiders, have two-section bodies.

Many kinds of field guides have been written like those in **Figure 21-10** and the field guide at the end of this chapter. Field guides about plants, fungi, fish, and nearly every other kind of organism are available. Most field guides have descriptions, illustrations of organisms, and information about habitats to help with identification. You can identify species from around the world by using the appropriate field guide.

Using Dichotomous Keys

A **dichotomous** (di KAH toh mus) **key** is a detailed list of characteristics used to identify organisms and includes scientific names. Dichotomous keys are arranged in steps with two descriptive statements at each step. Look at the dichotomous key for mites and ticks in **Table 21-2.** Notice that at each numbered step, the descriptions are labeled "a" and "b." To use the key, you must always begin with a choice from the first pair of descriptions. Notice that the end of each description is either the name of a species or directions to go to another step. If you use the dichotomous key properly, you will eventually end up with the correct name for your species.

Let's identify the soft tick in **Table 21-2.** Start at 1 of the key. Your tick is brown, so you go to 3. You measure your tick and find it is more than 5 mm in length, so you go on to 4. Your tick is brown with an oval, flattened body, so you choose "b."

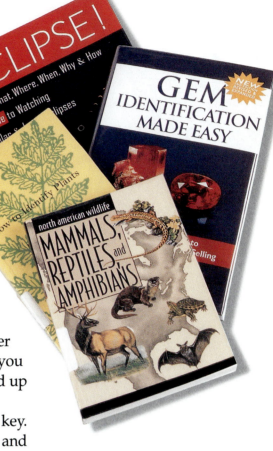

Figure 21-10 Field guides are useful when trying to identify things.

Table 21-2

Key to Some Mites and Ticks of North America

1. Animal color
  a. red, go to 2
  b. not red, go to 3

2. Body texture
  a. smooth; body globular and somewhat elongated; red freshwater mite, *Limnochares americana*
  b. dense velvety hair; body oval to rounded rectangle; velvet mite, *Trombidium* species

3. Body length
  a. 0.5 mm or less; two-spotted spider mite, *Tetranychus uriticae*
  b. more than 0.5 mm, go to 4

4. Body coloration
  a. dark brown with a small, whitish, patterned shield near the head; American dog tick, *Dermacentor* species
  b. brown; body is a flattened oval with a soft plate on the back; mammal soft tick, *Ornithodoros* species

Actual size: 5 mm

Figure 21-11 Each of these animals is a different species of mite or tick. **What things do they have in common?**

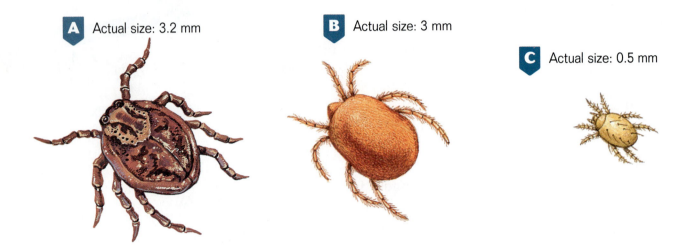

A Actual size: 3.2 mm

B Actual size: 3 mm

C Actual size: 0.5 mm

EARTH SCIENCE INTEGRATION ▶

The dichotomous key tells you that your tick is an example of an *Ornithodoros* species, which are mammal soft ticks.

Keys are useful in a variety of ways. It is important to know if a rock is igneous, metamorphic, or sedimentary when classifying fossils, for example. Minerals can be classified using a key that describes characteristics such as hardness, luster, color, streak, and cleavage. Why might you need to know several characteristics to classify a mineral or a living thing?

Section Assessment

1. List four reasons biologists use scientific names instead of common names in their communications.

2. Why can common names cause confusion?

3. What is the function of a dichotomous key?

4. **Think Critically:** Why would you infer that two species that look similar share a common evolutionary history?

5. **Skill Builder**
   Classifying Classify the ticks and mites marked A, B, and C in **Figure 21-11,** using the dichotomous key in **Table 21-2.** If you need help, refer to Classifying in the **Skill Handbook** on page 985.

Science **Journal**
Select a field guide for grasses, trees, insects, or mammals. Select two organisms in the field guide that closely resemble each other. Compare them and explain how they differ using labeled diagrams.

Using a Dichotomous Key

Materials
• Paper and pencil

Scientists who classify organisms have made many keys that allow you to identify unknown organisms. Try this activity to see how it is done.

What You'll Investigate

How a dichotomous key can be used to identify native cats in the United States.

Goals

• **Learn** to use a dichotomous key.
• **Identify** two native cats of North America.

Procedure

1. **Observe** the cats pictured below.

2. Begin with 1 of the key to the right. **Identify** the cat labeled A.

3. On your paper, write the common and scientific name for the cat and list all of its traits given in the key.

4. Use the same procedure to **identify** the species of the cat labeled B.

Conclude and Apply

1. According to the key, how many species of native cats reside in North America?

2. How do you know that this key doesn't contain all the species of native cats in the world?

3. **Infer** why you couldn't identify a lion using this key.

4. **Explain** why it wouldn't be a good idea to begin in the middle of a key instead of with the first step.

Key to Native Cats of North America

1. Tail length
   a. short, go to 2
   b. long, go to 3

2. Cheek ruff
   a. no cheek ruff; long ear tufts tipped with black; coat distinctly mottled; lynx, *Lynx canadensis*
   b. broad cheek ruffs; ear tufts short; coat with indistinct spots; bobcat, *Lynx rufus*

3. Coat
   a. plain colored, go to 4
   b. patterned, go to 5

4. Coat color
   a. yellowish to tan above with white to buff below; mountain lion, *Felis concolor*
   b. all brown or black; jaguarundi, *Felis yagouaroundi*

5. Coat pattern
   a. lines of black-bordered brown spots; ocelot, *Felis pardalis*
   b. irregular tan and black, go to 6

6. Animal size
   a. large cat; rows of black rosettes or rings unevenly distributed; jaguar, *Panthera onca*
   b. small cat; four dark-brown stripes on the back and one on the neck; some irregularly shaped spots; margay, *Felis wiedii*

A   **B**

FIELD GUIDE *to Insects*

FIELD *ACTIVITY*

For a week, use this field guide to help you identify insect orders. Look in different places and at different times of day for insects. In your Science Journal, record the order of insect found, along with the date, time, and place. *Why do you think there are so many kinds of insects?*

I t's brown and creepy, and has wings and six legs. If you call it a bug, you may be correct, but if you said it was an insect, you definitely would be correct. Insects belong to a large group of animals called the arthropods. They are related to shrimp, spiders, lobsters, and centipedes. There are more insect species than all other animal species on Earth. Insects are found from the tropics to the tundra. Some are aquatic all or part of their lives. There are even insects that live inside other animals. Insects play important roles in the environment. Many are helpful, but others are destructive.

How Insects Are Classified

An insect's body is divided into three parts: head, thorax, and abdomen. The head has a pair of antennae and eyes and paired mouthparts. Three pairs of jointed legs and, sometimes, wings are attached to the thorax. They have a hard covering over their entire body. Some insects shed this covering so that they can grow. Insects are classified into smaller groups called orders. By observing an insect and recognizing certain features, you can identify the order it belongs to. This field guide presents ten insect orders.

Insect Orders

Dermaptera Earwigs

- A pair of pincerlike structures extends from the end of the abdomen.
- They are usually active at night and hide under litter or in any dark, protected place during the day.
- Earwigs may damage plants.

Common Earwig

Coleoptera Beetles

- A pair of thick, leathery, sometimes-knobby wings meets in a straight line and covers another pair of wings, the thorax, and all or most of the abdomen.
- Most beetles are considered serious pests, but some feed on other insects and others are scavengers.

This is the largest order of insects. There are many sizes, shapes, and colors of beetles. Not all beetles are called beetles. For example, ladybugs, fireflies, June bugs, and weevils are beetles.

Convergent Ladybug Beetle

Male Stag Beetle

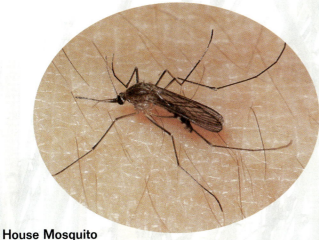

Common Housefly

Diptera Flies—Mosquitoes

- They are small insects with large eyes.
- They have two pair of wings but only one pair is visible.
- Mouths are adapted for piercing and sucking, or scraping and lapping

Many of these insects are food for larger animals. Some spread diseases, others are pests, and some eat dead and decaying things. They are found in many different environments.

House Mosquito

Odonata Dragonflies—Damselflies

- They have two pairs of transparent, many-veined wings that are nearly equal in size and never folded against the insect's body.
- A pair of large eyes are on its head.
- They have a long, thin abdomen.

These insects are usually seen near bodies of water. All members of this group catch small insects, such as mosquitoes, while in flight.

Twelve Spotted Skimmer Dragonfly

Isoptera Termites

- Adults are small, dark brown or black, and may have wings.
- Immature forms are small, soft-bodied, pale yellow or white, and wingless.
- Termites live in colonies in the ground or in wood.

The adults are sometimes confused with ants. The thorax and abdomen of a termite look like one body part, but a thin waist separates the thorax and abdomen of an ant. Although most people consider termites to be destructive insects, they play an important role in recycling trees and other woody plants. Termites can digest wood because certain bacteria and protists live in their digestive tracts.

Pacific Coast Termites

Carolina Praying Mantis

American Cockroach

Dictyoptera Cockroaches—Mantises

- They have long, thin antennae on the head.
- The front wings are smaller than back wings; back wings are thin and fanlike when opened.
  - Front legs of a mantis are adapted for grasping; the other two pairs of legs are similar to those of a cockroach.

Praying mantises are called beneficial insects because they eat other, often harmful, insects. Cockroaches are pests wherever humans live.

Hymenoptera

Ants—Bees—Wasps

- They have two pairs of transparent wings, if present.
- They are found in many different environments, either in colonies or alone.

Members of this order may be so small that they can be seen only with a magnifier. Others may be nearly 35 mm long. They are important because they pollinate flowers, and some prey on harmful insects. Honeybees make honey and wax. Despite common beliefs, not all bees and wasps can sting.

American Bumble Bee

Black Carpenter Ant

Paper Wasp

Lepidoptera Butterflies—Moths

- They have two pairs of wings with colorful patterns created by thousands of tiny scales.
- A moth's antennae are feathery; a butterfly's antennae are thin and each has a small knob on the tip.
- An adult's mouth-parts are adapted as a long, coiled tube for drinking nectar.
- Moths are active at night; butterflies are active on warm, sunny days.

Caterpillars are immature butterflies and moths. They eat plants, fabrics made from animal hair, and stored grains and nuts.

Yellow Woolly Bear Moth

Buckeye Butterfly

Periodic Cicada

Water Boatman

Hemiptera Bugs

- Front wings are thick and leathery near the insect's head and thin at the tip.
- Wing tips usually overlap when folded over the insect's back and cover a smaller pair of thin wings.

The prefix of this order, *Hemi-*, means "half" and describes the front pair of wings. Some bugs live on land and others are aquatic. Some bugs are pests, while others are beneficial insects.

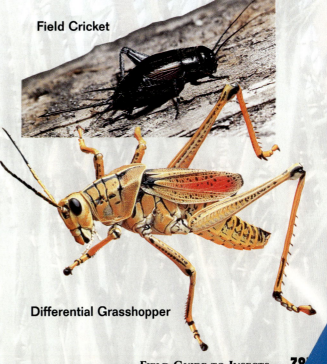

Field Cricket

Differential Grasshopper

Orthoptera
Grasshoppers—Crickets—Katydids

- They have large, hind legs adapted for leaping.
- They usually have two pairs of wings; outer pair is hard and covers a transparent pair.

Many of these insects "sing" by rubbing one body part against another. Males generally do the singing. These insects are considered pests because swarms of them can destroy a farmer's crops in a few days.

For a **preview** of this chapter, study this Reviewing Main Ideas before you read the chapter. After you have studied this chapter, you can use the Reviewing Main Ideas to **review** the chapter.

The Glencoe MindJogger, Audiocassettes, and CD-ROM provide additional opportunities for review.

Section
21-1

WHAT IS CLASSIFICATION?

To **classify** means to group ideas, information, or objects based on their similarities. **Taxonomy** is the science of classification. Aristotle developed the first classification system, but it was confusing. Over time, other systems were created. Linnaeus gave taxonomy **binomial nomenclature,** which is the two-word naming system for organisms, still used today. The two-word species name is the organism's scientific name.

The first word is the genus; the second word is the specific name. Methods of classification are important because they help us to see how groups of organisms are related, to identify organisms, and to find their scientific names. *Why was Aristotle's system confusing?*

Reading Check ✓

All organisms can be classified using only three features. Why can't these features be used to classify dogs? What features could you use to classify dogs?

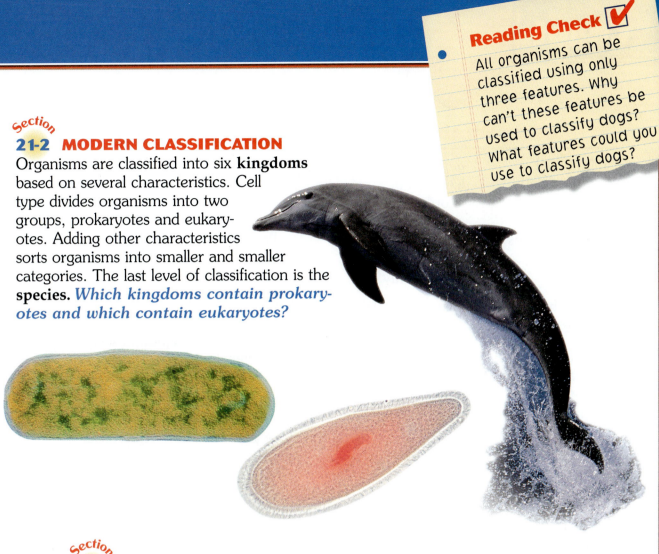

Section 21-2 MODERN CLASSIFICATION

Organisms are classified into six **kingdoms** based on several characteristics. Cell type divides organisms into two groups, prokaryotes and eukaryotes. Adding other characteristics sorts organisms into smaller and smaller categories. The last level of classification is the **species.** *Which kingdoms contain prokaryotes and which contain eukaryotes?*

Section 21-3 IDENTIFYING ORGANISMS

Scientific names give descriptive information about species. Each species has its own unique name. Species names are used worldwide. Communication among scientists and others is easier and clearer with scientific names. Field guides and **dichotomous keys** are used to identify specific organisms. Identification of organisms is important in the study of living organisms. *Why do you always start with the number one entry of a dichotomous key?*

Chapter 21 Assessment

Using Vocabulary

a. binomial
   nomenclature
b. class
c. classify
d. dichotomous key
e. division
f. family
g. genus
h. kingdom
i. order
j. phylogeny
k. phylum
l. species
m. taxonomy

Distinguish between the terms in each of the following sets.

1. kingdom, species
2. division, phylum
3. dichotomous key, binomial nomenclature
4. classify, taxonomy
5. class, family

Checking Concepts

Choose the word or phrase that best answers the question.

6. Which group has the most members?
   A) family
   B) kingdom
   C) genus
   D) order

7. In what category do the most similar organisms belong?
   A) family
   B) class
   C) genus
   D) species

8. Which of the following are all many celled organisms?
   A) animals
   B) bacteria
   C) fungi
   D) protists

9. What is the closest relative of *Canis lupus*?
   A) *Quercus alba*
   B) *Equus zebra*
   C) *Felis tigris*
   D) *Canis familiaris*

10. What does the first word in a two-word scientific name of an organism identify?
    A) kingdom
    B) species
    C) phylum
    D) genus

11. To which kingdom do mushrooms belong?
    A) animal
    B) eubacteria
    C) fungi
    D) plant

12. What is the evolutionary history of an organism?
    A) taxonomy
    B) biology
    C) phylogeny
    D) chemistry

13. What are the simplest eukaryotes?
    A) animals
    B) fungi
    C) eubacteria
    D) protists

14. What are trees and flowers?
    A) animals
    B) plants
    C) fungi
    D) protists

15. What are cells without a nucleus?
    A) eukaryotes
    B) phylogeny
    C) species
    D) prokaryotes

Thinking Critically

16. Explain what binomial nomenclature is and why it is important.

17. Name each of the six kingdoms, and identify a member of each kingdom.

18. Write a short dichotomous key to identify five of your classmates. Use such things as sex, hair color, eye color, and age in your key. Each person's first and last name will be their scientific name.

19. Discuss the relationship between tigers and lions, members of the genus *Panthera*.

20. Scientific names often describe a characteristic of the organism. What does *Lathyrus odoratus* tell you about a sweet pea?

Developing Skills

If you need help, refer to the **Skill Handbook**.

21. **Concept Mapping:** Using information in Sections 21-1 and 21-2, make an events chain concept map to show events from Aristotle to modern classification.

22. **Comparing and Contrasting:** Compare the number and variety of organisms in a kingdom and in a genus.

23. **Classifying:** Use the Key to Native Cats of North America to identify these cats.

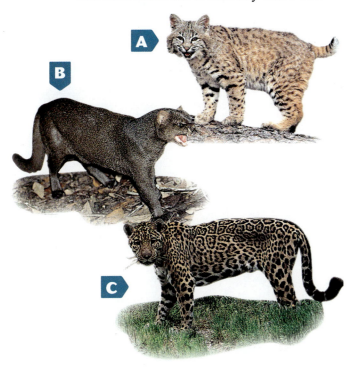

24. **Making and Using Graphs:** Make a circle graph using the data listed in the table below.

Number of Species of Organisms

Kingdom	Number of Species
Protists	51 000
Fungi	100 000
Plants	285 000
Animals	2 000 000

THE PRINCETON REVIEW

Test-Taking Tip

You Are Smarter Than You Think Nothing on the science tests that you will take this year is so difficult that you can't understand it. You can learn to master any of it. Be self-confident and just keep practicing your test-taking skills.

Test Practice

Use these questions to test your Science Proficiency.

1. You are examining a cell under a microscope. Which of the following observations lets you know that the cell is **NOT** from the Kingdom Eubacteria?
   A) Its nucleus is surrounded by a membrane.
   B) The cell has a wall.
   C) The cell is small.
   D) Flagella are attached to the cell wall.

2. Two organisms look different from each other, but a taxonomist suspects they are members of the same species. Why would the taxonomist come to this conclusion?
   A) They fight with each other.
   B) They come from the same country.
   C) They seem to get along well.
   D) They mate and produce fertile offspring.

3. The blue jay, *Cyanocitta cristata*, is most closely related to which of the following birds?
   A) green jay, *Cyanocorax yncas*
   B) Stellar's jay, *Cyanocitta stelleri*
   C) eastern bluebird, *Sialia sialis*
   D) bluethroat, *Luscinia svecica*

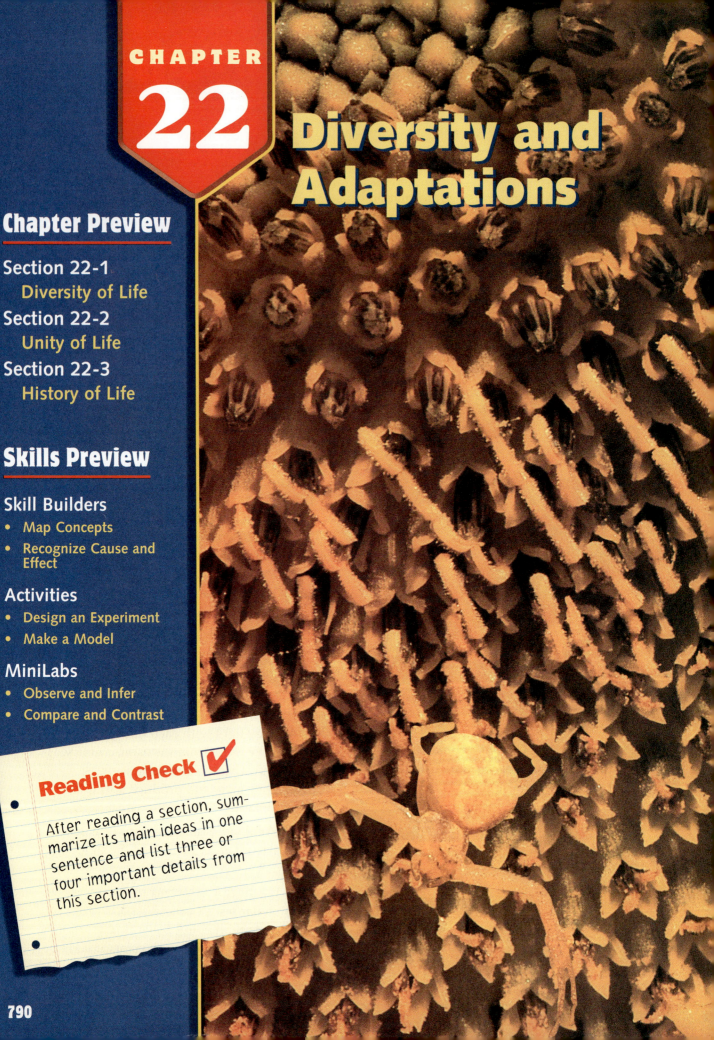

22

Diversity and Adaptations

Chapter Preview

Skills Preview

Skill Builders
- Map Concepts
- Recognize Cause and Effect

Activities
- Design an Experiment
- Make a Model

MiniLabs
- Observe and Infer
- Compare and Contrast

Reading Check ✔

After reading a section, summarize its main ideas in one sentence and list three or four important details from this section.

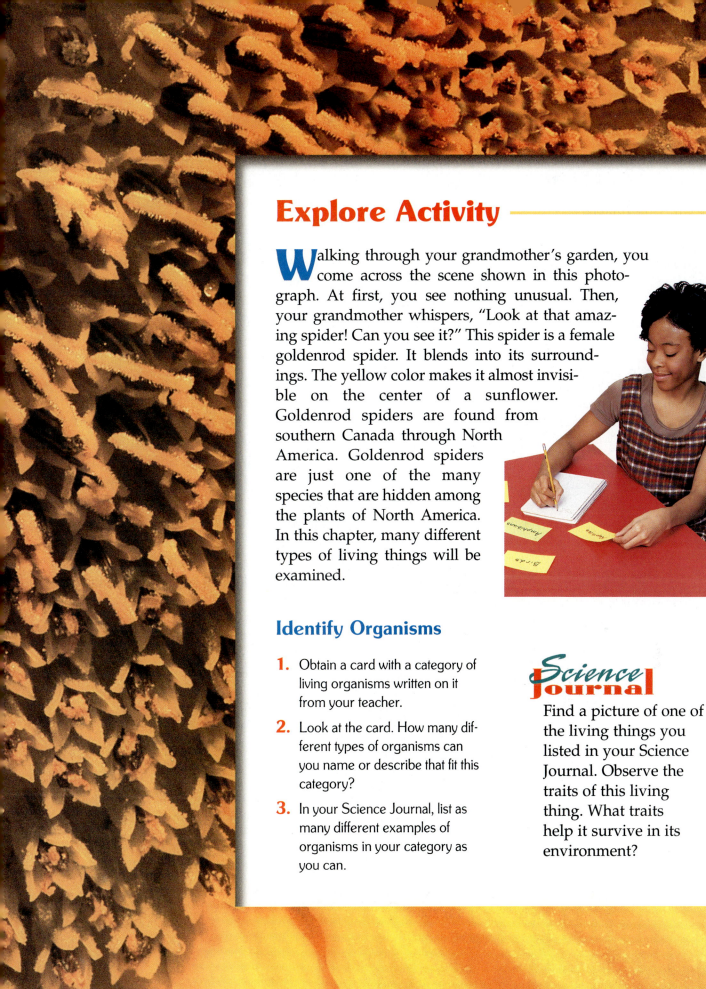

Explore Activity

Walking through your grandmother's garden, you come across the scene shown in this photograph. At first, you see nothing unusual. Then, your grandmother whispers, "Look at that amazing spider! Can you see it?" This spider is a female goldenrod spider. It blends into its surroundings. The yellow color makes it almost invisible on the center of a sunflower. Goldenrod spiders are found from southern Canada through North America. Goldenrod spiders are just one of the many species that are hidden among the plants of North America. In this chapter, many different types of living things will be examined.

Identify Organisms

1. Obtain a card with a category of living organisms written on it from your teacher.

2. Look at the card. How many different types of organisms can you name or describe that fit this category?

3. In your Science Journal, list as many different examples of organisms in your category as you can.

Science Journal

Find a picture of one of the living things you listed in your Science Journal. Observe the traits of this living thing. What traits help it survive in its environment?

22•1 Diversity of Life

What **You'll Learn**

- Why some environments have high biodiversity
- How organisms are adapted to their environments

Vocabulary
biodiversity
adaptation

Why **It's Important**

- Learning the connection between environments and the organisms that live there will help you make better decisions about Earth's resources.

Life's Endless Variety

Earth is filled with an enormous number of different living things. Life can be found almost everywhere on Earth—in the air, on water, on land, underground, and in the soil. Why do you think so many different forms of life exist on Earth?

How many different types of animals and plants did you name in the Explore Activity? Perhaps you named people, dogs, cats, birds, squirrels, bees, and other familiar organisms in your environment. No matter how many kinds of living things you named, they will be only a small portion of the many organisms known.

How do scientists keep track of all these organisms? All living things on the planet can be classified into major categories called kingdoms. Within these kingdoms, approximately 1.4 million different organisms have been identified and named. Scientists estimate that many more millions of different organisms are yet to be discovered. Some scientists estimate that the total of all life on Earth may be somewhere between 3 million and 10 million different organisms. The graph in **Figure 22-1** shows that plants, insects, and other animals show the most numbers of organisms that we know. Are you surprised to learn that insects represent more than half of all known organisms?

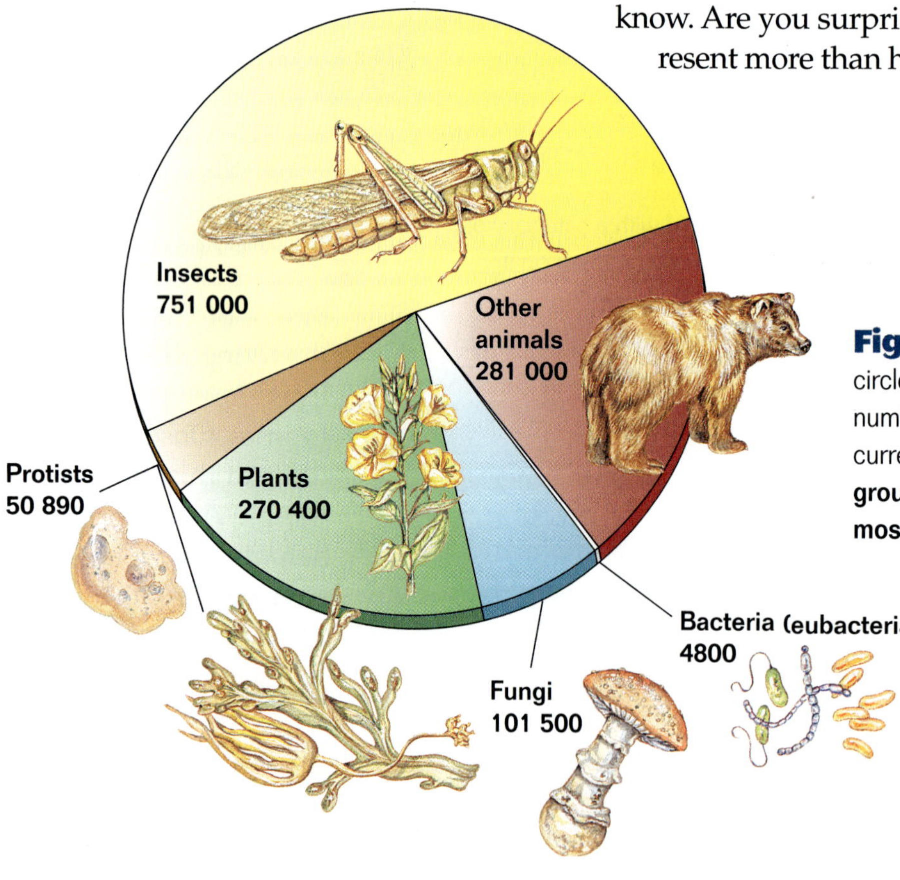

Insects
751 000
Other
animals
281 000
Protists
50 890
Plants
270 400
Bacteria (eubacteria and archaebacteria)
4800
Fungi
101 500

Figure 22-1 This circle graph illustrates the number of different organisms currently known. **Which group of organisms has the most members? The fewest?**

Figure 22-2 The tropical rain forest (A) has a plentiful supply of food, water, and shelter. Therefore, it is home to many different animals and plants, including the blue-crowned motmot (B) and the eyelash viper (C).

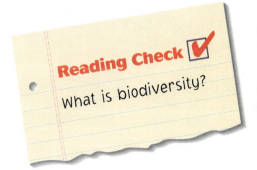

Rain Forest Diversity

You're now in the tropical rain forest, staring at all of the amazing plants and animals. The forest is thick with vines, mosses, orchids, and trees, trees, trees. Insects buzz all around. Brightly colored birds fly from branch to branch. Other animals feed and rest in the treetops.

Tropical rain forests are full of life. These environments have a high number of species. Biological diversity or **biodiversity** (bi oh duh VUR suh tee) is the measure of the number of different species in an area. Tropical rain forests have more different types of living things than any other places on Earth. They have a high biodiversity.

Why do tropical rain forests have such high biodiversity? To answer this question, think about an environment that contains fewer species, such as a desert. In the desert, temperatures are high and not much rain falls. Some deserts have little plant life. What kinds of animals might be able to survive in this environment? Where would they live? What would they eat?

In tropical areas of the world, temperatures remain warm and steady all year, and rainfall is high. These conditions are perfect for the growth of tropical plants. In the rain forest, you might find more than 200 different kinds of plants growing in an area the size of a football field. Living among these plants are many insects, birds, mammals, reptiles, and amphibians such as the ones shown in **Figure 22-2.** These animals use the plants for food and shelter. You can see that tropical environments have high biodiversity because food, water, and shelter are plentiful.

Reading Check

What is biodiversity?

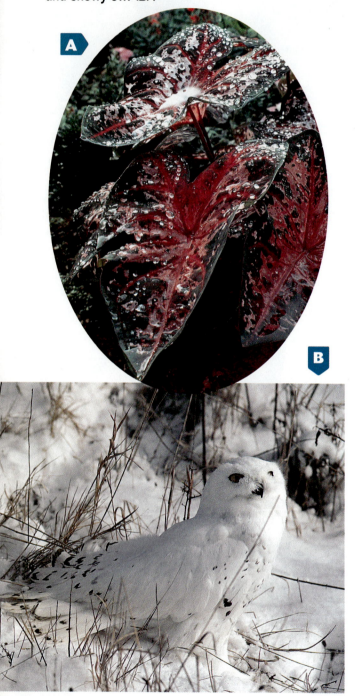

Figure 22-3 Plants and animals show a variety of adaptations for survival. **What evidence of adaptations do you see in this caladium plant (A) and snowy owl (B)?**

Diversity and Adaptation

From the snake in the rain forest, to a deep-sea fish, to a lizard in the desert, Earth is filled with living things that seem to fit into their environments. Their colors, shapes, sizes, and behaviors suit them to live in their surroundings. Any body shape, body process, or behavior that helps an organism survive in its environment and carry out its life processes is called an **adaptation.**

As you can see in **Figure 22-3,** species of organisms have different adaptations that help them survive. Some adaptations include physical features, such as the body shape and color of a snowy owl or a waxy cuticle on leaves that prevents water loss. These features cause the owl to blend into its environment and hide it from predators. Some animals that have coloration that helps them blend into the environment also may have behaviors that help protect them. The bobwhite quail and viper remain absolutely still in times of danger. As a result, these animals are not easily seen by their predators.

Adapting to the Environment

How do you think an organism living in the frozen Arctic would be different from one that lives in the rain forest or the desert? Why would it have different adaptations? An organism's environment includes all of the living things in its surroundings. It also includes the nonliving things such as water, sunlight, and soil. For example, kangaroo rats live in the deserts where there is little water. On hot days, they remain in their burrows where the air is moist. Kangaroo rats also have body adaptations that prevent water loss. They are able to change the dry seeds they eat into water. These mammals neither sweat nor pant as other animals do to keep cool, and their kidneys are adapted so that they rid their bodies of waste with little loss of water. These are all adaptations the kangaroo rat has to its particular surroundings. Some organisms such as the duck in **Figure 22-4** can move to find a suitable environment.

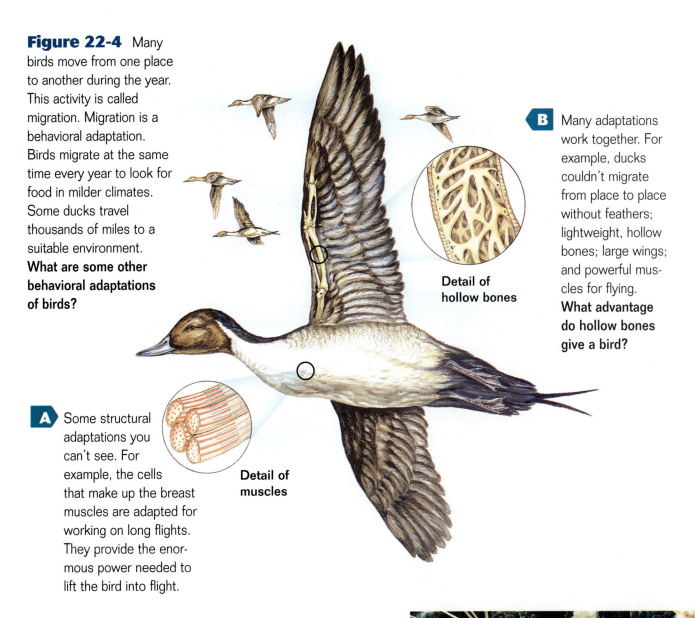

Figure 22-4 Many birds move from one place to another during the year. This activity is called migration. Migration is a behavioral adaptation. Birds migrate at the same time every year to look for food in milder climates. Some ducks travel thousands of miles to a suitable environment. **What are some other behavioral adaptations of birds?**

B Many adaptations work together. For example, ducks couldn't migrate from place to place without feathers; lightweight, hollow bones; large wings; and powerful muscles for flying. **What advantage do hollow bones give a bird?**

Detail of hollow bones

A Some structural adaptations you can't see. For example, the cells that make up the breast muscles are adapted for working on long flights. They provide the enormous power needed to lift the bird into flight.

Detail of muscles

Figure 22-5 shows a close-up view of an adaptation of a cactus plant. Cacti live in desert environments where water is in short supply. Thick, waxy coatings on the stems of cactus plants help prevent the cactus from drying up. This is an adaptation for conserving water.

Animals in the Arctic

In the Arctic, the ground is covered with snow and ice for months. For several weeks each winter, the sun never even rises above the horizon. Large areas of ice melt with the arrival of spring and summer, but the ground never thaws. Animals that live here are adapted for this harsh, cold climate of the Arctic.

Figure 22-5 A waxy outer layer and sharp spines are protective adaptations for cacti and many other plants.

Mini Lab

Identifying Adaptations of Fish

Procedure

1. Obtain a set of four adaptation cards from your teacher.
2. Look at the cards. On a sheet of paper, draw a picture of a fish that matches the features given to you.
3. On a separate sheet of paper, draw the type of environment your fish could survive in.

Analysis

1. Describe the adaptations of your fish.
2. Explain how the adaptations of your fish make it well suited to its environment.

Figure 22-6 Polar bears are efficient swimmers. They have been spotted more than 100 km from the closest land. **How can polar bears survive in such cold water?**

The thick, white hair of the polar bear, shown in **Figure 22-6,** not only helps it blend into its icy, snowy surroundings, it also protects it against the cold. Its hair is both hollow and transparent. The air inside the hair helps the bears float in the ice water and provides insulation against the cold air. Such hair acts as a greenhouse. It allows the limited heat from the sunlight to pass through the hair, where it is taken in by the polar bear's black skin and trapped by its fur. Polar bears also have hair on the bottoms of their feet for added warmth.

Sea otters and seals have fur so thick that the cold arctic water never even touches their skin. As seen in **Figure 22-7,** musk oxen have hair on the neck, chest, and rump that may be 0.6 m to 1 m long. This long hair protects them against the cold temperatures of the arctic winter, in addition to protecting them against the mosquitoes that are abundant in the Arctic in the summer.

Figure 22-7 Musk oxen are named for the musk glands located under their eyes. When attacked, they rub the gland on their legs. This releases an unpleasant odor that discourages many enemies from approaching.

*inter*NET
CONNECTION

Visit the Glencoe Science Web Site at **www.glencoe.com/ sec/science/ca** for more information about polar bears.

Organisms are adapted for the environments they live in. What is your environment? Can you name some adaptations of native plants and animals in your area that help them to survive and carry out their life processes? In the next section, you will learn how organisms have changed through time.

Section Assessment

1. Define the term *biodiversity*.
2. Explain why tropical rain forests have high biodiversity.
3. What are adaptations? Give an example of one.
4. **Think Critically:** What adaptations would an animal living in a desert need to survive?
5. **Skill Builder**
   Observing and Inferring Think of an organism, not a pet, that is familiar to you. Make a list of its traits. Next to each trait, describe how it helps the organism survive in its environment. If you need help, refer to Observing and Inferring in the **Skill Handbook** on page 992.

Using Math

Scientists have identified and named approximately 1 032 000 different species of animals. If 751 000 of these are insects, what percentage do insects make up in the total animal population? Show all of your work.

Using Field Guides

A bird with a red head and black wings (right) lands on a tree. It hammers into the bark with its beak. You're pretty sure it's a woodpecker, but what kind?

One place to find out is a field guide, such as the *National Geographic Society Field Guide to the Birds of North America*. Field guides are handbooks that help identify living things, from mushrooms to mammals. They contain descriptions and photographs or illustrations, as well as information about where organisms live. Field guides are useful tools for making sense of the often-bewildering diversity of life on Earth.

Some field guides are organized around easily identifiable characteristics, such as shape or color. A field guide to flowers might group yellow flowers in one section, red in another, and so on. Other guides group together species that may look different but belong to the same scientific family.

Using field guides is a bit like detective work. You follow clues, gradually narrowing your search until you can finally answer the question: "What *is* that?"

Red-headed Woodpecker
(*Melanerpes erythrocephalus*)

Description: L 9¼" (24 cm) Entire head, neck, and throat are bright red in adults, contrasting with blue-black back and snowy-white underparts. Juvenile is brownish; acquires red head during gradual winter molt. Look for distinctive white inner wing patches and white rump.
Call: A loud *queark*.
Habitat: Inhabits open woods, farmlands, bottomlands, parks, backyards. Forages on tree trunks and on the ground for insects, berries, acorns; occasionally seen catching flies.
Nesting: Bores nest holes in dead trees, fence posts, telephone poles.
Range: The Red-headed Woodpecker has become rare in the northeast, partly due to habitat loss and competition for nest holes. Somewhat more numerous in the rest of their range. In map above, orange shows year-round range, green the breeding range.

Science JOURNAL

Spend 15 minutes observing nature. Describe five plants or animals you see. Make sketches and note colors, shapes, and sizes. Then, using field guides, try to identify the organisms on your list. If you have a beetle on your list, good luck —there are nearly 300 000 different kinds!

Unity of Life

Why are they like that?

You probably would never confuse an eagle with a humming-bird. Both have wings, beaks, feathers, and other familiar features of birds, but they are different in size, shape, and where they live. On the other hand, you might have trouble recognizing different kinds of birds unless you were an experienced bird-watcher. Many groups of birds look alike. Why are some groups more similar than others? How do new types form? Through the study of living and once-living organisms, scientists try to find the answers.

Organisms are adapted to the environments in which they live. How do these adaptations happen? Individual organisms are not identical to each other, even if they belong to the same group, as illustrated in **Figure 22-8.** In every group, variations, or differences, occur in the traits of that group.

A Mallard duck

B Wood duck

Figure 22-8 Only an experienced bird-watcher may be able to recognize all three types of birds as ducks, especially if they are in flight.

C Northern pintail duck

Adaptation Through Natural Selection

In a population of gray squirrels, for example, individuals may have slightly different colors of fur. Most will have brown-gray fur color. A few will have dark fur, and some will have light fur.

Now, imagine this same population of squirrels in an environment that changed. Suppose the environment changed so that squirrels with dark fur are better able to survive than squirrels with a lighter fur color because predators are not able to see squirrels with darker fur as easily. Dark squirrels would be better off in this environment. They would be more likely to survive and have offspring, as shown in **Figure 22-9.** This process, in which organisms with characteristics best suited for the environment survive, reproduce, and pass these traits to their offspring, is called **natural selection.**

Now, think about the process of natural selection happening over many, many years. With each generation, more and more dark squirrels will survive and pass their coat color on to their offspring. Squirrels with lighter fur don't survive and so produce fewer offspring. The population changes. Every generation, the population consists of more dark squirrels than the one before it. This process of natural selection is the main way changes happen in a population.

VISUALIZING Natural Selection

Figure 22-9 A population of squirrels can change through natural selection.

A In all species, individual organisms within a population have differences, or variations.

B In this population, some squirrels may be alert and hide more quickly when predators come near.

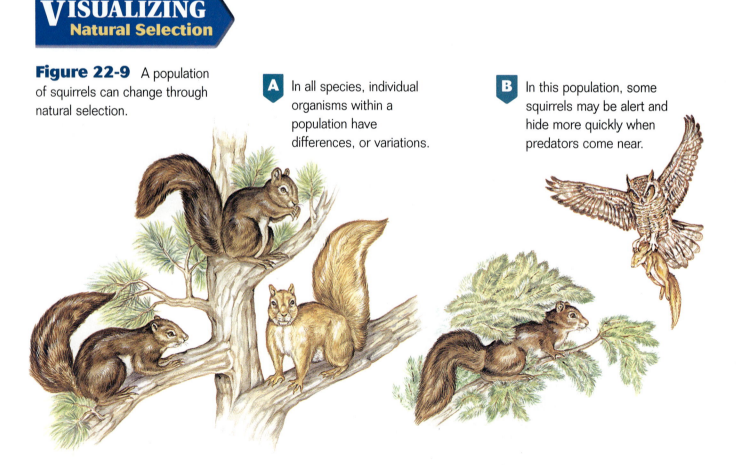

Natural selection can explain why polar bears are white, why some other bears are brown, and why some insects that live in the leaves of a tree are green. Think of how the snowy owl came to look the way it does. Individuals with traits most favorable for a specific environment survive and pass on these traits to their offspring. Natural selection, therefore, means that organisms with traits best suited to their environments are more likely to survive. The four general principles involved in natural selection are listed in **Table 22-1.**

Table 22-1

Principles of Natural Selection

1. Organisms produce more offspring than can survive.

2. Variations are found among individuals of a group of organisms.

3. Some variations make it possible for members of a population to survive and reproduce more successfully.

4. Over time, offspring of individuals with helpful variations make up more and more of a population.

C Organisms that survive reproduce and pass on their traits.

D There is still variation, but the population has a higher percentage of individuals with beneficial variations.

The Origin of New Species

If you've ever watched nature programs showing lions and tigers in the wild, you've seen the animals hunting, washing themselves, and caring for their young. You may have seen these same behaviors in a house cat. Maybe you've also noticed that all types of cats—lions, tigers, bobcats, and others—have similar features. How did the various species of cats form, and why do they share so many features?

Scientists define a species as a group of organisms that look alike and reproduce. One way a new species can form is if a large population of organisms becomes separated into smaller populations. They no longer breed with others of their kind. A barrier, such as a mountain range or river, can cause this separation. **Figure 22-10** shows an example. ☑

A New Species Develops

Let's look at a population of lizards. Suppose a river divides the whole population into two smaller populations. Lizards in one group can no longer mate with lizards in the other groups. They can mate only among themselves. Over time, each small population will adapt to its own environment. Because each environment is a little bit different, each small population will develop different adaptations. Over time, the populations may become so different from each other that offspring couldn't be produced even if the lizards could again mate with one another. Each small population of lizards has become a new species. Because the different species of lizards

Reading Check ☑
What is a species?

Figure 22-10 One way new species form is for a population to be separated. **What other factors could contribute to forming new species?**

A The members of this population of lizards all look alike and are able to interbreed.

in this example all arose from one population, we can say that they share a **common ancestor** (AN ses tur). Each of the new lizard species now has its own specific traits. But, all the species share some traits that they inherited from their common ancestor.

Evidence for Change over Time

It is not always possible to see everything you'd like to study. Objects may be too tiny or too far away for you to see. Processes may happen too quickly or too slowly for us to observe. That's the problem with natural selection. It occurs in all species, but it usually occurs so slowly that it's not possible to see the process in action. How can scientists be sure that species have changed over time? They rely on several types of evidence. They compare physical traits of species that are similar. They study the DNA and proteins of species for clues to how closely they are related. They look at fossils. Now, you can take a closer look at each of these types.

CHEMISTRY
INTEGRATION

DNA
The DNA molecule is made up of five common elements: hydrogen, oxygen, carbon, nitrogen, and phosphorus. These elements are combined in different chemical groups and arranged in two chains. These chains twist around each other in a double spiral, like a twisted ladder. What words do the letters "DNA" represent?

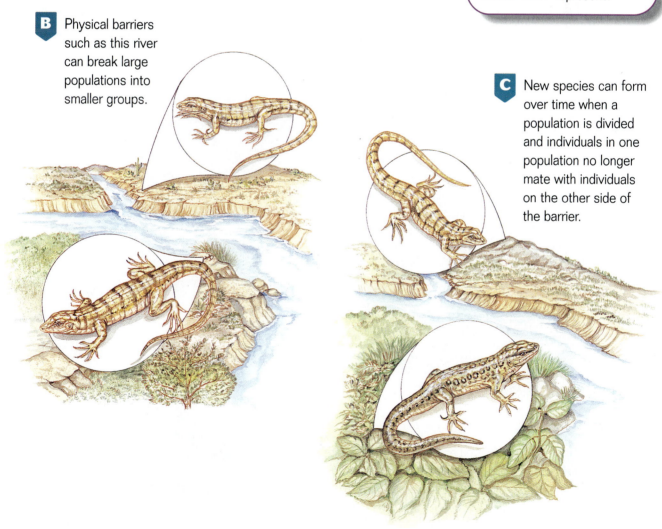

B Physical barriers such as this river can break large populations into smaller groups.

C New species can form over time when a population is divided and individuals in one population no longer mate with individuals on the other side of the barrier.

Modeling a Fossil

Procedure

1. A mold fossil is formed when an organism leaves an impression in clay or mud. When the mold is later filled in, a cast fossil can be formed.

2. To make a model of a fossil, pour plaster of paris into the milk container until it is half full.

3. When the plaster begins to thicken, use a small paintbrush and vegetable oil to coat some small objects and press them into the plaster.

4. After the plaster has hardened, remove the objects. You have now made a mold.

5. Next, paint the entire layer of hard plaster with a generous coating of vegetable oil. Pour another layer of colored plaster to fill in the mold.

6. After the plaster hardens, tear away the milk container. Use a butter knife or putty knife to carefully pry apart the two layers of plaster. The colored layer shows your cast.

Analysis

Which fossil showed the most details of the objects you used, the mold or the cast?

Fossils Show Change over Time

Although dinosaurs have been extinct for millions of years, they come to life in the movies. Do you think those giant, roaring creatures on screen are anything like real dinosaurs were? How do scientists and the movie producers know how dinosaurs looked and acted? Scientists have learned a lot about the ancient reptiles by studying their fossils. **Fossils** are the remains or traces of ancient life.

Fossils give scientists the most direct evidence that species change over time. For example, fossils of trilobites (TRI luh bites) show that change occurred in their structure over time, as illustrated in **Figure 22-11**. Trilobites are extinct relatives of animals you know today such as lobsters, crabs, and insects. Early trilobites had generalized body structures with few segments. Fossils of later trilobites show many differences in shape. Through the study of fossils, scientists have shown that trilobites changed over time.

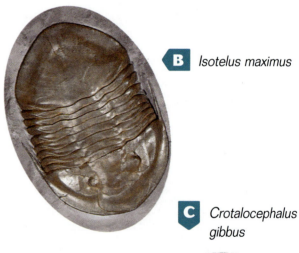

B *Isotelus maximus*

A *Modocia typicales*

C *Crotalocephalus gibbus*

Figure 22-11 Trilobites changed over time. *Modocia typicales* (A) lived around 500 million years ago. *Isotelus maximus* existed about 450 million years ago, and *Crotalocephalus gibbus* (C) were on Earth around 400 million years ago.

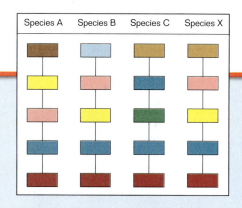

Figure 22-12 Timber wolves and dogs such as this Alaskan husky are closely related. **What physical similarities can you see between these two animals?**

DNA Shows Relationships

Appearances can trick you. Some species such as the wolf and dog in **Figure 22-12** look a lot alike but aren't closely related. Scientists need something besides physical appearance to help them find out how closely related species are. DNA determines the traits of organisms. The more similar the DNAs of two species are, the more closely they are related. For example, in comparing the DNA of modern breeds of dogs, wolves, and foxes, the gray wolf was found to be the closest relative of the domestic dog.

Problem Solving

Comparing Protein Sequences

DNA can be used to show how organisms are related. Scientists also use other chemicals found in living things to show how closely related two species are. One type of chemical they study is protein. Proteins perform a variety of jobs in living things. Some are used in the building of living material, such as bones, muscles, and skin. Others help living things grow, digest foods, and fight diseases. Scientists can learn about the relationships between species by studying the structure of proteins. Each protein is made of building blocks put together in a specific order. In closely related species, similar proteins have a similar order of building blocks. In species that are more distantly related, the same proteins have different arrangements of building blocks.

The illustration shows the structure of a type of protein used in digestion found in three unknown bird species (Species A, Species B, and Species C) and in a known bird species (Species X). The colored blocks represent the building blocks of the digestive protein. Compare the structure of the proteins in all four species.

Think Critically: Which bird species (A, B, C) do you think is most closely related to Species X? Why did you reach your decision?

Anatomy and Ancestry

If you were a biologist studying the many species of cichlid (SIH klud) fish in Africa's Lake Victoria, you would see differences in the jaws and teeth of these fish. You also would see differences in their color. Some of these differences are shown in **Figure 22-13.** Some species have small mouths and sharp teeth for eating insects. Others have mouths adapted for scraping algae. Still others are adapted for eating the scales of other fish. However, despite the differences, all 170 species of cichlids in the lake have many more things in common.

Scientists compare similarities and differences in the body structures of all living things. This gives them clues to how species may have changed over time. After comparing the

Figure 22-13 All the fish below are ciclids. The differences in the head shapes of these fish allow them to eat different things and feed in different ways. Two species may feed on insects but do so in different ways.

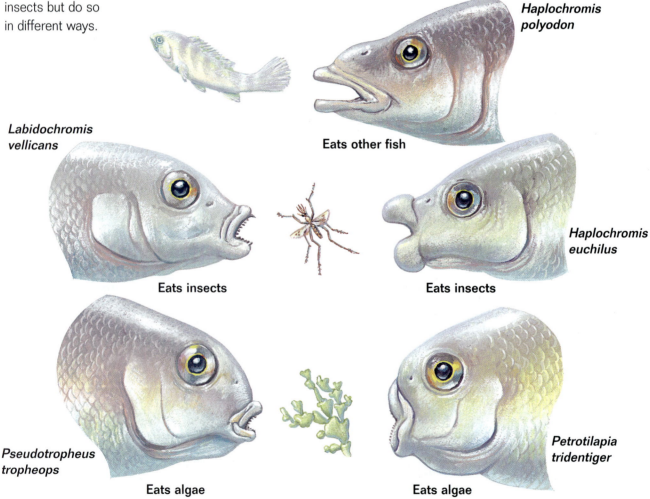

Haplochromis polyodon

Eats other fish

Labidochromis vellicans

Eats insects

Haplochromis euchilus

Eats insects

Pseudotropheus tropheops

Eats algae

Petrotilapia tridentiger

Eats algae

anatomy of many species, scientists conclude that all species may have come from a common ancestor.

Another example of similarities in anatomy between two organisms is seen in **Figure 22-14.** Do you see these similarities? If you said yes, then you made the type of observation that scientists use to find relationships among organisms. Scientists view these similarities as evidence that two populations of organisms developed from a common ancestor.

Figure 22-14
Archaeopteryx (A) has many similarities to *Ornitholestes* (B), a small dinosaur. *Archaeopteryx* is considered a close relative of the ancestor of modern birds. **What do the similarities between these two organisms tell you about the probable ancestor of *Archaeopteryx*?**

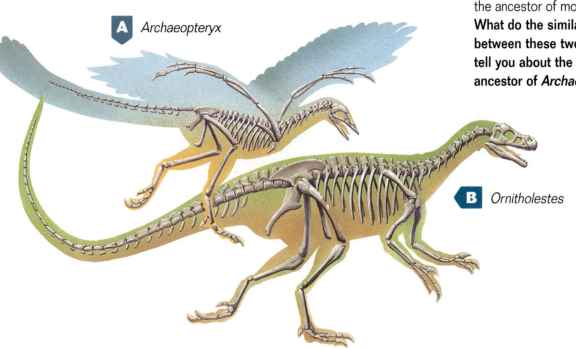

A *Archaeopteryx*

B *Ornitholestes*

Section Assessment

1. Explain natural selection. What are the four general principles involved in natural selection?

2. Briefly describe how natural selection plays a role in how species adapt to the environment.

3. What is a common ancestor?

4. **Think Critically:** Explain how fossils can show that species change over time.

5.  **Skill Builder**
   Concept Mapping Make an events chain concept map that describes how camouflage adaptations may arise in a population of birds. If you need help, refer to Concept Mapping in the **Skill Handbook** on page 986.

Science Journal
Some scientists hypothesize that dinosaurs and birds are closely related. Imagine you are a scientist who wants to examine this hypothesis. In your Science Journal, describe methods you would use to investigate the relationship between dinosaurs and birds.

Simulating Selection

Natural selection causes a population to change. In this activity, you will design an experiment to discover how camouflage adaptations—those adaptations that allow organisms to blend into the environment—happen through natural selection.

Possible Materials

- Bag of small-sized jelly beans in assorted colors (approximately 100 beans)
- Meterstick
- Paper
- Pencil
- Green rug or another solid-colored rug
- Watch with second hand

Recognize the Problem

How does natural selection work?

Form a Hypothesis

Any body shape, structure, or coloration of an organism that helps it blend in with its surroundings is a camouflage adaptation. Make a hypothesis about how natural selection can explain camouflage adaptations.

Goals

- **Model** natural selection in a population of insects.
- **Explain** how natural selection produces camouflage adaptations.

Safety Precautions

Do not eat any jelly beans used in this activity.

Test Your Hypothesis

Plan

1. With a partner, **discuss** the process of natural selection. How does natural selection cause species to change?

2. In this activity, one student will play the role of the bird that eats insects (jelly beans) that live in grass. With your partner, think about how you can model natural selection.

3. With your partner, **make a list** of the different steps you might take to model natural selection.

4. You might start the experiment with a particular insect population. How many insects (jelly beans) will be in your starting population? How will you show variation in your starting population?

5. Think about how many generations of insects you will use in the experiment.

6. What data will you collect? Will you need a data table for this experiment? If so, **design a table** in your Science Journal for recording data.

7. Decide what happens to individual organisms if they have favorable variations for a particular environment? What happens if an organism has unfavorable variations? Think about these questions when designing your experiment.

8. **Review** your list of steps to make sure that the experiment makes sense and that all of the steps are in logical order.

Do

1. Make sure that your teacher approves your plan before you proceed.

2. Carry out the experiment as planned.

3. While doing the experiment, **record** your observations and **complete** your data table in your Science Journal.

Analyze Your Data

1. **Observe** which types of insects the bird in your experiment was able to locate most quickly. Why?

Draw Conclusions

1. Did your population of insects change over time? **Explain** your answer.

2. How can your experiment be used to **explain** camouflage adaptations in organisms?

A Trip Through Geologic Time

Have you ever seen a movie or read a book about time travel? What if you could travel back in time into Earth's past? What kinds of interesting plants and animals would you see? Time travel will always be science fiction rather than science fact. But, in a way, scientists can travel back through time by studying fossils. Fossils are evidence of ancient life. Fossils help scientists form a picture of the past. They provide a history for life on Earth. Let's go along on the journey through Earth's history.

The Fossil Record

Earth's rocky crust is a vast graveyard that contains the fossil remains of species that have lived throughout Earth's history. Large fossils are carefully removed from the ground as shown in **Figure 22-15.** All of the fossils that scientists have recovered from the ground make up the **fossil record.** The fossil record for life on Earth is a rich one. Fossils from almost every major group of plants and animals are part of the fossil record.

However, the fossil record doesn't show a complete history. Not every species is represented in the fossil record. It is much more common for an organism to decay without ever becoming a fossil.

Figure 22-15 These men (A) are carefully uncovering a *Hadrosaur* fossil at an excavation site on a Navajo reservation. Fossils give scientists information that can be used to make models of dinosaurs, such as this *Hadrosaur* (B).

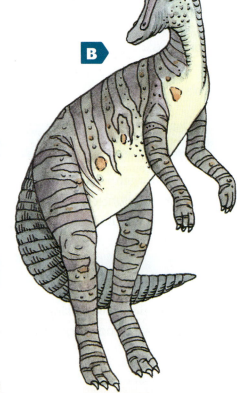

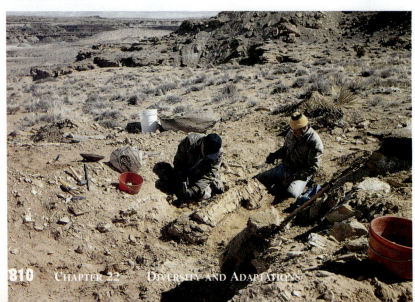

Geologic Time Scale

By studying the fossil record, scientists have put together a sort of diary for life on Earth called the **geologic time scale.** The geologic time scale helps scientists keep track of when a species appeared on Earth or when it disappeared from Earth.

You can see the geologic time scale in **Table 22-2.** As you can see, the geologic time scale is divided into four large periods of time called eras, and each era is subdivided into periods. The beginning or end of each time period marks an important event in Earth's history, such as the appearance or disappearance of a group of organisms. The fossil record of life on Earth gives scientists strong evidence that life has changed over time. ✔

EARTH SCIENCE
◀ INTEGRATION

Reading Check ✔

How many eras are included in the geologic time scale?

Table 22-2

Geologic Time Scale				
Era	**Period**	**Million years ago**	**Major evolutionary events**	**Representative organisms**
Cenozoic	Quaternary	1.6	First humans	
Cenozoic	Tertiary	66.4		
Mesozoic	Cretaceous	146	Large dinosaurs First flowering plants	
Mesozoic	Jurassic	208	First birds First mammals	
Mesozoic	Triassic	245		
Paleozoic	Permian	290		
Paleozoic	Pennsylvanian	323	First conifer trees; first reptiles and insects	
Paleozoic	Mississippian	362		
Paleozoic	Devonian	408	First amphibians and land plants; first bony fish	
Paleozoic	Silurian	439	First fish with jaws	
Paleozoic	Ordovician	510	First vertebrates, armored fish without jaws	
Paleozoic	Cambrian	540	Simple invertebrates	
	Precambrian		First fossilized animals and plants; protozoa, sponges, coral and algae	
			First fossil bacteria	
		4000		

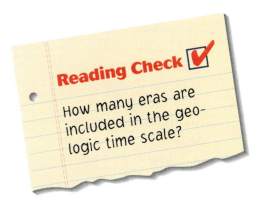

Compsognathus, a meateater, was one of the smallest dinosaurs at 60 cm long. *Sauropods* were the biggest dinosaurs at 40 m long. How many times longer was a *Sauropod* than a *Compsognathus*?

Extinction of Species

Why don't you see dinosaurs at the zoo? These large reptiles ruled Earth for more than 100 million years, but they're all gone now. Among the dinosaurs were the largest land animals, such as the plant-eating *Brachiosaurus* and the meateating *Tyrannosaurus rex*. Yet, despite the great success and long history of the dinosaurs, all of them became extinct about 66 million years ago. So did many other land and sea animals.

Scientists aren't surprised that dinosaurs are now extinct. That's because about 99 percent of all species that have ever existed are now extinct. Usually, extinction is a natural event. Earth's environments are constantly changing. When a species can't adapt to changes in its environment, it becomes extinct.

Figure 22-16 The second-largest mass extinction event in Earth's history occurred 66 million years ago at the end of the Cretaceous period. One half of all living things—including many dinosaurs— became extinct around this time.

Mass Extinctions

The extinction event that killed the dinosaurs around 66 million years ago was a mass extinction. A **mass extinction** is a large-scale disappearance of many species within a short time.

The extinction of the dinosaurs was not the only mass extinction event in Earth's history. Other large extinctions have occurred. The most severe mass extinction happened about 245 million years ago. Scientists estimate that nearly 96 percent of all animal species became extinct at this time. Most were animals without backbones, such as clams, jellyfish, sponges, and trilobites. Most fish and land species survived.

What causes mass extinctions? Scientists are not sure about the exact causes of all the mass extinctions. One idea that has been hypothesized for the extinction of the dinosaurs is that large asteroids slammed into Earth. According to this hypothesis, the collision sent huge clouds of dust into the atmosphere. Over time, the clouds blocked out sunlight. The result would have been a cooling of the environment. Over a brief period of time, species of dinosaurs and other organisms probably would not have been able to adapt quickly enough to survive.

Loss of Biodiversity

Mass extinctions are not just a part of the past. Extinctions also have been occurring within the last few thousand years. For instance, large mammals such as mammoths and mastodons, shown in **Figure 22-17,** disappeared from North America about the time the first humans appeared here.

Today, scientists are discovering that human activity is rapidly causing more species to become extinct. Humans use large areas of land for many reasons. Some of these uses are changing or limiting the habitat for many organisms. The tropical rain forests, where biodiversity is high, are in the greatest danger from changes from humans. Many rain forest species have not yet been discovered or named. If these species are lost, people may lose possible sources of food or new medicines.

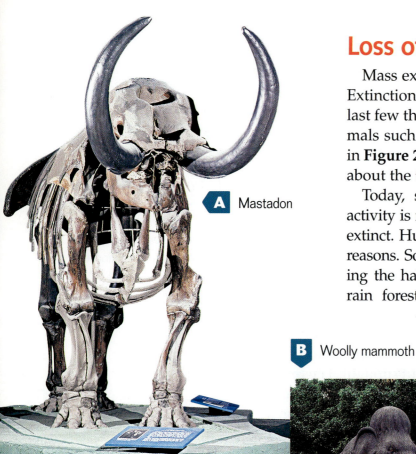

A Mastadon

B Woolly mammoth

Figure 22-17 Many organisms, such as the mastodon and the mammoth, disappeared from Earth for reasons not completely understood.

Section Assessment

1. What is the fossil record?
2. What is the geologic time scale?
3. What is a mass extinction? Give an example.
4. **Think Critically:** How might the extinction of a single plant species from a forest affect other organisms that live there?
5. **Skill Builder**
   Recognizing Cause and Effect Have you ever wondered why something happened? Do the **Chapter 22 Skill Activity** on page 1015 to look for possible cause-and-effect relationships.

Using Math

The Precambrian era represents about 4.1 billion years of Earth's 4.6-billion-year history. What percent of the total does this represent?

Dinosaur Size

Fossils can be used to estimate the size of a dinosaur. The models made from fossil observations also can be used to estimate dinosaur size.

What You'll Investigate

How can you estimate the mass of a dinosaur?

Goals

- **Estimate** the mass of a dinosaur using a model.

Procedure

1. **Make a data table** in your Science Journal. Include type of dinosaur, its scale, and volume of water displaced in your table.

2. Obtain a plastic dinosaur model. Fill in your data table. A good scale to use is a 1:40 scale, meaning that each dimension of the model—length, width, and height—is 1/40 of the dinosaur's actual size.

3. Almost **fill** the pail with water. Carefully place the pail in the utility pan. Fill the pail to the brim, taking care not to let any water spill over into the utility pan. **CAUTION:** *Clean up water spills immediately.*

4. **Submerge** the dinosaur model in the water, allowing the water to flow out of the pail and into the utility pan.

5. Carefully remove the pail from the utility pan.

6. Pour the water from the utility pan into a graduated cylinder. The volume of the water displaced is equal to the volume of the dinosaur model.

7. **Record** your measurement in your data table.

8. To find the mass of the actual dinosaur in grams, multiply the volume of the model by the cube of the scale. If the scale is 1:40 and the model has a volume of 10 mL, you would multiply 10×40^3 ($10 \times 40 \times 40 \times 40$). To find the mass in kilograms, divide by 1000.

Materials

- Plastic dinosaur model
- Plastic graduated cylinder
- Marking pen
- Calculator
- Water
- Small pail
- Utility pan

Conclude and Apply

1. Assuming that the density of a live dinosaur is similar to that of water, **estimate** the mass of your dinosaur in kilograms.

2. Male Indian elephants have a mass of about 5500 kg. What can you **infer** about the approximate size of some dinosaurs?

For a **preview** of this chapter, study this Reviewing Main Ideas before you read the chapter. After you have studied this chapter, you can use the Reviewing Main Ideas to **review** the chapter.

The Glencoe MindJogger, Audiocassettes, and CD-ROM provide additional opportunities for review.

Section

22-1 DIVERSITY OF LIFE

Biodiversity is the measure of the number of different species in an area. This term is used to describe the variety of plants, animals, and other species. Biodiversity changes and is dependent upon the environment. *Why do tropical rain forests have high biodiversity?*

ADAPTATION

An **adaptation** is any structure or behavior that helps a species survive in its environment. Some adaptations involve physical features, such as body shape and color. Others involve behaviors such as animals being able to migrate. *What are some adaptations of fish?*

Reading Check ✔

Predict an adaptation that animals living in urban areas might develop over the next century.

Section 22-2 UNITY OF LIFE

Natural selection is a process in which organisms with characteristics best suited for the environment survive, reproduce, and pass these traits to their offspring. Such a process cannot be directly observed. Evidence for this change over time includes **fossils,** DNA, and similarities in anatomy. *How are similarities in anatomy and ancestry thought to be related?*

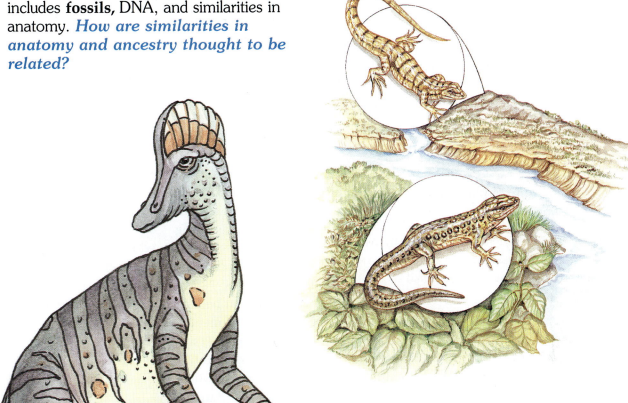

Section 22-3 HISTORY OF LIFE

The **geologic time scale** shows when species appeared and disappeared during Earth's history. The geologic time scale is divided into four large intervals of time called eras, and each era is subdivided into periods. *When were the dinosaurs the dominant land animals on Earth?*

Chapter 22 Assessment

Using Vocabulary

a. adaptation
b. biodiversity
c. common ancestor
d. fossil
e. fossil record
f. geologic time scale
g. mass extinction
h. natural selection

Match each phrase with the correct term from the list of Vocabulary words.

1. traces or remains of ancient life
2. numbers of different species in an area
3. mechanism for species' change over time
4. dolphin's flipper or a bird's wing
5. diary of life on Earth

Checking Concepts

Choose the word or phrase that best answers the question.

6. What is the disappearance of many species in a short time called?
   A) natural selection
   B) adaptation
   C) fossil
   D) mass extinction

7. What is the hollow hair on a polar bear an example of?
   A) fossil formation
   B) an adaptation
   C) biodiversity
   D) mass extinction

8. What are dinosaur bones examples of?
   A) species
   B) adaptations
   C) fossils
   D) biodiversity

9. Which of the following can form new species when split into smaller groups?
   A) fossils
   B) adaptations
   C) populations
   D) biodiversity

10. Species adapt to the environment through the processes of mutation and which of the following?
    A) natural selection
    B) biodiversity
    C) mass extinction
    D) fossil formation

11. Which of the following rabbits will best survive in the Arctic during winter?
    A) a brown rabbit
    B) a black rabbit
    C) a white rabbit
    D) a black-and-white rabbit

12. What is the most direct evidence that species change over time?
    A) similar anatomies
    B) DNA
    C) fossils
    D) mass extinctions

13. About what percent of all species that have ever existed are now extinct?
    A) 25 percent
    B) 50 percent
    C) 75 percent
    D) 99 percent

14. Which of the following organisms adapted to their environment?
    A) ones that are extinct
    B) ones that are not reproducing
    C) ones that are surviving and reproducing
    D) those that formed fossils

15. Which of the following terms describes any body shape, body process, or behavior that helps an organism survive in its environment?
    A) biodiversity
    B) extinction
    C) mass extinction
    D) adaptation

Thinking Critically

16. Which of the following variations would be most beneficial to a bird living in a wetland: webbed feet, clawed feet, feet with toes for gripping branches? Explain.

17. If a scientist had DNA samples from four organisms, how could he find out which organisms were related?

18. What types of adaptations would be beneficial to an organism living in the desert?

19. Use the idea of natural selection to explain why polar bears are white and why some other bears are brown.

20. Horseshoe crabs are an example of an organism that has changed very little through time. What factors might have kept these organisms from changing?

Developing Skills

If you need help, refer to the Skill Handbook.

21. Observing and Inferring: Look at the graph below. Scientists hypothesize that millions more microscopic species exist than we now know. Why do you think the number of microscopic species known to science is so low?

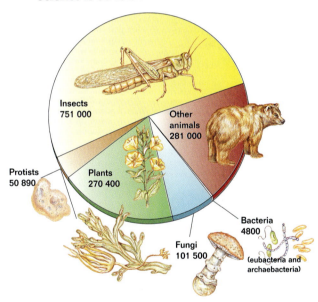

Insects 751 000

Other animals 281 000

Protists 50 890

Plants 270 400

Bacteria 4800

Fungi 101 500

(eubacteria and archaebacteria)

22. Recognizing Cause and Effect: A new predator is introduced into a population of rabbits. Rabbits with longer back legs have an advantage because they can run faster. Using the concept of natural selection, explain what might happen to the rabbit population over time.

23. Interpreting Illustrations: Study the geologic time scale on page 811. Make a table that lists when the following groups of organisms appeared on Earth: amphibians, fish, land plants, mammals, reptiles, birds, and simple animals.

Test-Taking Tip

Don't Be Afraid to Ask for Help Ask for advice on things you don't understand. If you're practicing for a test and you find yourself stuck, unable to understand why you got a question wrong, or unable to do it in the first place, ask for help.

Test Practice

Use these questions to test your Science Proficiency.

1. Why do tropical rain forests have a large number of animal species?
   A) Temperatures remain warm and steady all year and rainfall is high.
   B) Temperatures fluctuate greatly and rainfall is high.
   C) Temperatures remain warm all year and rainfall is low.
   D) Temperatures remain cool and steady all year and rainfall is high.

2. Fossils enable scientists to study how species have changed over time. Which of the following statements about the fossil record is true?
   A) The fossil record shows a complete history of Earth.
   B) A fossil represents every species on Earth.
   C) It is more common for an organism to decay without ever becoming a fossil.
   D) Fossils from almost every major group of plants and animals are part of the fossil record.

Life and the Environment

Chapter Preview

Skills Preview

Skill Builders
• Classify

Activities
• Graph

MiniLabs
• Infer

Reading Check ✔

Define several terms that begin with the prefix *a* (meaning "without"), such as *abiotic*.

Explore Activity

Mountain goats rely on winter winds to uncover food plants buried beneath the snow. Surefooted and strong, they scale high cliffs to get their next meal. A mountain goat's range consists of high terrain where few other animals dare to tread. This reduces competition from different organisms for food. How does the number of related organisms in an area affect each individual? You share your science classroom with other students. How much space is available to each student?

Measure Space

1. Use a meterstick to measure the length and width of the classroom.

2. Multiply the length times the width to find the area of the room in square meters.

3. Count the number of individuals in your class. Divide the number of square meters in the classroom by the number of individuals.

Science Journal

In your Science Journal, record how much space each person has. Determine the amount of space each person would have if the number of individuals in your class doubled. Predict how having that amount of space would affect you and your classmates.

The Living and Nonliving Environment

The Biosphere

Think of all the organisms on Earth. Millions of species exist. Where do all these organisms live? Living things can be found 11 000 m below the surface of the ocean and on tops of mountains 9000 m high. The part of Earth that supports organisms is known as the **biosphere** (BI uh sfihr). The biosphere seems huge, but it is actually only a small portion of Earth. The biosphere includes the topmost portion of Earth's crust, all the waters that cover Earth's surface, and the surrounding atmosphere. Overall though, the thickness could be compared to the thickness of the skin of an apple.

Within the biosphere, many different environments can be found. For example, red-tailed hawks are found in environments where tall trees live near open grassland. The hawks nest high in the trees and soar over the land in search of rodents and rabbits to eat. In environments with plenty of moisture, such as the banks of streams, willow trees provide food and shelter for birds, mammals, and insects. All organisms interact

Figure 23-1 The biosphere is the region of Earth that contains all living organisms. An ecologist is a scientist who studies relationships among organisms and between organisms and the physical features of the biosphere.

with the environment. The science of **ecology** is the study of the interactions that take place among organisms and between organisms and the physical features of the environment. Ecologists, such as the one in **Figure 23-1,** are the scientists who study interactions between organisms and the environment.

Abiotic Factors

A forest environment is made up of trees, birds, insects, and other living things that depend on one another for food and shelter. But, these organisms also depend on factors that surround them such as soil, sunlight, water, temperature, and air. These factors—the nonliving, physical features of the environment—are called **abiotic factors.** Abiotic—*a* meaning "not" and *biotic* meaning "living"—factors have effects on living things and often determine the organisms that are able to live in a certain environment. Some abiotic factors are shown in **Figure 23-2.**

Figure 23-2 Abiotic factors help determine which species can survive in an area.

A **Soil**
Soil consists of minerals mixed with decaying, dead organisms. It contains both living and nonliving components.

B **Light**
Seasonal events, such as flowering in plants or migration of birds, are often triggered by a change in the number of hours of daylight.

C **Water**
Many organisms live in water, such as this lake in Pennsylvania, rather than air.

D **Temperature**
Temperatures change with daily and seasonal cycles. Desert-dwelling rattlesnakes, like this sidewinder in the Colorado desert, are active only in the cool, early morning hours. During the hottest part of the day, they rest in the shade.

Water

Water is an important abiotic factor. The bodies of most organisms are 50 to 95 percent water. Water is an important part of cytoplasm and the fluid that surrounds cells. Respiration, photosynthesis, digestion, and other important life processes can take place only in the presence of water.

Soil

The type of soil in a particular location helps determine which plants and other organisms live in that location. Most soil is a combination of sand, clay, and humus. Soil type is determined by the relative amounts of sand, clay, and humus in the soil. Humus is the decayed remains of dead organisms. The greater the humus content, the more fertile the soil.

Light and Temperature

The abiotic factors of light and temperature also impact the environment. Through the process of photosynthesis, the radiant energy of sunlight is transformed into chemical energy that drives virtually all of life's processes. The availability of sunlight is a major factor in determining where green plants and other photosynthetic organisms live, as shown in **Figure 23-3.** Sunlight does not penetrate far into deep water. Most green algae benefit from living near the surface. In a similar situation, because little sunlight reaches the shady darkness of the forest floor, plant growth there is limited.

Figure 23-3 Many wildflowers that live on the forest floor, such as these padres shooting stars and Johnny jump-ups, produce seeds early in the spring. At this time, they receive the maximum amount of sunlight. When the leaves are fully out on the trees, they receive little direct sun.

Biotic Factors

Abiotic factors do not provide everything an organism needs for survival. Mushrooms would not be able to grow without the decaying bodies of other organisms to feed on. Honeybees could not survive without pollen from flowers. Some species of owls and woodpeckers prefer to nest in the hollow trunks of dead trees. Organisms depend on other organisms for food, shelter, protection, or reproduction. Living or once-living organisms in the environment are called **biotic factors.**

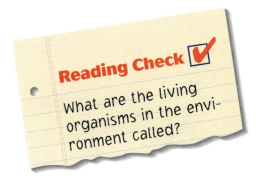

Reading Check ✓

What are the living organisms in the environment called?

Levels of Biological Organization

The living world is highly organized. Atoms are arranged into molecules, which are in turn organized into cells. Cells form tissues, tissues form organs, and organs form systems. Similarly, the biotic and abiotic factors studied by ecologists can be arranged into layers of organization, as shown in **Figure 23-4.**

Figure 23-4 The living world is organized into several levels.

Organism
An organism is a single individual from a population.

Population
A population is all of the individuals of one species that live and reproduce in the same area at the same time.

Community
A community is made up of populations of different species that interact in some way.

Ecosystem
An ecosystem consists of communities and the abiotic factors that affect them.

Biosphere
The biosphere is the highest level of biological organization. It is made up of all the ecosystems on Earth.

Figure 23-5 This coral reef is an example of an ecosystem. It is made up of hundreds of populations of organisms, as well as ocean water, sunlight, and other abiotic factors.

Populations

Individual organisms of the same species that live in the same place and can produce young form a **population.** Members of several populations on a coral reef are seen in **Figure 23-5.** Members of populations of organisms compete with each other for food, water, mates, and space. The resources of the environment and how the organisms use these resources determine how large a population can be.

Communities

Most populations of organisms do not live alone. They live and interact with populations of other organisms. Groups of populations that interact with each other in a given area form a **community.** Populations of organisms in a community depend on each other for food and shelter and for other needs.

Ecosystem

An **ecosystem** is made up of a biotic community and the abiotic factors that affect it. The rest of this chapter will discuss in more detail the kinds of interactions that take place between abiotic and biotic factors in an ecosystem.

Section Assessment

1. What is the difference between an abiotic factor and a biotic factor? Give at least five examples of each.

2. What is the difference between a population and a community? A community and an ecosystem?

3. **Think Critically:** Could oxygen in the atmosphere be considered an abiotic factor? Why or why not? What about carbon dioxide?

4. **Skill Builder**
   Observing and Inferring Each person lives in a population as part of a community. Describe your population and community. If you need help, refer to Observing and Inferring in the **Skill Handbook** on page 992.

Using Computers

Spreadsheet Obtain two months of temperature and rainfall data from your local newspaper or the Internet. Enter the data in a spreadsheet and then average the totals for temperature and the totals for rainfall. What kind of climate do you think you have based on your calculations? If you need help, refer to page 1010.

Soil Composition

Soil is more than minerals mixed with the decaying bodies of dead organisms. It contains other biotic and abiotic factors.

What You'll Investigate

What are the components of soil?

Goals

- **Determine** what factors are present in soil.

Materials

- Small paper cups containing freshly dug soil (3)
- Newspaper
- Beaker of water
- Hand lens
- Jar with lid
- Scale

Procedure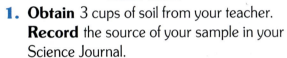

1. **Obtain** 3 cups of soil from your teacher. **Record** the source of your sample in your Science Journal.

2. **Pour** one of your samples onto the newspaper. **Sort** through the objects in the soil. Try to separate abiotic and biotic items. Use a hand lens to help identify the items. **Describe** your observations in your Science Journal.

3. Carefully place the second sample in the jar, disturbing it as little as possible. Quickly fill the jar with water and screw the lid on tightly. Without moving the jar, **observe** its contents for several minutes. **Record** your observations in your Science Journal.

4. **Weigh** the third sample. **Record** the weight in your Science Journal. Leave the sample undisturbed for several days, then weigh it again. **Record** the second weight in your Science Journal.

Conclude and Apply

1. Can you **infer** the presence of any organisms? Explain.

2. **Describe** the abiotic factors in your sample. What biotic factors did you **observe?**

3. Did you **record** any change in the soil weight over time? If so, why?

23•2 Interactions Among Living Organisms

What You'll Learn

▶ The characteristics of populations
▶ The types of relationships that occur among populations in a community
▶ The habitat and niche of a species in a community

Vocabulary
population density
limiting factor
carrying capacity
symbiosis
habitat
niche

Why It's Important

▶ You must directly or indirectly interact with other organisms to survive.

Characteristics of Populations

As shown in **Figure 23-6,** populations can be described by their characteristics. These include the size of the population, spacing (how the organisms are arranged in a given area), and density (how many individuals there are in a specific area). Suppose you spent several months observing a population of field mice living in a pasture. You would probably observe changes in the size of the population. Older mice die, baby mice are born, some are eaten by prey, and some mice wander away to new homes. The size of a population—the number of individual organisms it contains—is always changing, although some populations change more rapidly than others. In contrast to a mouse population, the number of pine trees in a forest changes fairly slowly, but a forest fire could quickly reduce the population of pine trees in the forest.

Figure 23-6 Populations have several characteristics that define them.

Each dot represents 1000 people

A Spacing
A characteristic of populations is spacing. In some populations, such as the oak trees of an oak-hickory forest, individuals are spaced fairly evenly throughout the area.

B Density
Human population density is higher in and around cities than in rural areas. **Which part of the United States has the highest population density?**

Population Density

At the beginning of this chapter, when you figured out how much space is available to each student in your classroom, you were measuring another population characteristic. The size of a population that occupies an area of limited size is called **population density.** The more individuals there are in a given amount of space, as seen in **Figure 23-7,** the more dense the population. For example, if 100 mice live in an area of a square kilometer, the population density is 100 mice per km^2.

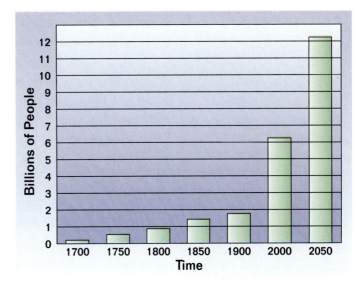

Figure 23-7 The size of the human population is increasing at a rate of about 1.6 percent per year. At the present time, it is about 6 billion. In 2050, the population will be about 12 billion.

Limiting Factors

Populations cannot continue to grow larger and larger forever. In any ecosystem, there are limits to the amount of food, water, living space, mates, nesting sites, and other resources available. A **limiting factor** is any biotic or abiotic factor that restricts the number of individuals in a population. A limiting factor can also indirectly affect other populations in the community. For example, a drought might restrict the growth of seed-producing plants in a forest clearing. Fewer plants means that food may become a limiting factor for a mouse population that feeds on the seeds. Food also may become a limiting factor for hawks and owls that feed on the mice, as well as for the deer in **Figure 23-8.**

Competition is the struggle among organisms to obtain the resources they need to survive and reproduce. As population density increases, so does competition among individuals.

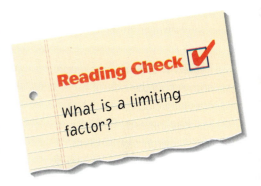

Reading Check

What is a limiting factor?

Figure 23-8 In many parts of the United States, deer populations, such as this one in northern Wisconsin, have become large enough to exceed the environment's ability to produce adequate food. Individuals starve or, weakened from lack of food, fall victim to disease.

Carrying Capacity

Suppose a population of robins continues to increase in size, year after year. At some point, food, nesting space, or other resources become so scarce that some individuals may not be able to survive or reproduce. When this happens, the environment has reached its carrying capacity, as seen in **Figure 23-9. Carrying capacity** is the largest number of individuals an environment can support and maintain for a long period of time. If a population begins to exceed the environment's carrying capacity, some individuals will be left without adequate resources. They may die or be forced to move elsewhere.

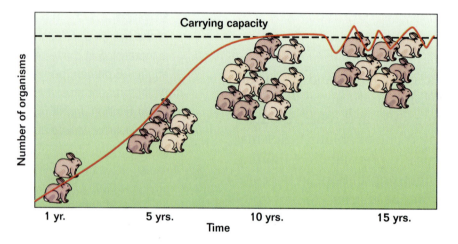

Figure 23-9 This graph shows how the size of a population increases until it reaches the carrying capacity of its environment. At first, growth is fairly slow. It speeds up as the number of adults capable of reproduction increases. Once the population reaches carrying capacity, its size remains fairly stable. **Why don't most populations achieve their biotic potential?**

Biotic Potential

What would happen if there were no limiting factors? A population living in an environment that supplies more than enough resources for survival will continue to grow. The maximum rate at which a population increases when there is plenty of food, water, ideal weather, and no disease or enemies is its biotic potential. However, most populations never reach their biotic potential, or do so for only a short period of time. Eventually, the carrying capacity of the environment is reached and the population stops increasing.

Interactions in Communities

Populations are regulated not only by the supply of food, water, and sunlight, but also by the actions of other populations. The most obvious way one population can limit another is by predation (prih DAY shun). One organism feeds on another. Owls and hawks are predators that feed on mice. Mice are their prey. Predators are biotic factors that limit the size of prey populations. Predation also helps to maintain the health of a prey population. Old, ill, or young individuals are more often captured than strong healthy animals. Thus, the overall health of the prey population improves. **Figure 23-10** shows how some predators work together to hunt their food.

Figure 23-10 Hyenas work together to hunt their food. This is called cooperation and helps all members of their population survive.

Symbiosis

Many types of relationships exist between organisms in ecosystems. Many species of organisms in nature have close, complex relationships in order to survive. When two or more species live close together, their relationship is called a symbiotic relationship. **Symbiosis** (sihm bee OH sus) is any close relationship between two or more different species.

Using Math

Calculating Population Growth

Example Problem: Estimates show the total human population will be about 6 billion in the year 2000. This number is thought to increase by 1.6 percent each year. What will the population be in the year 2005?

Problem-Solving Steps

1. What is known? Current population is 6 000 000 000. Yearly increase is 1.6%.
2. What is unknown? The population in 2001, 2002, 2003, 2004, and 2005.
3. **Solution:** Calculate the population increase for one year. Then, repeat the process four more times using the answer you came up with as a starting point.

$$
\begin{array}{r}
6\ 000\ 000\ 000 \\
\times\ 0.016 \\
\hline
36\ 000\ 000\ 000 \\
60\ 000\ 000\ 000 \\
\hline
96\ 000\ 000\ \text{more people}
\end{array}
\qquad
\begin{array}{r}
6\ 000\ 000\ 000 \\
+\ 96\ 000\ 000 \\
\hline
6\ 096\ 000\ 000\ \text{people in 2001}
\end{array}
$$

The estimated population in the year 2005 is 6 495 607 732 people.

Practice Problem

An endangered species of fish currently has a population of 136 individuals. If the population increases by two percent every year, how many individuals will there be in three years?

Strategy Hint: When calculating percentages, remember to move your decimal two spaces to the left (0.02).

Mini Lab

Observing Symbiosis

Procedure

1. Carefully wash then examine the roots of a legume plant and a nonlegume plant.

2. Examine a prepared microscope slide of the bacteria that live in the roots of legumes.

Analysis

1. What differences do you observe in the roots of the two plants?

2. The bacteria help legumes thrive in poor soil. What type of symbiotic relationship is this? Explain.

Not all relationships benefit one organism at the expense of another as in predation. Symbiotic relationships can be identified by the type of interaction between organisms, as shown in **Figure 23-11.** Many types of symbiotic relationships occur between organisms. These are usually described by how each organism in the relationship is affected by the relationship.

A symbiotic relationship that benefits both species is called mutualism. An example of mutualism is the lichen. Each lichen species is made up of a fungus and an alga or cyanobacterium. The fungus provides a protected living space, and the alga or bacterium provides the fungus with food.

Figure 23-11 Many examples of symbiotic relationships occur in nature.

B Tropical orchids grow on the trunks of trees. The tree provides the orchid with a sunlit living space high in the forest canopy. This relationship is an example of commensalism because the orchid benefits from the relationship without harming or helping the tree.

A The partnership between the desert yucca plant and the yucca moth is an example of mutualism. Both species benefit from the relationship. The yucca depends on the moth to pollinate its flowers. The moth depends on the yucca for a protected place to lay its eggs and a source of food for its larvae.

C Tapeworms are parasites that feed inside the intestines of some mammals. This one was found inside a cat.

In shallow tropical seas, brightly colored anemone fish find protection from predators by swimming among the stinging tentacles of sea anemones. The presence of the fish does not affect the anemone in a harmful or beneficial way. Commensalism is a symbiotic relationship that benefits one partner but does not harm or help the other.

Parasitism is a symbiotic relationship that benefits the parasite and does definite harm to the parasite's host. Many parasites live on or in the body of the host, absorbing nutrients from the host's body fluids. Tapeworms live as parasites in the intestines of mammals. Mistletoe is a parasitic plant that penetrates tree branches with its roots.

Habitats and Niches

In a community, every species plays a particular role. Each also has a particular place to live. The physical location where an organism lives is called its **habitat.** The habitat of an earthworm is soil. The role of an organism in the ecosystem is called its **niche.** The niche of an earthworm is shown in **Figure 23-12.** What a species eats, how it gets its food, and how it interacts with other organisms are all parts of its niche. An earthworm takes soil into its body to obtain nutrients. The soil that leaves the worm enriches the soil. The movement of the worm through soil also loosens it and aerates it, creating a better environment for plant growth.

Figure 23-12 Each organism in an ecosystem uses and affects its environment in particular ways. **What role does the earthworm play in the environment?**

EARTH SCIENCE
◄ **INTEGRATION**

Section Assessment

1. Describe how limiting factors can affect the organisms in a population.

2. Describe the difference between a habitat and a niche.

3. **Think Critically:** A parasite can obtain food only from its host. Most parasites weaken but do not kill their hosts. Why?

4. **Skill Builder**
   Predicting There are methods used to determine the size of a population without counting each organism. Do the **Chapter 23 Skill Activity** on page 1016 to learn how to infer population size.

Using Math

In a 12 m² area of weeds, 46 dandelion plants, 212 grass plants, and 14 bindweed plants are growing. What is the population density per square meter of each species?

Identifying a Limiting Factor

Possible Materials

- Bean seeds
- Small planting containers
- Soil
- Water
- Labels
- Trowel or spoon
- Aluminum foil
- Sunny window or other light source
- Refrigerator or oven

Organisms depend on many biotic and abiotic factors in their environment to survive. When these factors are limited or are not available, it can affect an organism's survival. By experimenting with some of these limiting factors, you will see how organisms depend on all parts of their environment.

Recognize the Problem

How do abiotic factors such as light, water, and temperature affect the germination of seeds?

Form a Hypothesis

Based on what you have learned about limiting factors, make a hypothesis about how one specific abiotic factor may affect the germination of a bean seed. Be sure to consider factors that you can change easily.

Goals

- **Observe** the effects of an abiotic factor on the germination and growth of bean seedlings.

- **Design** an experiment that demonstrates whether or not a specific abiotic factor limits the germination of bean seeds.

Safety Precautions

Wash hands after handling soil and seeds.

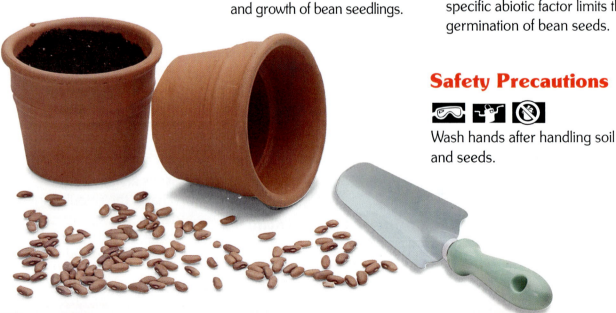

Test Your Hypothesis

Plan

1. As a group, agree upon and write out a hypothesis statement.

2. Decide on a way to test your group's hypothesis. Keep available materials in mind as you plan your procedure. **List** your materials.

3. **Prepare** a data table in your Science Journal.

4. Remember to **test** only one variable at a time and use suitable controls.

Do

1. Make sure your teacher has approved your plan before you proceed.

2. Carry out the experiment as planned.

3. While the experiment is going on, write down any observations that you make and complete the data table in your Science Journal.

5. **Read** over your entire experiment to make sure that all steps are in logical order.

6. **Identify** any constants, variables, and controls in your experiment.

7. Be sure the factor you test is measurable.

Analyze Your Data

1. **Compare** your results with those of other groups.

2. **Infer** how the abiotic factor you tested affected the germination of bean seeds.

3. **Graph** your results in a bar graph that compares the number of bean seeds that germinated in the experimental container with the number of seeds that germinated in the control container.

Draw Conclusions

1. **Identify** which factor had the greatest effect on the seeds.

2. **Determine** whether you could substitute one factor for another and still grow the seeds.

23•3 Matter and Energy

What You'll Learn

- How energy flows through ecosystems
- The cycling of matter in the biosphere

Vocabulary

food chain
food web
ecological pyramid
water cycle
nitrogen cycle

Why It's Important

- You depend on the recycling of matter and energy to survive.

Energy Flow Through Ecosystems

As you can see, life on Earth is not simply a collection of living organisms. Even organisms that seem to spend most of their time alone interact with other members of their species. They also interact with other organisms. Most of the interactions between members of different species are feeding relationships. They involve the transfer of energy from one organism to another. Energy moves through an ecosystem in the form of food. Producers are organisms that capture energy from the sun. They use the sun's energy for photosynthesis to produce chemical bonds in carbohydrates. Consumers are organisms that

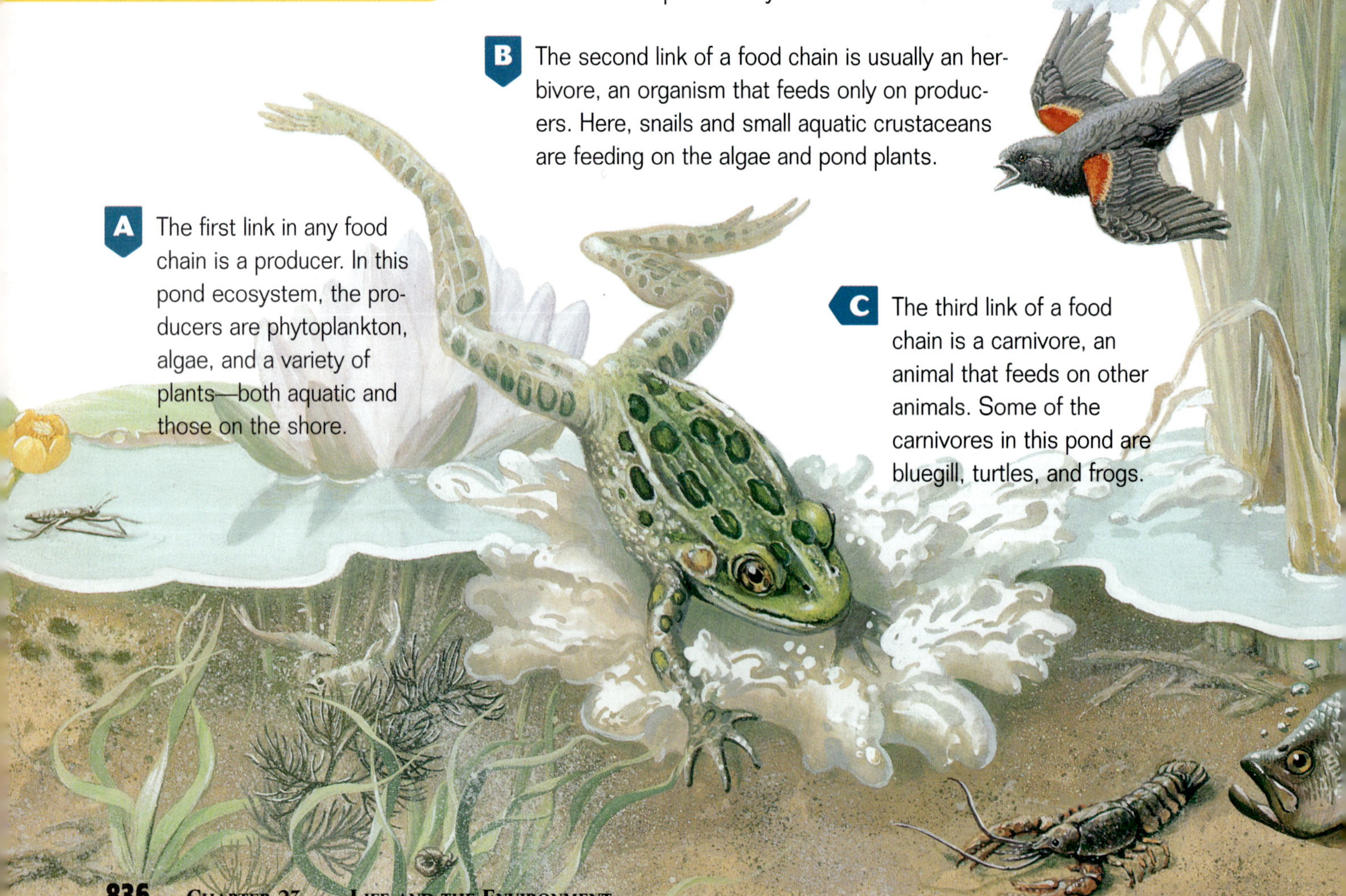

Figure 23-13 In any community, energy flows from producers to consumers. Follow several food chains in the pond ecosystem shown here.

B The second link of a food chain is usually an herbivore, an organism that feeds only on producers. Here, snails and small aquatic crustaceans are feeding on the algae and pond plants.

A The first link in any food chain is a producer. In this pond ecosystem, the producers are phytoplankton, algae, and a variety of plants—both aquatic and those on the shore.

C The third link of a food chain is a carnivore, an animal that feeds on other animals. Some of the carnivores in this pond are bluegill, turtles, and frogs.

obtain energy when they feed on producers or other consumers. The transfer of energy does not end there. When organisms die, other organisms called decomposers obtain energy when they break down the bodies of the dead organisms. This movement of energy through a community can be drawn as food chains, and food webs.

Food Chains and Food Webs

A **food chain** is a simple way of showing how energy in the form of food passes from one organism to another. The pond community pictured in **Figure 23-13** shows examples of several aquatic food chains. When drawing a food chain, arrows between organisms indicate the direction of energy transfer. An example of a pond food chain would be as follows.

phytoplankton → insects → bluegill → bass

Food chains usually have three or four links. Most have no more than five links. This is due to the decrease in energy available at each link. The amount of energy left by the fifth link is only a small portion of the total amount of energy available at the first link. This is because at each transfer of energy, a portion of the energy is lost as heat due to the activities of the organisms as they search for food and mates.

D The fourth link of a food chain is a top carnivore, which feeds on other carnivores. Examples of these consumers in this pond are large fish such as crappies and bass.

E When an organism dies in any ecosystem, bacteria and fungi, which are decomposers, feed on the dead organism, breaking down the remains of the organism.

Figure 23-14 A food web includes many food chains. It provides a more accurate model of the complex feeding relationships in a community than a single food chain does.

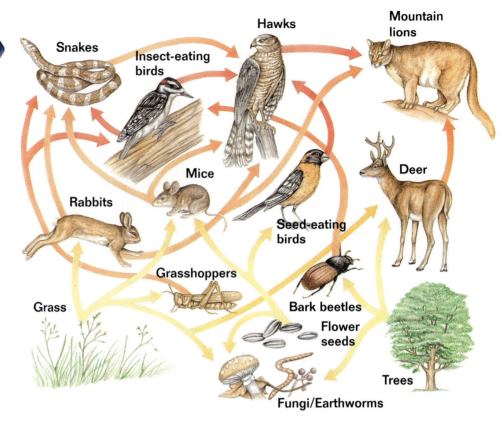

Single food chains are too simple to describe the many interactions among organisms in an ecosystem. Many food chains exist in any ecosystem. A **food web** is a series of overlapping food chains, as seen in **Figure 23-14.** This concept provides a more complete model of the way energy moves through a community. Food webs are also more accurate models because they show the many organisms that feed on more than one level in an ecosystem.

Ecological Pyramids

Almost all the energy used in the biosphere comes from the sun. Producers capture and transform only a small part of the energy that reaches Earth's surface. When an herbivore eats a plant, some of the energy in the plant is passed on to the herbivore. However, most of it is given off into the atmosphere as heat. The same thing happens when a carnivore eats an herbivore. This transfer of energy can be modeled by an **ecological pyramid.** The bottom of an ecological pyramid represents the producers of an ecosystem. The rest of the levels represent successive organisms in the food chain. ☑

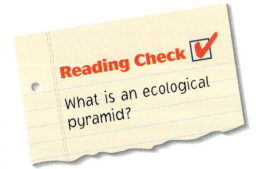

Reading Check ☑

What is an ecological pyramid?

Energy Pyramid

The flow of energy from grass to the hawk in **Figure 23-15** can be illustrated by an energy pyramid. An energy pyramid compares the energy available at each level of the food chain in an ecosystem. Just as most food chains have three or four links, a pyramid of energy usually has three or four levels. Only about ten percent of the energy available at each level of the pyramid is available to the next level. By the time the top level is reached, the amount of energy is greatly reduced.

The Cycles of Matter

The energy available at each link in the food chain is constantly renewed by sunlight. But, what about the physical matter that makes up the bodies of living organisms? The laws of conservation of mass and energy state that matter on Earth is never lost or gained. It is used over and over again. In other words, it is recycled. The carbon atoms present in your body right now have been on Earth since the planet formed billions of years ago.

Figure 23-15
An energy pyramid illustrates that energy decreases at each successive feeding step. **Why aren't there more levels in an energy pyramid?**

Problem Solving

Changes in Antarctic Food Webs

The food chain in the ice-cold Antarctic Ocean is based on phytoplankton—microscopic algae that float near the water's surface. The algae are eaten by tiny shrimp-like krill, which are consumed by baleen whales, squid, and fish. The fish and squid are eaten by toothed whales, seals, and penguins. In the past, humans have hunted baleen whales. Now with laws against it, there is hope that the population of baleen whales will increase. How will an increase in the whale population affect this food web? Which organisms compete for the same source of food?

Think Critically

1. Populations of seals, penguins, and krill-eating fish increased in size as populations of baleen whales declined. Why?

2. What might happen if the number of baleen whales increases, but the amount of krill does not?

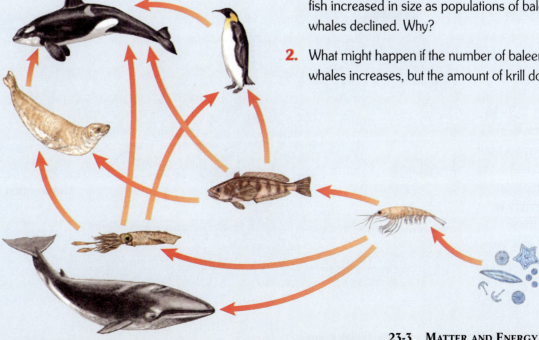

Mini Lab

Modeling the Water Cycle

Procedure

1. With a marker, make a line halfway up on a plastic cup. Fill the cup to the mark with water.
2. Cover the top with plastic wrap and secure it with a rubber band or tape.
3. Put the cup in direct sunlight. Observe the cup for three days. Record your observations.
4. Remove the plastic wrap and observe it for a week.

Analysis

1. What parts of the water cycle did you observe in this activity?
2. What happened to the water level in the cup when the plastic wrap was removed?

They have been recycled untold billions of times. Many important materials that make up your body cycle through ecosystems. Some of these materials are water, carbon, and nitrogen.

The Water Cycle

Water molecules on Earth are on a constant journey, rising into the atmosphere, falling to land or the ocean as rain or snow, and flowing into rivers and oceans. The **water cycle** involves the processes of evaporation, condensation, and precipitation.

When energy, such as heat, is added to a liquid, its molecules begin to move faster. The more energy the molecules absorb, the faster they move, until they are moving so fast they break free and rise into the atmosphere. The liquid evaporates, or changes from a liquid to a gas. The heat of the sun causes water on the surface of Earth to evaporate and rise into the atmosphere as water vapor.

Figure 23-16

A water molecule that falls as rain can follow several paths through the water cycle. **Identify as many of these paths as you can in this diagram.**

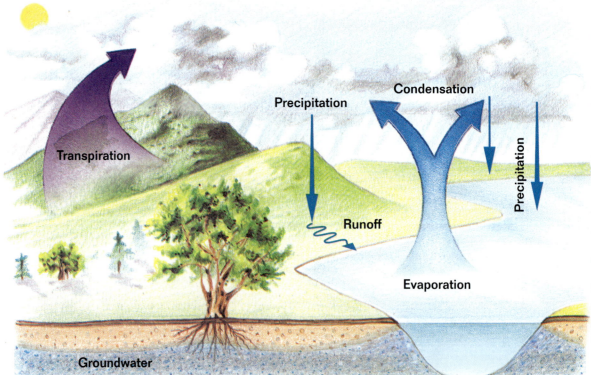

Carbon Dioxide

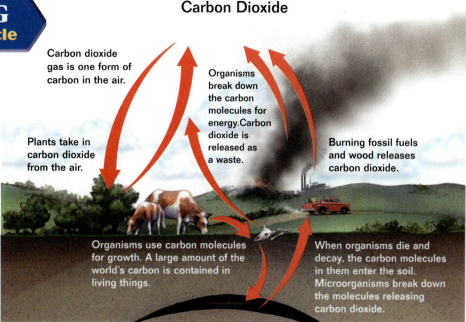

Figure 23-17 Carbon is cycled between the atmosphere and living organisms. **Why is the carbon cycle important?**

Carbon dioxide gas is one form of carbon in the air.

Organisms break down the carbon molecules for energy. Carbon dioxide is released as a waste.

Plants take in carbon dioxide from the air.

Burning fossil fuels and wood releases carbon dioxide.

Organisms use carbon molecules for growth. A large amount of the world's carbon is contained in living things.

When organisms die and decay, the carbon molecules in them enter the soil. Microorganisms break down the molecules releasing carbon dioxide.

As the water vapor rises, it encounters colder and colder air temperatures. As the molecules of water vapor become colder, they slow down. Eventually, the water vapor changes back into tiny droplets of water. It condenses, or changes from a gas to a liquid. These water droplets clump together to form clouds. When the droplets become large and heavy enough, they fall back to Earth as rain, or precipitation. This process is illustrated in **Figure 23-16.**

The Carbon Cycle

What do you have in common with all organisms? You all contain carbon. Earth's atmosphere contains about 0.03 percent carbon in the form of a gas called carbon dioxide. The movement of the element carbon through Earth's ecosystem is called the carbon cycle.

The carbon cycle begins with plants. During photosynthesis, plants remove carbon from the air and use it along with sunlight and water to make carbohydrates. These carbohydrates are used by other organisms and then returned to the atmosphere through cellular respiration, combustion, and erosion. See **Figure 23-17.** Once the carbon is returned to the atmosphere, the cycle begins again.

The Nitrogen Cycle

Nitrogen is an important element that is used by organisms to make proteins. Even though nitrogen gas makes up 78 percent of the atmosphere, most living organisms cannot use nitrogen in this form. It has to be combined with other elements through a process that is called nitrogen fixation.

*inter*NET
CONNECTION

Visit the Glencoe Science Web Site at **www.glencoe.com/ sec/science/ca** for more information about food chains and food webs.

You can see in **Figure 23-18** how nitrogen is changed into usable compounds by bacteria associated with certain plants. A small amount is changed into nitrogen compounds by lightning. The transfer of nitrogen from the atmosphere to plants and back to the atmosphere or directly into plants again is the **nitrogen cycle.**

Phosphorus, sulfur, and other elements needed by living organisms also are used and returned to the environment. Just as we recycle aluminum, glass, and paper products, the materials that organisms need to live are recycled continuously in the biosphere.

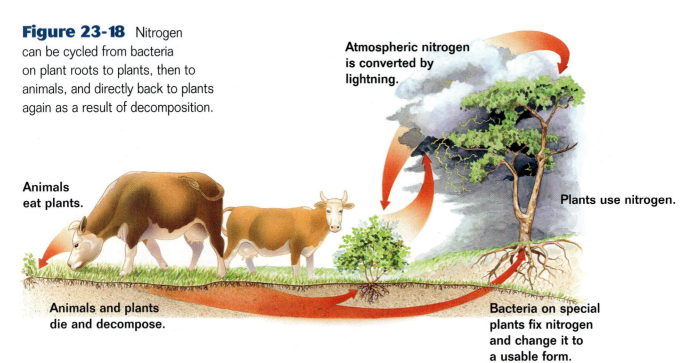

Figure 23-18 Nitrogen can be cycled from bacteria on plant roots to plants, then to animals, and directly back to plants again as a result of decomposition.

Atmospheric nitrogen is converted by lightning.

Plants use nitrogen.

Animals eat plants.

Animals and plants die and decompose.

Bacteria on special plants fix nitrogen and change it to a usable form.

Section Assessment

1. What is the difference between a food chain and a food web?
2. How does the cycling of matter affect a food chain?
3. **Think Critically:** Use your knowledge of food chains and the energy pyramid to explain why fewer lions than gazelles live on the African plains.
4. **Skill Builder**
   Classifying Look at the food web pictured in **Figure 23-14.** Classify each organism pictured as a producer, an herbivore, a carnivore, or a decomposer. If you need help, refer to Classifying in the **Skill Handbook** on page 985.

Science Journal In your Science Journal, compare the water cycle, carbon cycle, and nitrogen cycle. Use this information to discuss the processes that are involved in each cycle and how each cycle is important to living organisms.

Never Cry Wolf
by Farley Mowat

In the book *Never Cry Wolf*, Canadian biologist Farley Mowat details his yearlong expedition learning about wolves and surviving on the frozen tundra of northern Canada. When Mowat set up camp in a remote wilderness area, he didn't know he would end up eating mice to prove a point. Mowat was hired by the Canadian Wildlife Service to investigate and live among the wolves to help solve the country's growing "*Canis lupus* problem." Hunters were reporting that packs of bloodthirsty wolves were slaughtering caribou by the thousands and contributing to their extinction.

Mowat's Discovery

This action-packed book is more than just an adventure story. It's also the report of a stunning scientific discovery. Instead of fierce killers, Mowat found wolves to be gentle, skillful providers and devoted protectors of their young. Mowat challenged the idea that wolves were causing the decline in the caribou population. He showed that his wolf population fed almost exclusively on mice during the warmer summer months when the mouse population skyrocketed. To prove that a large mammal could survive on mice, he ate them himself. Following the publication of *Never Cry Wolf*, Mowat's conclusions about the habits and behaviors of wolves were criticized by people clinging to the old image of wolves as vicious killers.

Filled with beautiful images of animals in their natural setting, *Never Cry Wolf* describes one person's struggle to preserve a vanishing species. Mowat's heroic efforts to document never-before-seen behaviors in wild wolves focused international attention on wolves, which are threatened with extinction in North America and elsewhere. In 1983, Mowat's groundbreaking book was made into an entertaining movie.

Science JOURNAL

Never Cry Wolf was made into a movie based on the book. In your Science Journal, explain how books and movies like *Never Cry Wolf* can be used to persuade or to change a person's attitude toward a subject.

For a **preview** of this chapter, study this Reviewing Main Ideas before you read the chapter. After you have studied this chapter, you can use the Reviewing Main Ideas to **review** the chapter.

The Glencoe MindJogger, Audiocassettes, and CD-ROM provide additional opportunities for review.

Section 23-1 THE LIVING AND NONLIVING ENVIRONMENT

The region of Earth in which all organisms live is the **biosphere.** The nonliving features of the environment are **abiotic factors,** and the organisms in the environment are **biotic factors. Populations** and **communities** make up an **ecosystem. Ecology** is the study of interactions among organisms and their environment. *How does the relationship between an organism, a population, and a community affect an ecosystem?*

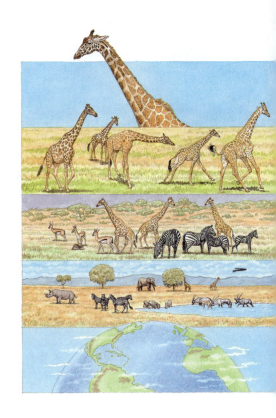

Section 23-2 INTERACTIONS AMONG LIVING ORGANISMS

A **population** can be described by characteristics that include size, spacing, and density. Any biotic or abiotic factor that limits the number of individuals in a population is a **limiting factor.** A close relationship between two or more species is a symbiotic relationship. The place where an organism lives is its **habitat,** and its role in the environment is its **niche.** *How could two similar species of birds live in the same area and nest in the same tree without occupying the same niche?*

Reading Check ✓

Translate the informa-
tion in **Figure 23-14** into
a diagram. Clearly show
the relationships among
the links in a food chain.

^{Section}
23-3 MATTER AND ENERGY

Food chains and **food webs**
are models that describe the feeding
relationships in a community. An
energy pyramid describes the flow of
energy through a community. Energy
is distributed at each level of the food
chain but is replenished by the sun.
Matter is never lost or
gained but is recycled.
*If the rabbits, birds,
mice, beetles, and
deer were removed
from the food web
shown in this figure,
which organisms
would be affected
and how?*

Career
CONNECTION

Isidro Bosh, Aquatic Biologist

As an aquatic biologist, Isidro Bosh
studies ocean invertebrates such as sea urchins, sea
slugs, and sponges. He is interested in how
these animals live in tough environmental
conditions, such as cold polar oceans
and the dark deep sea with its high
pressure. He has explored the oceans
in everything from huge research vessels to small, inflatable rafts. He also has
explored tropical coral reefs and giant kelp
forests. *Why is it important to study how
animals adapt to tough environments?*

Chapter 23 Assessment

Using Vocabulary

a. abiotic factor
b. biosphere
c. biotic factor
d. carrying capacity
e. community
f. ecological pyramid
g. ecology
h. ecosystem
i. food chain
j. food web
k. habitat
l. limiting factor
m. niche
n. nitrogen cycle
o. population
p. population density
q. symbiosis
r. water cycle

Match each phrase with the correct term from the list of Vocabulary words.

1. any living thing in the environment
2. number of individuals of a species living in the same place at the same time
3. all the populations in an ecosystem
4. series of overlapping food chains
5. where an organism lives in an ecosystem

Checking Concepts

Choose the word or phrase that best answers the question.

6. Which of the following is a biotic factor?
   A) animals
   B) air
   C) sunlight
   D) soil

7. What are coral reefs and oak-hickory forests examples of?
   A) niches
   B) habitats
   C) populations
   D) ecosystems

8. What is made up of all populations in an area?
   A) niche
   B) habitat
   C) community
   D) ecosystem

9. What does the number of individuals in a population occupying an area of a specific size describe?
   A) clumping
   B) size
   C) spacing
   D) density

10. Which of the following is an example of an herbivore?
    A) wolf
    B) moss
    C) tree
    D) rabbit

11. Which level of the food chain has the most energy?
    A) omnivores
    B) herbivores
    C) decomposers
    D) producers

12. What is a relationship in which one organism is helped and the other is harmed?
    A) mutualism
    B) parasitism
    C) commensalism
    D) symbiosis

13. Which of the following is **NOT** cycled in the biosphere?
    A) nitrogen
    B) soil
    C) water
    D) carbon

14. Which of the following is a model that shows how energy is lost as it flows through an ecosystem?
    A) pyramid of biomass
    B) pyramid of numbers
    C) pyramid of energy
    D) niche

15. What does returning wolves to Yellowstone National Park add to the food web?
    A) producer
    B) herbivore
    C) top carnivore
    D) decomposer

Thinking Critically

16. What would be the advantage to a human or other omnivore of eating a diet of organisms that are lower rather than higher on the food chain?

17. Why are viruses considered parasites?

18. What does carrying capacity have to do with whether or not a population reaches its biotic potential?

19. Why are decomposers vital to the cycling of matter in an ecosystem?

20. Describe your own habitat and niche.

Developing Skills

If you need help, refer to the **Skill Handbook.**

21. **Classifying:** Classify each event in the water cycle as the result of either evaporation or condensation.

    A) A puddle disappears after a rainstorm.

    B) Rain falls.

    C) A lake becomes shallower.

    D) Clouds form.

22. **Making and Using Graphs:** Use the following data to graph the population density of a deer population over the years. Plot the number of deer on the *y*-axis and years on the *x*-axis. Propose a hypothesis to explain what might have happened to cause the changes in the size of the population.

Arizona Deer Population	
Year	Deer per 400 hectares
1905	5.7
1915	35.7
1920	142.9
1925	85.7
1935	25.7

23. **Observing and Inferring:** A home aquarium contains water, an air pump, a light, algae, a goldfish, and algae-eating snails. What are the abiotic factors in this environment? Which of these items would be considered a population? A community?

24. **Concept Mapping:** Use the following information to draw a food web of organisms living in a goldenrod field. *Goldenrod sap is eaten by aphids, goldenrod nectar is eaten by bees, goldenrod pollen is eaten by beetles, goldenrod leaves are eaten by beetles, stinkbugs eat beetles, spiders eat aphids, assassin bugs eat bees.*

THE PRINCETON REVIEW

Test-Taking Tip

Skip Around, If You Can Just because the questions are in order doesn't mean you have to answer them that way. You may want to skip over hard questions and come back to them later. Answer all the easier questions first to guarantee you more points toward your score.

Test Practice

Use these questions to test your Science Proficiency.

1. According to the table, at which point are there more deer than available food?
   A) 1
   B) 2
   C) 3
   D) 4

2. In the water cycle, how is water returned to the atmosphere?
   A) evaporation
   B) condensation
   C) precipitation
   D) fixation

3. What are the food relationships among all organisms in the same environment called?
   A) food chain
   B) ecological pyramid
   C) food web
   D) energy pyramid

4. In an energy pyramid, which level has the most available energy?
   A) first
   B) second
   C) third
   D) fourth

CHAPTER
24

Ecosystems

Chapter Preview

Section 24-1
How Ecosystems Change

Section 24-2
Land Environments

Section 24-3
Water Environments

Skills Preview

Skill Builders
- Map Concepts
- Compare and Contrast

Activities
- Observe

MiniLabs
- Observe
- Infer

Reading Check ✔

As you read about succession, record words and phrases that indicate a time sequence, such as *long ago, gradually,* and *as time passed.*

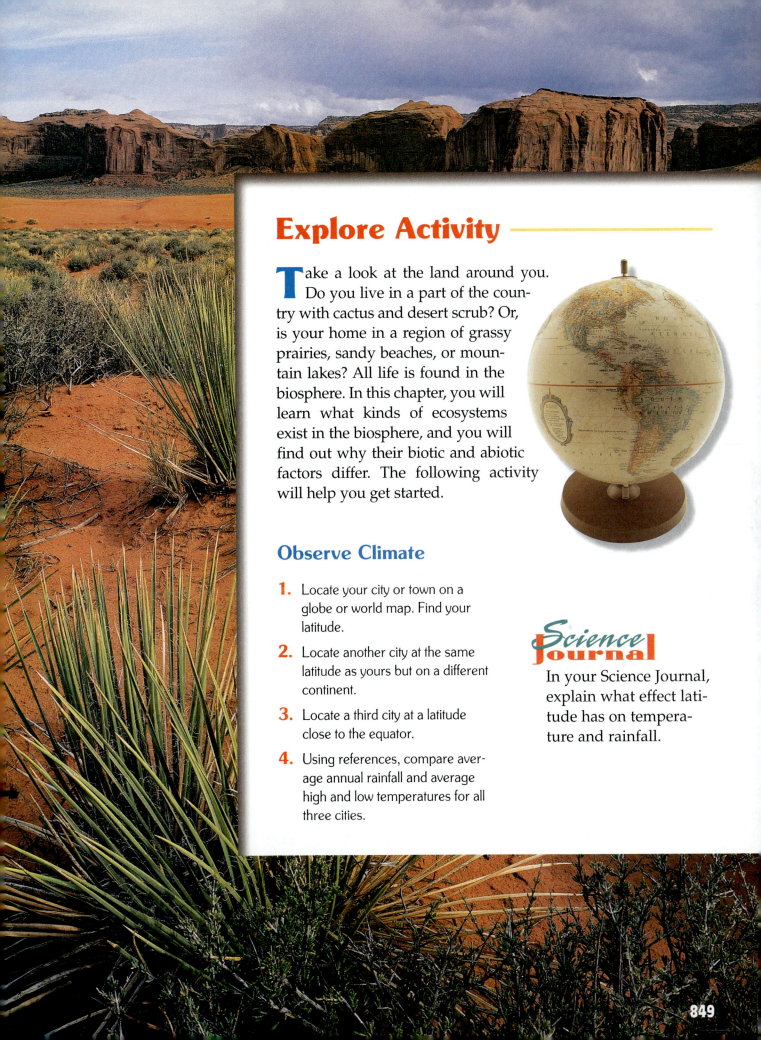

Explore Activity

Take a look at the land around you. Do you live in a part of the country with cactus and desert scrub? Or, is your home in a region of grassy prairies, sandy beaches, or mountain lakes? All life is found in the biosphere. In this chapter, you will learn what kinds of ecosystems exist in the biosphere, and you will find out why their biotic and abiotic factors differ. The following activity will help you get started.

Observe Climate

1. Locate your city or town on a globe or world map. Find your latitude.

2. Locate another city at the same latitude as yours but on a different continent.

3. Locate a third city at a latitude close to the equator.

4. Using references, compare average annual rainfall and average high and low temperatures for all three cities.

Science Journal

In your Science Journal, explain what effect latitude has on temperature and rainfall.

24·1 How Ecosystems Change

What You'll Learn

► How ecosystems change over time
► How new communities arise in areas that were bare of life
► How to compare and contrast pioneer communities and climax communities

Vocabulary

ecological succession
primary succession
pioneer community
secondary succession
climax community

Why It's Important

► Your ecosystem is changing right now.

Ecological Succession

Imagine hiking through a forest. Huge trees tower over the trail. You know it can take many years for trees to grow this large, so it's easy to think of the forest as something that has always been here. But, this area has not always been covered with trees. Long ago, it may have been a pond full of fish and frogs surrounded by water-loving plants. As time passed, the decomposed bodies of plants and animals slowly filled in the pond until it eventually became a lush, green meadow full of grass and wildflowers. Gradually, over many more years, seeds blew in, trees began to grow, and a forest developed. The process of gradual change from one community of organisms to another is called **ecological succession.** The changes associated with succession usually take place in a fairly predictable order and involve animals, plants, and other organisms.

VISUALIZING Succession

Figure 24-1 The following are the stages in primary succession.

A Life on this bare rock begins with a pioneer community of lichens. These hardy organisms produce acids that help to break down the rock. The acids release chemicals and nutrients from the rock that can then be absorbed by the lichens. The decaying bodies of dead lichens contribute to soil formation.

B Mosses and ferns gradually replace the lichens. These plants can grow even in extremely poor, thin soil. As they die, their decomposed bodies add humus to the soil. Insects and other small animals appear.

Primary Succession

Think about conditions around an erupting volcano. Incredibly hot, molten lava flows along the ground, destroying everything in its path. As the lava cools, it forms new land. Soil is formed from bare rock. Similar events happen to this newly formed land. Particles of dust and ash fall to the ground. The forces of weather and erosion break up the lava rock. A thin layer of soil begins to form. Birds, wind, and rain deposit more dust, along with bacteria, seeds, and fungal spores. Plants start to grow and decay. A living community has begun to develop.

Ecological succession that begins in a place that does not have soil is called **primary succession.** The first community of organisms to move into a new environment is called the **pioneer community,** as shown in **Figure 24-1.** Members of pioneer communities are usually hardy organisms that can survive drought, extreme heat and cold, and other harsh conditions. Pioneer communities change the conditions in their environments. These new conditions support the growth of other types of organisms that gradually take over.

CHEMISTRY
INTEGRATION

Freezing Water
Freezing temperatures are harmful to living organisms because water is the main component of cells. As water freezes, it expands. Infer what happens to cells if ice crystals form inside them.

C As the soil layer thickens, its ability to absorb and hold water improves. Grasses, wildflowers, and other plants that require richer, more moist soil begin to take over. Butterflies, bees, and caterpillars come to feed on the leaves and flowers. When these plants die, they also enrich the soil, which will become home to earthworms and other large soil organisms.

D Thicker, richer soil supports the growth of shrubs and trees. More insects, birds, mammals, and reptiles move into the area. After hundreds or thousands of years of gradual change, what was once bare rock has become a forest.

Figure 24-2 The tangled growth of weeds and grasses in untended yards and vacant lots, on abandoned farms, and along country roadsides is the beginning stage of secondary succession.

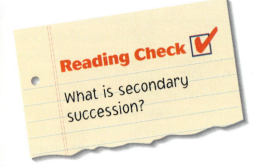

Reading Check ✔

What is secondary succession?

*inter*NET
CONNECTION

Visit the Glencoe Science Web Site at **www. glencoe.com/sec/ science/ca** for more information about the Yellowstone fires and how they contributed to succession.

Secondary Succession

What happens when a forest is destroyed by a fire or a city building is torn down? After a forest fire, nothing is left except dead trees and ash-covered soil. Once the rubble of a demolished building has been taken away, all that remains is bare soil. But, these places do not remain lifeless for long. The soil may already contain the seeds of weeds, grasses, and trees. More seeds are carried to the area by wind and birds. As the seeds germinate and plants begin to grow, insects, birds, and other wildlife move in. Ecological succession has begun again. Succession that begins in a place that already has soil and was once the home of living organisms is called **secondary succession,** shown in **Figure 24-2.** ✔

Climax Communities

Succession involves changes in abiotic factors as well as biotic factors. You have already seen how lichens, mosses, and ferns change the environment by helping to form the rich, thick soil needed for the growth of shrubs and trees. Shrubs and trees also cause changes in abiotic factors. Their branches shade the ground beneath them, reducing the temperature. Shade also reduces the rate of evaporation, increasing the moisture content of the soil. Amount of sunlight, temperature, and moisture level determine which species will grow in soil.

The redwood forest shown in **Figure 24-3** is an example of a community that has reached the end of succession. As long as the trees are not cut down or destroyed by fire or widespread disease, the species that make up the redwood community tend to remain the same. When a community has reached the final stage of ecological succession, it is called a **climax community.** Because primary succession begins in areas with no life at all, it can take hundreds or even thousands of years for a pioneer community to develop into a climax community. Secondary succession is a shorter process, but it still may take a century or more.

Comparing Communities

As you have seen, pioneer communities are simple. They contain only a few species, and feeding relationships usually can be described with simple food chains. Climax communities are much more complex. They may contain hundreds of thousands of species, and feeding relationships usually involve complex food webs. Interactions among the many biotic and abiotic factors in a climax community create a more stable environment that does not change much over time. Climax communities are the end product of ecological succession. A climax community that has been disturbed in some way will eventually return to the same type of community, as long as all other factors remain the same. However, it may take a century or more for the community to return to its former state.

Figure 24-3 This forest of redwood trees in California is an example of a climax community. Redwoods live for hundreds of years. They create shade on the ground beneath them. Needles constantly fall from their branches. Eventually, they form an acidic soil that allows the growth of young redwoods but prevents the growth of many other types of plants.

Section Assessment

1. What is ecological succession?
2. What is the difference between primary and secondary succession?
3. What is the difference between pioneer and climax communities?
4. **Think Critically:** What kind of succession will take place on an abandoned, unpaved country road? Why?
5.  **Skill Builder**
   Sequencing Describe the sequence of events in primary succession. Include the term *climax community.* If you need help, refer to Sequencing on page 986.

Science Journal In your Science Journal, draw a food chain for a pioneer community of lichens and a food web for the climax community of an oak-maple forest. Write a short paragraph comparing the two communities.

On The Internet

Activity 24•1

Endangered and Threatened Species

A species becomes endangered when its numbers are so low that it is in danger of extinction in the near future. The list of threatened and endangered species in the United States and around the world is constantly growing due to a variety of reasons. In 1998, about 965 species in the United States were listed as endangered or threatened.

Recognize the Problem

What endangered or threatened species have been identified for your region of the country?

Form a Hypothesis

Form a hypothesis to explain some of the reasons why the organisms identified as threatened or endangered in your region are on the list.

Goals
- **Obtain** and **organize** data.
- **Infer** relationships between the plant or animal and its environment.
- **Use the Internet** to collect and compare data from other students.

Data Sources
Go to the Glencoe Science Web Site at **www.glencoe. com/sec/science/ca** to find links to information about endangered plants and animals around the country. You also will find information posted by other students from around the country.

Species Data

Organism Genus species	Threatened or Endangered	Length of Time on List	Recovery Plan	General Information

Test Your Hypothesis

Plan

1. Find links to information on the Glencoe Science Web Site. You can also find information on endangered species at the local library or a local zoo.

2. Prepare a data table similar to the one below to record your findings.

3. If possible, observe one of the endangered or threatened species you've identified either in a zoo or in the wild.

Do

1. **Describe** the habitat and range of the organism you chose to study.

2. **Identify** any steps being taken to protect the organism. Outline the recovery plan written for one of the organisms in your region.

3. **Post** the information you collected in the table provided for this activity on the Glencoe Science Web Site.

4. **Check** the postings by other students for more information on your organism and on other organisms.

Analyze Your Data

1. Brainstorm possible reasons why your organism is threatened or endangered.

2. What factors were you able to identify as reasons for the organism becoming endangered?

3. Was your hypothesis supported by the information you collected? **Explain** your answer.

Draw Conclusions

1. What might help the organism you are studying survive the changes in conditions or other changes that have occurred in its range that caused its numbers to decrease.

2. How successful have any techniques established to protect the organism been?

3. Did you find more threatened or endangered species of plants or animals in your region? What explanation might there be for your findings?

4. What steps do you think should be taken, if any, to protect endangered or threatened species in your region? What objections might be raised for the steps taken to protect a species?

What You'll Learn

► How climate influences land environments
► The six biomes that make up land environments on Earth
► The adaptations of plants and animals found in each biome

Vocabulary
biome
tundra
taiga
temperate deciduous forest
tropical rain forest
grassland
desert

Why It's Important

► Resources that you need to survive are found in a variety of biomes.

Factors That Determine Climate

What does a desert in Arizona have in common with a desert in Africa? They both have water-conserving plants with thorns, lizards, heat, little rain, and poor soil. How are the plains of the American West like the veldt of central Africa? Both regions have dry summers, wet winters, and huge expanses of grassland that support grazing animals such as elk and antelope. Many widely separated regions of the world have similar ecosystems. Why? Because they have similar climates. Climate is the general weather pattern in an area. The factors that determine a region's climate include temperature and precipitation.

Temperature

The sun supplies life on Earth not only with light energy for photosynthesis, but also with heat energy for warmth. The temperature of a region is regulated primarily by the amount of sunlight that reaches it. In turn, the amount of sunlight is determined by an area's latitude and elevation.

Latitude

As **Figure 24-4** shows, not all parts of Earth receive the same amount of energy from the sun. When you conducted the Explore Activity at the beginning of this chapter, you probably concluded that temperature is affected by latitude.

Figure 24-4 Because Earth is tilted on its axis, the angle of the sun's rays changes during the year. These changes create the seasons. The tilt of Earth's axis does not have as much of an effect on regions near the equator.

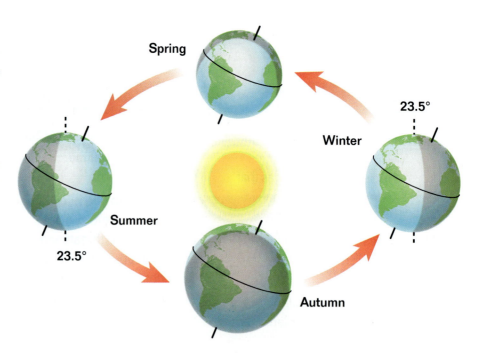

Spring

23.5°

Winter

Summer

23.5°

Autumn

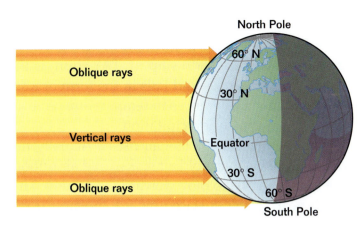

Figure 24-5 Because Earth is curved, oblique rays of sunlight reaching higher latitudes near the poles are more spread out. These rays are therefore weaker than the sunlight reaching lower latitudes near the equator. Climates near the equator are warmer, and those near the poles are colder.

The nearer a region is to the north or south pole, the higher its latitude, the smaller the amount of energy it receives from the sun, as seen in **Figure 24-5,** and the colder its climate.

Seasonal changes in sunlight also have an effect on the temperature of a climate. Because Earth is tilted on its axis, the angle of the sun's rays changes as Earth moves through its yearly orbit. During winter in the northern hemisphere, regions north of the equator are tilted away from the sun. Rays of sunlight are spread over a larger area, reducing their warming effect. As a result, winter temperatures are colder than summer temperatures.

Elevation

A region's elevation, or distance above sea level, also has an influence on temperature. Earth's atmosphere acts as insulation that traps some of the heat that reaches Earth's surface. At higher elevations, the atmosphere is thinner, so more heat escapes back into space. As a result, the higher the elevation, the colder the climate. The climate on a mountain will be cooler than the climate at sea level at the same latitude. Higher elevations affect plant growth, as seen in **Figure 24-6.**

EARTH SCIENCE
◄ **INTEGRATION**

Using Math

Earth is tilted at an angle of 23.5°. Without using a protractor, sketch an angle that measures about 23.5°. Then, check your angle by measuring it with a protractor.

Figure 24-6 These Rocky Mountain bristlecone pines show the effects of higher elevations on plants. These trees are shaped by the wind and stunted by the cold, harsh conditions.

Precipitation

Water is one of the most important factors affecting the climate of an area. Precipitation (prih sihp uh TAY shun) is the amount of water that condenses and falls in the form of rain, snow, sleet, hail, and fog. Differences in temperature have an important effect on patterns of precipitation.

Have you heard the expression "Hot air rises"? Actually, hot air is pushed upward whenever cold air sinks. Cold air is more dense than hot air, so it tends to move toward the ground. This pushes warm air near Earth's surface upward. In warm tropical regions near the equator, the air, land, and oceans are constantly being heated by the direct rays of the sun. As the cooler air sinks, the warm air is pushed upward into the atmosphere. This warm air carries large amounts of water vapor from the oceans. When the air reaches a high enough altitude in the atmosphere, the water vapor it contains cools and condenses as rain. While the air rises, it also moves slowly toward either the north or south pole. The air loses virtually all of its moisture by the time it reaches a latitude of about 30°. Because of this pattern, deserts are common at latitudes near 30° in both the northern and southern hemispheres. Latitudes between 0° and 22° receive much larger amounts of rain.

The Rain Shadow Effect

The presence of mountain ranges also has an effect on rainfall patterns. As **Figure 24-7** shows, air that is moving toward a mountain range is forced upward by the shape of the land. As warm air is forced upward, it cools, condensing the water vapor it contains and creating rain or snow. By the time the air has passed over the mountains, it has lost its moisture. The region on the opposite side of the mountain range receives very little rain because it is in a "rain shadow" created by the mountains.

Figure 24-7 Moist air moving into California from the Pacific Ocean is forced upward when it reaches the Sierra Nevada Mountains. As air rises, it cools and loses its moisture in the form of rain or snow. By the time the air reaches Nevada and Utah, on the other side of the mountains, it is dry. This area is in the mountains' "rain shadow." It receives so little rain that it has become a desert.

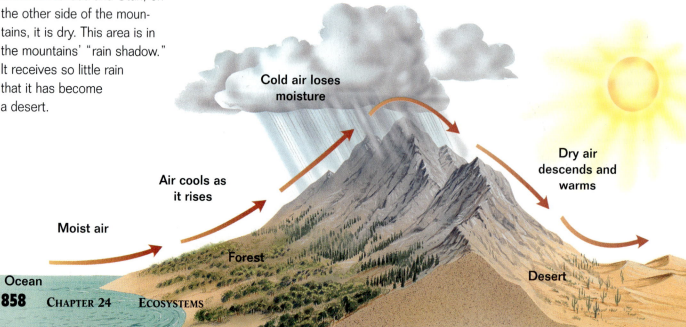

Cold air loses moisture

Air cools as it rises

Dry air descends and warms

Moist air

Forest

Ocean

Desert

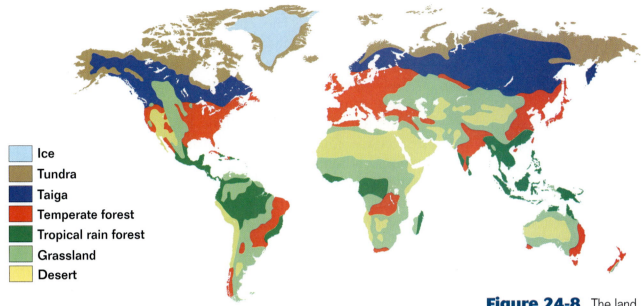

Ice
Tundra
Taiga
Temperate forest
Tropical rain forest
Grassland
Desert

Figure 24-8 The land portion of the biosphere can be divided into several biomes. Tundra, taiga, temperate forest, tropical rain forest, grassland, and desert are the most commonly known. **Which biome is most common in the United States?**

Land Biomes

As you will see in the **Field Guide to Biomes** at the end of this chapter, regions with similar climates tend to have ecosystems with climax communities of similar structure. Tropical rain forests are climax communities found near the equator, where temperatures are warm and rainfall is plentiful. Coniferous forests grow where winter temperatures are cold and rainfall is moderate. Large geographic areas that have similar climates and ecosystems are called **biomes** (BI ohmz). The six most common biomes are mapped in **Figure 24-8.**

Tundra

At latitudes surrounding the north pole lies a biome that receives little precipitation but is covered with ice most of the year. The **tundra** (TUN dra) is a cold, dry, treeless region, sometimes called a cold desert, where winters are six to nine months long. For some of those months, the land remains dark because the sun never rises above the horizon. For a few days during the short, cold summer, the sun never sets. Precipitation averages less than 25 cm per year, and winter temperatures drop to −40°C, so water in the tundra soil remains frozen solid during the winter. During the summer, only the top few inches thaw.

Try at Home

Mini Lab

Comparing Tundra and Taiga

Procedure

1. Compare the latitudes where tundra is found in the northern hemisphere with the same latitudes in South America.

2. Compare the latitudes where taiga is found in the northern hemisphere with the same latitudes in South America.

Analysis

Are either of these biomes found in South America? Explain why or why not.

Below the thawed surface is a layer of permanently frozen soil called permafrost. The cold temperatures slow down the process of decomposition, so the soil is also poor in nutrients.

Tundra plants are resistant to drought and cold. They include species of lichens known as reindeer moss, true mosses, grasses, and small shrubs, as seen in **Figure 24-9.** During the summer, mosquitoes, blackflies, and other biting insects are abundant. Many birds, including ducks, geese, various shorebirds, and songbirds, migrate to the tundra to nest during the summer. Hawks, snowy owls, mice, voles, lemmings, arctic hares, caribou, and musk oxen are also found there.

Taiga

Just below the tundra, at latitudes between about 50°N and 60°N, and stretching across Canada, northern Europe, and Asia, lies the world's largest biome. The **taiga** (TI guh), as shown in **Figure 24-10,** is a cold region of cone-bearing evergreen trees. This biome is also called the northern coniferous forest. Although the winter is long and cold, the taiga is warmer and wetter than the tundra. Precipitation is mostly snow and averages 35 cm to 100 cm each year.

Figure 24-9 Land is so flat in the tundra that water does not drain away. Because the frozen soil also prevents water from soaking into the soil, part of the tundra becomes wet and marshy during the summer. Frozen soil also prevents trees and other deep-rooted plants from growing in the tundra biome.

Figure 24-10 The climax community of the taiga is dominated by fir and spruce trees. Mammal populations include moose, black bears, lynx, and wolves.

Permafrost is found in northern areas of the taiga. The ground thaws completely during the summer, making it possible for trees to grow. There are few shrubs and grasses, primarily because the forests of the taiga are so dense that little sunlight penetrates through the trees. Lichens and mosses grow on the forest floor.

Temperate Deciduous Forest

Temperate forests are found in both the northern and southern hemispheres, at latitudes below about 50°. Temperate regions usually have four distinct seasons each year. Precipitation ranges from about 75 cm to 150 cm and is distributed evenly throughout the year. Temperatures range from below freezing during the winter to 30°C or more during the warmest days of summer.

Many coniferous forests exist in the temperate regions of the world, particularly in mountainous areas. However, most of the temperate forests in Europe and North America are dominated by climax communities of deciduous trees, which lose their leaves every autumn. These forests, like the one in **Figure 24-11,** are called **temperate deciduous forests.** In the United States, they are found primarily east of the Mississippi River. ☑

The loss of leaves in the fall signals a dramatic change in the life of the deciduous forest. Food becomes less abundant, and the leafless trees no longer provide adequate shelter for many organisms. Some animals, particularly birds, migrate to warmer regions during the winter. Other organisms reduce their activities and their need for food by going into hibernation until spring.

Reading Check ☑

Where are temperate deciduous forests found?

Figure 24-11 The mild climate and rich soil of the temperate deciduous forest support a wide variety of organisms. Animal life includes deer, foxes, squirrels, mice, snakes, and a huge number of bird and insect species. **Why do you think the temperate forests support a wide variety of organisms?**

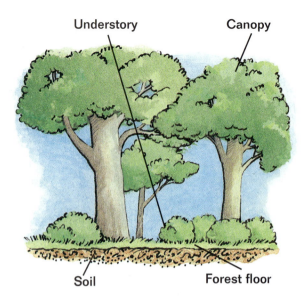

Figure 24-12 All forests are made up of layers with distinctly different biotic and abiotic factors.

Layers of Vegetation

Forests form layers of vegetation, as illustrated in **Figure 24-12.** At the top of the forest is the canopy, which consists of the leafy branches of trees. The *canopy* shades the ground below and provides homes for birds, insects, mammals, and many other organisms.

Beneath the canopy and above the forest floor is the shrub layer, or *understory*. The understory is made up of shorter plants that tolerate shade, along with organisms that depend on these plants for food and shelter.

The forest floor is dark and moist. It is home to many insects, worms, and fungi, as well as plants that can survive in dim light. Leaves, twigs, seeds, and the bodies of dead animals that fall to the forest floor either decompose or are eaten.

Problem Solving

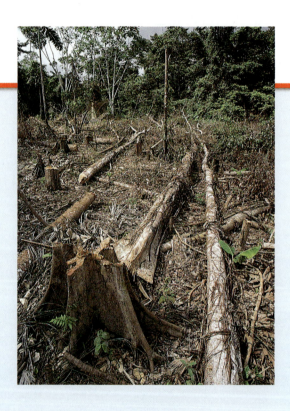

Saving the Rain Forests

Many of the world's rain forests are being destroyed for economic reasons. Logging and farming provide income for people living in these areas. When a section of rain forest is cleared, trees that can be used as lumber are removed and sold. The remaining plants are cut down and burned, the ash is used to fertilize the soil, and food crops are planted. After a couple of years, the soil becomes too poor to produce a harvest, so the land is abandoned and another patch of forest is cleared.

People can make a living from the rain forest in other ways. Latex, a material used in surgical gloves, rubber bands, tires, and shoes, is the sap of rubber trees. Carefully tapping the trees provides a continual harvest without harming the forest. Many rain forest plants produce edible fruits, nuts, and oils that can be harvested year after year, without the need for clearing land. Harvesting these plants, rather than clearing land on which other crops can be grown for only a short time, could provide people with a sustainable income.

Think Critically: Suppose a family could earn the same amount of money in two different ways. One is to clear several hectares of rain forest, sell the timber, and grow food crops for two years. The other is to harvest latex and edible fruits and nuts from a larger area of rain forest for four years. Which course of action would you recommend? Why? Give reasons why the family might choose the other method.

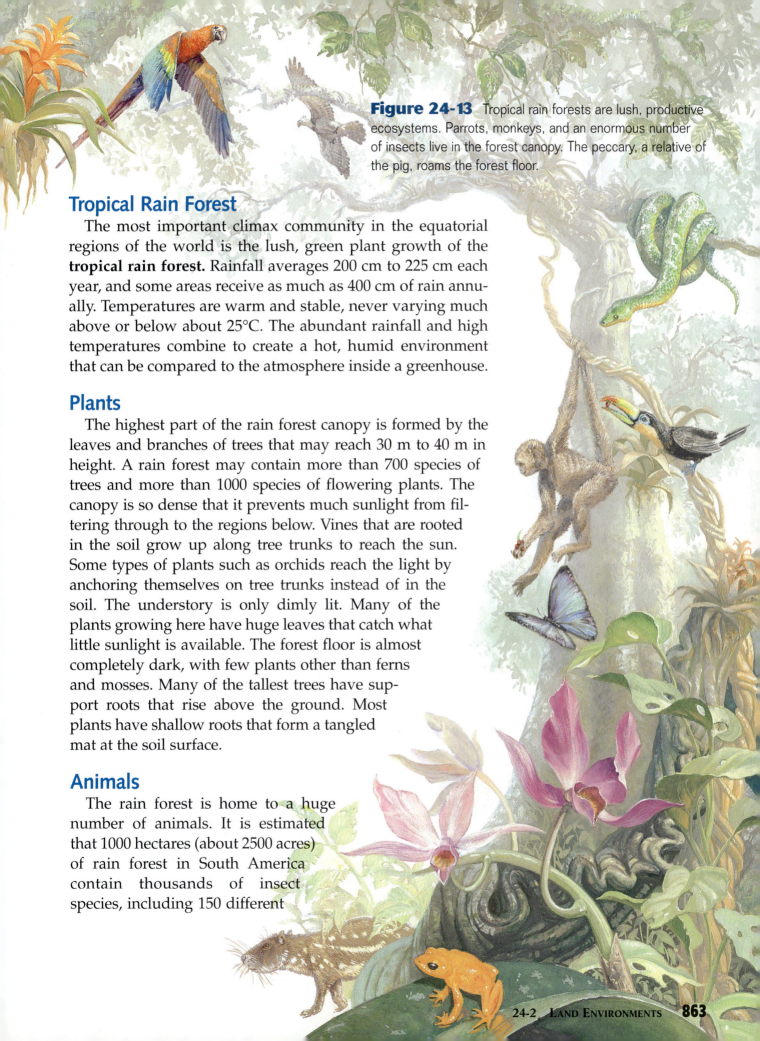

Figure 24-13 Tropical rain forests are lush, productive ecosystems. Parrots, monkeys, and an enormous number of insects live in the forest canopy. The peccary, a relative of the pig, roams the forest floor.

Tropical Rain Forest

The most important climax community in the equatorial regions of the world is the lush, green plant growth of the **tropical rain forest.** Rainfall averages 200 cm to 225 cm each year, and some areas receive as much as 400 cm of rain annually. Temperatures are warm and stable, never varying much above or below about 25°C. The abundant rainfall and high temperatures combine to create a hot, humid environment that can be compared to the atmosphere inside a greenhouse.

Plants

The highest part of the rain forest canopy is formed by the leaves and branches of trees that may reach 30 m to 40 m in height. A rain forest may contain more than 700 species of trees and more than 1000 species of flowering plants. The canopy is so dense that it prevents much sunlight from filtering through to the regions below. Vines that are rooted in the soil grow up along tree trunks to reach the sun. Some types of plants such as orchids reach the light by anchoring themselves on tree trunks instead of in the soil. The understory is only dimly lit. Many of the plants growing here have huge leaves that catch what little sunlight is available. The forest floor is almost completely dark, with few plants other than ferns and mosses. Many of the tallest trees have support roots that rise above the ground. Most plants have shallow roots that form a tangled mat at the soil surface.

Animals

The rain forest is home to a huge number of animals. It is estimated that 1000 hectares (about 2500 acres) of rain forest in South America contain thousands of insect species, including 150 different

Using Math

Make a bar graph that shows the average yearly precipitation in each of the land biomes.

kinds of butterflies. The same patch of forest also contains dozens of species of snakes, lizards, frogs, and salamanders, and hundreds of varieties of brightly colored birds, including parrots, toucans, cockatoos, and hummingbirds. Tree-dwelling mammals include monkeys, sloths, and bats. Ocelots and jaguars are tropical cats that prowl the forest floor in search of small mammals such as pacas and agoutis, or piglike peccaries, shown in **Figure 24-13.**

Grassland

Temperate and tropical regions that receive between 25 cm and 75 cm of precipitation each year and are dominated by climax communities of grasses are known as **grasslands.** Most grasslands have a dry season, when little or no rain falls, which prevents the development of forests. Virtually every continent has grasslands, like the one in **Figure 24-14,** and they are known by a variety of names. The prairie and plains of North America, the steppes of Asia, the veldts of Africa, and the pampas of South America are all grasslands.

Grass plants have extensive root systems, called sod, that absorb water when it rains and can withstand drought during long dry spells. The roots remain dormant during winter and sprout new stems and leaves when the weather warms in the spring. The soil is rich and fertile, and many grassland regions of the world are now important farming areas. Cereal grains such as wheat, rye, oats, barley, and corn, which serve as staple foods for humans, are types of grasses.

The most noticeable animals in grassland ecosystems are usually mammals that graze on the stems, leaves, and seeds of grass plants. Kangaroos graze in the grasslands of Australia. In Africa, common grassland inhabitants include wildebeests and zebras.

Figure 24-14 Grasslands, like this one in South Dakota, are hot and dry during the summer and cold and wet during the winter. They once supported huge herds of bison. Today, they are inhabited by pronghorn, gophers, ground squirrels, prairie chickens, and meadowlarks.

Desert

The **desert,** the driest biome on Earth, receives less than 25 cm of rain each year and supports little plant life. Some desert areas may receive no rain for years. When rain does come, it quickly drains away due to the sandy soil. Any water that remains on the ground evaporates rapidly, so the soil retains almost no moisture.

Because of the lack of water, desert plants are spaced widely apart, and much of the ground is bare. Some areas receive enough rainfall to support the growth of a few shrubs and small trees. Barren, windblown sand dunes are characteristic of the driest deserts, where rain rarely falls. Most deserts are covered with a thin, sandy or gravelly soil that contains little humus.

Adaptations of Desert Plants and Animals

Desert plants have developed a variety of adaptations for survival in the extreme dryness and hot and cold temperatures of this biome. Cactus plants, like the one in **Figure 24-15A,** with their reduced, spiny leaves, are probably the most familiar desert plants. Cacti have large, shallow roots that quickly absorb any water that becomes available.

Water conservation is important to all desert animals. Some, like the kangaroo rat, never need to drink water. They get all the moisture they need from the breakdown of food during digestion. Other adaptations involve behavior. Most animals are active only during the early morning or late afternoon, when temperatures are less extreme. Few large animals are found in the desert because there is not enough water or food to support them.

Figure 24-15 Desert organisms are adapted to hot, dry conditions.

A Giant saguaro cacti expand to store water after it rains.

B Desert iguanas, common in deserts of the southwestern United States and Mexico, prefer temperatures above 100°F.

Section Assessment

1. Name two biomes that receive less than 25 cm of rain each year.

2. Compare the adaptations of tundra organisms to their environment with those of a desert organism to its environment.

3. **Think Critically:** Compare and contrast the canopies of temperate deciduous forests and tropical rain forests.

4. **Skill Builder**
   Observing and Inferring Animals adapt to their environments in order to survive. Do the **Chapter 24 Skill Activity** on page 1017 to infer how some organisms adapt.

Using Computers

Database Create a database of information on Earth's land biomes. Include data on temperature range, precipitation, limiting factors, and descriptions of climax communities. If you need help, refer to page 1005.

Materials

- Graph paper
- Thermometer
- Tape measure
- Hand lens
- Notebook
- Binoculars
- Pencil
- Field guides

Studying a Land Environment

An ecological study includes observation and analysis of living organisms and the physical features of the environment.

What You'll Investigate

How do you study an ecosystem?

Goals

- **Observe** biotic and abiotic factors of an ecosystem.
- **Analyze** the relationships among organisms and their environment.

Procedure

1. **Choose** a portion of an ecosystem near your school or home as your area of study. You might choose to study a pond, a forest area in a park, a garden, or another area.

2. **Decide** the boundaries of your study area.

3. Using a tape measure and graph paper, **make a map** of your study area.

4. Using a thermometer, **measure and record** the air temperature in your study area.

5. **Observe** the organisms in your study area. Use field guides to identify them. Use a hand lens to study small organisms. Use binoculars to study animals you cannot get near. Also, look for evidence (such as tracks or feathers) of organisms you do not see.

6. Record your observations in a table like the one shown. Make drawings to help you remember what you see.

7. Visit your study area as many times as you can and at different times of the day for four weeks. At each visit, be sure to make the same measurements and record all observations. Note how biotic and abiotic factors interact.

Conclude and Apply

1. **Identify** relationships among the organisms in your study area, such as predator-prey or symbiosis.

2. **Diagram** a food chain or food web for your ecosystem.

3. **Predict** what might happen if one or more abiotic factors were changed suddenly.

4. **Predict** what might happen if one or more populations were removed from the area.

Environmental Data				
Date	Time of Day	Temperature	Organisms Observed	Observations and Comments

Protecting Antarctica

The Coldest Place on Earth

Antarctica is a vast continent of rock covered with ice and surrounded by ocean. It is the least changed landmass in the world, in part because it is an environment hostile to humans. Winters are dark and long, with temperatures dipping to –90°C. During winter, shelves of ice extend from the land out over the ocean, essentially doubling the size of the continent. The yearly freezing and thawing of this ice has important effects on worldwide weather patterns and is a force that drives ocean currents.

Antarctica's Resources

Although the land is barren, seals and penguins, like the ones at left, use the shores as breeding grounds, and the waters of the Antarctic Ocean teem with life. Under the surface of Antarctica lie untouched mineral resources. Coal and oil probably exist in enormous quantities, as do other minerals that have already been discovered.

Antarctica and its remarkable natural resources are fully protected by a treaty that was drawn up in 1959 and signed by 12 nations—the United States, Great Britain, Argentina, Chile, France, Belgium, Norway, Australia, New Zealand, Japan, South Africa, and what was then the USSR. The Antarctic Treaty made the entire continent "a natural reserve, devoted to peace and science." Military activities, hunting, mining, and other actions that might harm the environment and its wild inhabitants are banned.

Since 1959, the Antarctic Treaty has been expanded to promote even greater environmental protection, international cooperation, and freedom for scientific research. Thanks to this agreement, Antarctica will remain an essentially undisturbed wilderness far into the future.

*inter*NET
CONNECTION

Visit the Glencoe Science Web Site at **www.glencoe.com/sec/science/ca** to find out more about research in Antarctica.

Water Environments

Freshwater Biomes

You've learned that temperature and precipitation are the most important factors determining which species can survive in a land environment. The limiting factors in water environments are the amount of salt in the water, dissolved oxygen, water temperature, and sunlight. The amount of salts dissolved in the water is called salinity. Freshwater contains little or no dissolved salts, so it has a low salinity. Earth's freshwater biomes include flowing water like these rivers and streams, as well as still or standing water, such as lakes and ponds.

Rivers and Streams

Flowing freshwater environments range from small, swiftly flowing streams, like the one in **Figure 24-16A,** to large, slow rivers. The faster a stream flows, the clearer its water tends to be and the higher its oxygen content. Swift currents quickly wash loose particles downstream, leaving a rocky or gravelly bottom. The tumbling and splashing of swiftly flowing water mixes in air from the atmosphere, increasing the oxygen content of the water.

Most of the nutrients that support life in flowing-water ecosystems are washed into the water from land. In areas where the water movement slows down, such as wide pools in streams or large rivers, debris settles to the bot-

Figure 24-16

 Freshwater streams are important in the ecosystem.

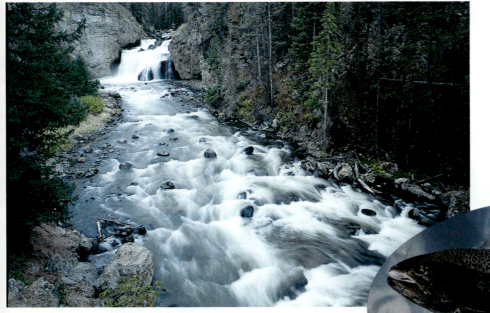

B The cold water, rapid current, and high oxygen content of this stream provide the kind of habitat required for fish like this rainbow trout.

Figure 24-17 Ponds and lakes differ in the types of communities inhabiting them. **What are some other differences between ponds and lakes?**

A The warm, sunlit waters of this pond are home to a large variety of organisms. Plants and algae form the basis of a food web that includes snails, insects, frogs, snakes, turtles, and fish.

tom. These environments tend to have higher nutrient levels and lower dissolved oxygen levels. They contain organisms such as freshwater mussels, minnows, and leeches that are not so well adapted for swiftly flowing water. They also tend to have more plant growth.

Lakes and Ponds

A lake or pond forms when a low place in the land fills with rainwater, snowmelt, or water from a stream. The waters of lakes and ponds hardly move at all. They contain more plant growth than flowing-water environments contain.

Ponds, like the one in **Figure 24-17A,** are smaller, shallow bodies of water. Because they are shallow, sunlight can usually penetrate all the way to the bottom, making the water warmer and promoting the growth of plants and algae. In fact, many ponds are almost completely filled with plant material, so the only clear, open water is at the center. Because of the lush growth in pond environments, they tend to be high in nutrients.

Lakes are larger and deeper than ponds. They tend to have more open water because most plant growth is limited to shallow areas along the shoreline. In fact, organisms found in the warm, sunlit waters of the lakeshore are often similar to those found in ponds.

Floating in the warm, sunlit water near the surface of freshwater lakes and ponds are algae and other microscopic organisms known all together as plankton. **Plankton** includes algae, plants, and other organisms. If you were to dive all the way to the bottom, you would discover few, if any, plants or algae growing. Colder temperatures and lower light levels limit the types of organisms that can live in deep lake waters. Most lake organisms are found along the shoreline and in the warm water near the surface. ✔

B The population density of the warm, shallow water of the lakeshore is high. Fewer types of organisms live in the deeper water.

Reading Check ✔

What is plankton?

Saltwater Biomes

About 95 percent of the water on the surface on Earth contains high concentrations of salts. The saltwater biomes include the oceans, seas, and a few inland lakes, such as the Great Salt Lake in Utah.

Estuaries

Virtually every river on Earth eventually flows into the ocean. The area where a river meets the ocean and contains a mixture of freshwater and salt water is called an **estuary.** Estuaries are located near coastlines and border the land. Salinity changes with the amount of freshwater brought in by rivers and streams, and with the amount of salt water pushed inland by the tides.

Estuaries like the one in **Figure 24-18** are extremely fertile, productive environments because freshwater streams bring in tons of nutrients from inland soils. Nutrient levels in estuaries are higher than those in freshwater or other saltwater ecosystems. Estuarine organisms include many species of algae, a few salt-tolerant grasses, shrimp, crabs, clams, oysters, snails, worms, and fish. Estuaries serve as important nursery grounds for many species of ocean fish.

Seashores

All of Earth's landmasses are bordered by ocean water. The fairly shallow waters along the world's coastlines contain a variety of saltwater ecosystems, all of which are influenced by the tides and by the action of waves. The gravitational pull of the sun and moon causes the tides to rise and fall twice each day in most parts of the world. The **intertidal zone** is the portion of the shoreline that is covered with water at high tide and exposed to the air during low tide. Organisms living in the intertidal zone must not only be adapted to dramatic changes in temperature, moisture, and salinity, but also be able to withstand the force of wave action. Two kinds of intertidal zones are shown in **Figure 24-19.**

Mini Lab

Modeling Freshwater Environments

Procedure

1. Cover the bottom of a 2-L bottle with about 2 cm of gravel, muck, and other debris from the bottom of a pond. If plants are present, add one or two to the bottle. Use a dip net to capture small fish, insects, or tadpoles.

2. Carefully pour pond water into the bottle until it is about two-thirds full. Seal the bottle.

3. Keep the bottle indoors at room temperature and out of direct sunlight.

Analysis

1. Using a hand lens, observe as many organisms as possible. Record your observations. After two or three days, return your sample to the original habitat.

2. Write a short paper describing the organisms in your sample ecosystem and explaining their interactions.

Figure 24-19 Organisms living in intertidal zones have adaptations to survive in these changing environments.

A Wave action keeps the sandy bottom in constant motion, and organisms that live on sandy shores, such as clams, crabs, and worms, burrow into the sand to avoid being washed away.

Open Ocean

Life abounds in the open ocean, where there is no land. The ocean can be divided into life zones based on the depth to which sunlight can penetrate the water. The lighted zone of the ocean is the upper 200 m or so. It is the home of the plankton that make up the foundation of the food chain in the open ocean. Below about 200 m, where sunlight cannot reach, is the dark zone of the ocean. Animals living in this region feed on material that floats down from the lighted zone, or they feed on each other.

B Algae, mussels, barnacles, snails, and other organisms adapted for clinging to the rocks are typically found on rocky shores. These organisms must be able to tolerate the heavy force of breaking waves.

Section Assessment

1. What are the similarities and differences between a lake and a stream?

2. What biotic or abiotic factor limits life on the floor of a tropical rain forest and the bottom of the deep ocean? Why?

3. **Think Critically:** Why do few plants grow in the waters of a swift-flowing mountain stream?

4.  **Skill Builder**
   Comparing and Contrasting Compare and contrast the effects of (1) temperature in the tundra and desert and (2) sunlight in deep-lake and deep-ocean waters. If you need help, refer to Comparing and Contrasting in the **Skill Handbook** on page 992.

Science Journal Write a paragraph in your Science Journal explaining how starting from the equator and moving toward the north pole is like climbing a mountain. Refer to abiotic factors in your explanation.

to BIOMES

Research the average monthly rainfall, high temperature, and low temperature for each month of the past year for the area where you live. Prepare a graph of data using the example below. Based on your findings, which biome graph most closely matches your data? What biome do you live in? What type of plant and animal life do you expect to find in your biome?

Have you ever wondered why you do not find polar bears in Florida or palm trees in Alaska? Organisms are limited to where they can live and survive due to temperature, amount of rainfall, and type of soil found in a region. A biome's boundaries are determined by climate more than anything else. Climate is a way of categorizing temperature extremes and yearly precipitation patterns. Use this field guide to identify some of the world's biomes and to determine which biome you live in.

Interpreting Land Biome Climates

The following graphs represent the climates of six different biomes. To read each biome graph, use the following information. Axis *A* shows the months of the year. Axis *B* shows the average amount of precipitation for each month. Axis *C* shows the average high and low temperature for each month.

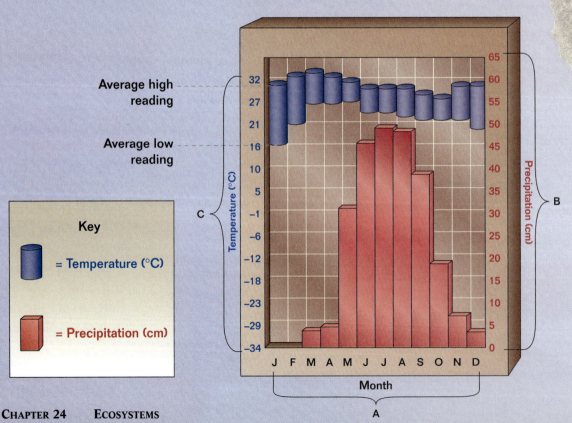

Biome: Tundra

- Seasons: long, harsh winters; short summers; very little precipitation
- Plants: mosses, lichens, grasses, and sedges
- Animals: weasels, arctic foxes, snowshoe hares, snowy owls, and hawks

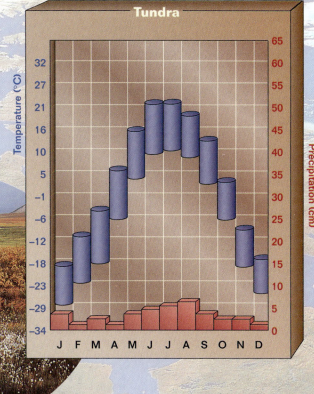

Tundra

Temperature (°C): 32, 27, 21, 16, 10, 5, -1, -6, -12, -18, -23, -29, -34

Precipitation (cm): 65, 60, 55, 50, 45, 40, 35, 30, 25, 20, 15, 10, 5, 0

J F M A M J J A S O N D

Taiga

Temperature (°C): 32, 27, 21, 16, 10, 5, -1, -6, -12, -18, -23, -29, -34

Precipitation (cm): 65, 60, 55, 50, 45, 40, 35, 30, 25, 20, 15, 10, 5, 0

J F M A M J J A S O N D

Biome: Taiga

- Seasons: cold, severe winters with much snow; short growing seasons
- Plants: conifers such as spruces, firs, and larches
- Animals: caribou, wolves, moose, bear, and summer birds

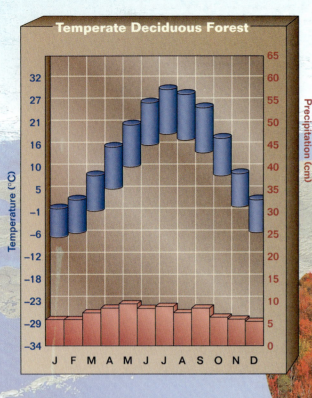

Temperate Deciduous Forest

Biome: Temperate Deciduous Forest

- Seasons: cold winters, hot summers, and moderate precipitation
- Plants: deciduous trees such as oak, hickory, and beech, which lose their leaves every autumn
- Animals: wolves, deer, bears, small mammals, and birds

Biome: Grassland

- Seasons: cold winters, hot summers with little precipitation
- Plants: grasses and a few trees
- Animals: grazing animals, wolves, prairie dogs, foxes, ferrets, snakes, lizards, and insects

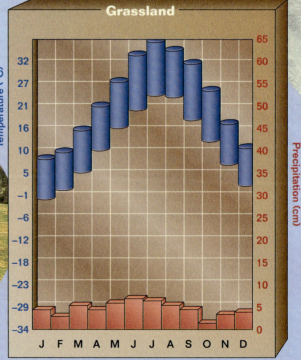

Grassland

Biome: Desert

- Seasons: warm to hot in daytime, cool in the evening, little precipitation
- Plants: cacti, yuccas, Joshua trees, and bunchgrasses
- Animals: small rodents, jackrabbits, birds of prey, and snakes

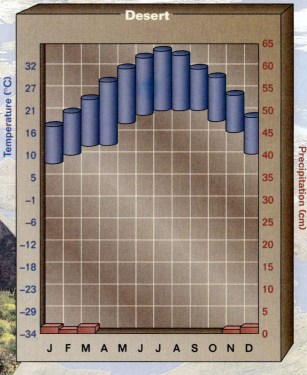

Desert

Temperature (°C): 32, 27, 21, 16, 10, 5, -1, -6, -12, -18, -23, -29, -34

Precipitation (cm): 65, 60, 55, 50, 45, 40, 35, 30, 25, 20, 15, 10, 5, 0

J F M A M J J A S O N D

Biome: Tropical Rain Forest

- Seasons: hot all year with precipitation almost every day
- Plants: trees and orchids
- Animals: birds, reptiles, insects, monkeys, and sloths

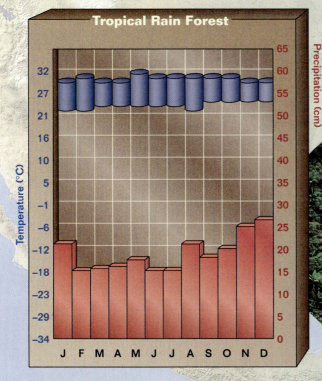

Tropical Rain Forest

Temperature (°C): 32, 27, 21, 16, 10, 5, -1, -6, -12, -18, -23, -29, -34

Precipitation (cm): 65, 60, 55, 50, 45, 40, 35, 30, 25, 20, 15, 10, 5, 0

J F M A M J J A S O N D

For a **preview** of this chapter, study this Reviewing Main Ideas before you read the chapter. After you have studied this chapter, you can use the Reviewing Main Ideas to **review** the chapter.

The Glencoe MindJogger, Audiocassettes, and CD-ROM provide additional opportunities for review.

Section 24-1 HOW ECOSYSTEMS CHANGE

The process of gradual change from one community of organisms to another is **ecological succession.** It involves changes in both abiotic and biotic factors. Succession can be divided into **primary** and **secondary succession. Pioneer communities** are the first to move into an environment, and **climax communities** are the final organisms to move in. *How can you explain that lawns usually do not go through succession?*

Section 24-2 LAND ENVIRONMENTS

Climate is the general weather pattern in an area. The factors that determine a region's climate are temperature and precipitation. Large geographic areas with similar climates and climax communities are biomes. The six major biomes are the **tundra, taiga, temperate deciduous forests, tropical rain forests, grasslands,** and **deserts.** *How does climate influence the type of biomes?*

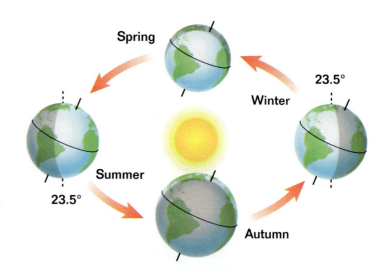

Spring

Winter

23.5°

Summer

23.5°

Autumn

Reading Check ✓

Diagram changes in an ecosystem as a series of causes and effects. You might start with this cause: an ecosystem's soil is thin and poor. What is a possible effect?

Section 24-3 WATER ENVIRONMENTS

The limiting factors in water environments include the amount of salt in the water, dissolved oxygen, water temperature, and sunlight. Freshwater ecosystems include rivers, streams, lakes, and ponds. Saltwater ecosystems include the oceans, seas, and a few inland lakes. An area where a river meets the ocean is called an **estuary.** All land on Earth is surrounded by ocean water. The **intertidal zone** is the portion of the shoreline that is covered with water at high tide and exposed to the air during low tide. The open ocean is divided into life zones based on the depth to which sunlight can penetrate the water. *Describe where estuaries form. How are they important?*

Using Vocabulary

a. biome
b. climax community
c. desert
d. ecological succession
e. estuary
f. grassland
g. intertidal zone
h. pioneer community
i. plankton
j. primary succession
k. secondary succession
l. taiga
m. temperate deciduous forest
n. tropical rain forest
o. tundra

Each of the following sentences is false. Make the sentence true by replacing the italicized word with a word from the list above.

1. *Primary succession* has occurred when one community of organisms replaces another.
2. *Plankton* are the first organisms to inhabit an area.
3. An *estuary* is a region with similar climate and climax communities.
4. A *biome* is an equatorial region that receives large amounts of rainfall.
5. A *tropical rain forest* is where freshwater mixes with salt water.

Checking Concepts

Choose the word or phrase that best answers the question.

6. What determines the climate of an area?
   A) plankton
   B) succession
   C) limiting factors
   D) abiotic factors
7. What are tundra and desert examples of?
   A) ecosystems
   B) biomes
   C) habitats
   D) communities
8. What is a treeless, cold, and dry biome called?
   A) taiga
   B) tundra
   C) desert
   D) grassland

9. Which is **NOT** a grassland?
   A) pampas
   B) veldts
   C) steppes
   D) estuaries
10. Mussels and barnacles have adapted to the wave action of what?
   A) sandy beach
   B) rocky shore
   C) open ocean
   D) estuary
11. Which biome contains the largest number of species?
   A) taiga
   B) temperate deciduous forest
   C) tropical rain forest
   D) grassland
12. What is the end result of succession?
   A) pioneer community
   B) limiting factor
   C) climax community
   D) permafrost
13. Which biome does **NOT** have trees as a climax community?
   A) tundra
   B) taiga
   C) tropical rain forest
   D) grassland
14. Which does **NOT** contain freshwater?
   A) lakes
   B) ponds
   C) rivers
   D) oceans
15. Which does **NOT** have flowing water?
   A) ponds
   B) rivers
   C) seashores
   D) streams

Thinking Critically

16. Would a soil sample from a temperate deciduous forest contain more or less humus than soil from a tropical rain forest? Explain.
17. A grassy meadow borders an oak-maple forest. Is one of these ecosystems undergoing succession? Why?
18. Describe how ecological succession eventually results in the layers of vegetation found in forests.
19. Why do many tropical rain forest plants make good houseplants?

Developing Skills

If you need help, refer to the **Skill Handbook**.

20. **Concept Mapping:** Make a concept map for water environments. Include these terms: *saltwater ecosystems, freshwater ecosystems, intertidal zone, lighted zone, dark zone, lake, pond, river, stream, flowing water,* and *standing water.*

21. **Making and Using Graphs:** Make a bar graph of the amount of rainfall per year in each biome.

Rainfall Amounts

Biome	Rainfall/Year
Deciduous forests	100 cm
Tropical rain forests	225 cm
Grasslands	50 cm
Deserts	20 cm

22. **Hypothesizing:** Make a hypothesis as to what would happen to succession in a pond if the pond owner removed all the cattails and reeds from around the pond edges every summer.

23. **Comparing and Contrasting:** Compare and contrast the adaptations of organisms living in swiftly flowing streams and organisms living in the rocky intertidal zones.

24. **Recognizing Cause and Effect:** Devastating fires, like the one in Yellowstone National Park in 1988, cause many changes to the land. Determine the effect of a fire to an area that has reached its climax community.

THE PRINCETON REVIEW

Test-Taking Tip

Where's the fire? Slow down! Go back over reading passages and double check your math. Remember that doing most of the questions and getting them right is always better than doing all the questions and getting lots of them wrong.

Test Practice

Use these questions to test your Science Proficiency.

1. What determines whether a land supports a deciduous forest or a grassland?
   A) temperature
   B) latitude
   C) precipitation
   D) length of growing season

2. What causes the vertical distribution of plants in a deep lake?
   A) color of the water
   B) depth that light can penetrate
   C) kind of plants in the lake
   D) kind of animals in the lake

3. How are primary succession and secondary succession similar?
   A) both begin where no soil is present
   B) both end in climax communities
   C) both begin with a pioneer community
   D) both develop where lava has cooled

4. What is the layer of vegetation that shades the ground below and provides homes for birds, insects, and mammals called?
   A) soil
   B) understory
   C) canopy
   D) forest floor

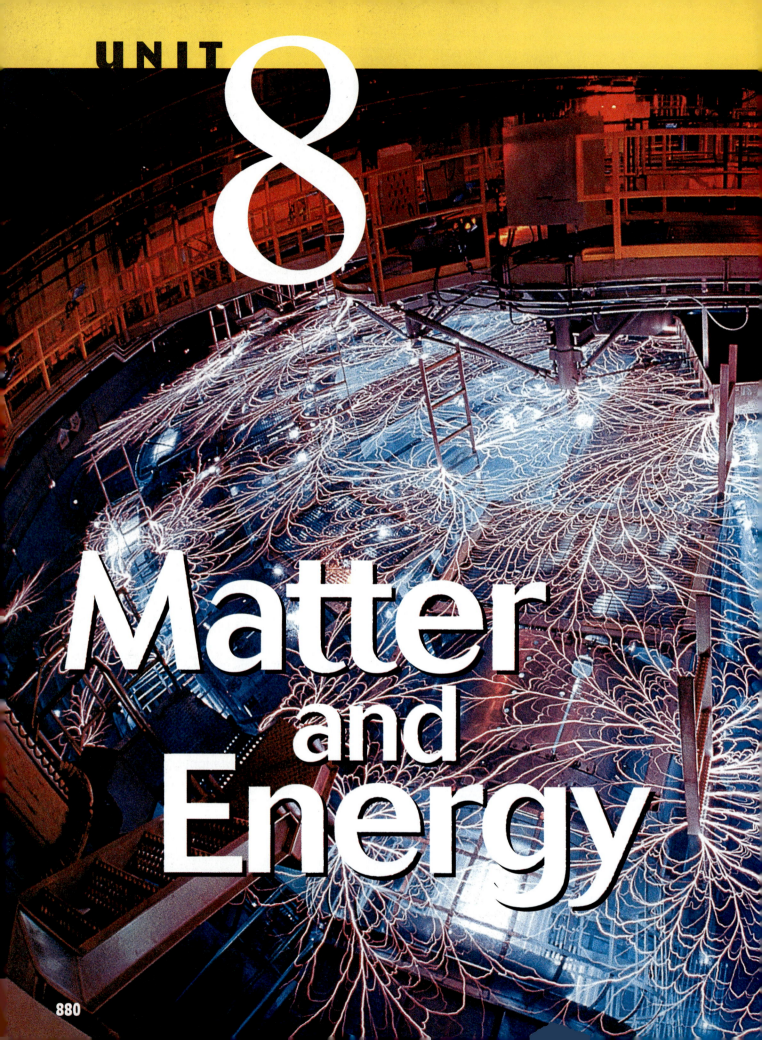

8

Matter and Energy

NATIONAL GEOGRAPHIC

What's Happening Here?

You might think the world is made of earth and water and air, but what are earth and water and air made of? Only in the 1980s did scientists glimpse what they had long reasoned was the building block of our world—the atom. Scientists now know the atom itself has parts. No one has ever seen these subatomic particles, yet scientists are studying them. At the Sandia National Laboratories in New Mexico, the building shakes and electric discharges create wild patterns of light during a trial of the "Z machine" (left). Dozens of scientists are working on this experiment to heat atoms to such temperatures that their subatomic particles fuse, or come together, and release energy.

If you have ever been knocked down by an ocean wave (below), you are familiar with another carrier of energy, the wave. What is energy, and where does it come from? How many different kinds of atoms are there, and how are their parts arranged? These are some of the questions you will explore in this unit.

interNET CONNECTION

Explore the Glencoe Science Web Site at **www.glencoe. com/sec/science/ca** to find out more about topics found in this unit.

CHAPTER 25

Matter

Chapter Preview

Skills Preview

Skill Builders
- Interpret Data
- Compare and Contrast

Activities
- Make and Use a Table
- Form a Hypothesis

MiniLabs
- Make a Model
- Observe and Infer

Reading Check ✓

Use the headings and sub-headings to make an outline as you read this chapter. Write a few important points under each subheading.

Explore Activity

You've just finished playing basketball. You're hot and thirsty. You reach for your bottle of water and, leaning back, squeeze out a long, thirst-quenching drink. Releasing your grip, you notice that the bottle is nearly empty. But, is the bottle really almost empty? According to the dictionary, empty means containing nothing. When you have finished all the water in the bottle, will it be empty? And, if it's full, what is it full of?

Observe Matter

1. Wad up a small piece of a dry paper towel or tissue paper and tape it to the bottom of the inside of a plastic drinking cup. When you turn the cup upside down, the towel or paper should remain inside the cup.

2. Fill a bowl or sink almost to the top with water. Hold the cup upside down over the water's surface. Slowly push the cup straight into the water as far as you can.

3. Slowly raise the cup straight out of the water. Remove the paper towel and examine it.

Science Journal

In your Science Journal, describe your experiment. Include a description of the paper after you removed it from the cup. Explain what you think happened. Was anything in the cup besides the paper? If so, what was it?

25•1 Structure of Matter

What You'll Learn

► What matter is
► What makes up matter
► The parts of an atom
► The models that are used for atoms

Vocabulary

matter
atom
law of conservation
    of matter
electron
nucleus
proton
neutron

Why It's Important

► Matter makes up your body, your environment, and the universe.

What is matter?

Did you decide that the bottle of water and the plastic cup in the Explore Activity were filled with air? Have you wondered what makes up the air around you? It's mostly nitrogen and oxygen. Nitrogen and oxygen are kinds of matter. Scientists define **matter** as anything that has mass and takes up space. So even if you can't see it or catch hold of it, air is matter.

What about the things you *can* see, taste, smell, and touch when you eat lunch in the cafeteria or walk around your neighborhood? These things are also made of matter. What about your own body? Yes, it's matter too. Through science, you will explore the many amazing kinds of matter that make up the universe—things as common as a flower or as spectacular as a supernova, both shown in **Figure 25-1.**

What isn't matter?

You can see the words on this page because of light. Does light have mass or take up space? What about the warmth from the sun or the heater in your classroom? Neither light nor heat take up any space. They don't have any mass either, so they are not forms of matter. Emotions, thoughts, and ideas also are not matter.

Figure 25-1   A flower in your backyard (A) and a supernova (a large exploding star) in a galaxy millions of light-years away (B) seem as different as night and day. But, the flower and supernova are the same in an important way—they're both matter. **How is matter defined?**

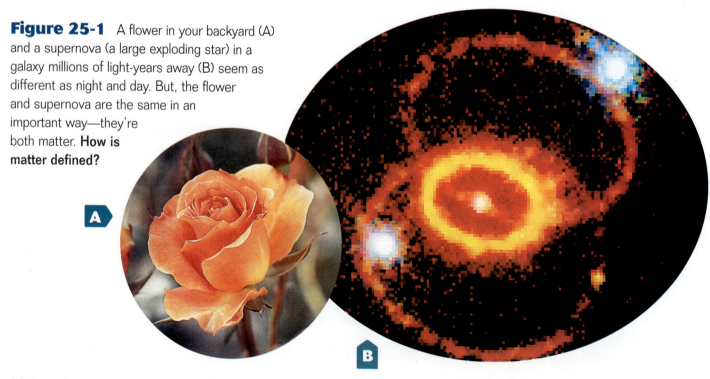

A

B

What makes up matter?

Suppose you cut a sheet of notebook paper into smaller and smaller pieces, as shown in **Figure 25-2.** Do the pieces seem to be made of the same matter as the large sheet you started with? If you could cut a small enough piece, would it still have the same properties as the large sheet of paper? Or, would it no longer be paper at all? People have asked questions like these—and wondered about what matter is made of—for centuries.

An Early Idea

Democritus, who lived from 460 to 370 B.C., was a Greek philosopher who thought the universe was made of empty space and tiny bits of stuff. He believed that the bits of stuff were so small they could no longer be divided into smaller pieces. He called these tiny pieces of stuff atoms. In fact, the term *atom* comes from a Greek word that means "cannot be divided." In science today, an **atom** is defined as a small particle that makes up most types of matter. Democritus thought that different types of atoms exist for every type of matter. His idea proved to be a small step in understanding the structure of matter that continues today.

Lavoisier's Contribution

Antoine Lavoisier (la VWAH see ay), a French chemist who lived about 2000 years after Democritus, was also curious about matter—especially when it changed from one form to another. Before Lavoisier, people thought matter could appear and disappear during changes such as burning and rusting. You might have thought the same thing—that matter can disappear—if you've ever watched wood burn to embers, then ashes in a fireplace. But, Lavoisier showed that wood and the oxygen it combines with during burning have the same mass as the ash, water, and

Figure 25-2

Paper is made up of carbon, hydrogen, and oxygen. So, if you could cut paper into small enough pieces, it wouldn't be paper at all. **What common type of matter is made up of only hydrogen and oxygen?**

Oxygen
+

**Water vapor
and
carbon dioxide**
+

Figure 25-3 When wood burns, matter is not lost. The total mass of the wood and the oxygen it combines with equals the total mass of the water vapor, carbon dioxide, and ashes produced. **When you burn wood in a fireplace, what is the source of the oxygen?**

carbon dioxide (KAR bun di AHK side) produced, as shown in **Figure 25-3.** In the same way, iron and oxygen have the same mass as the rust they form. From Lavoisier's work came the **law of conservation of matter.** This law states that matter is neither created nor destroyed, only changed in form.

Models of the Atom

Scientists often use models for things that are too small to be seen and observed easily, as well as things that are too complicated or too large to be understood easily. Throughout history, scientists have created and used models to help find out what atoms are made of and how they act.

One way to make a model is to make a small version of something larger. For example, if you wanted to design a new kind of sailboat, would you just come up with a design, build a full-sized boat, and hope it would float? It would be smarter—and safer—to first build and test a small model of your design. Then, if it doesn't float, you can change your design and build another model. You can keep trying until the model works. As with the model sailboat, scientists' models are changed as new information is gained.

Dalton's Atomic Model

In the early 1800s, an English schoolteacher and chemist named John Dalton studied the experiments of Lavoisier and many others. Dalton thought that an atomic model could explain the results of these experiments. He named his model *the atomic theory of matter.* Dalton's atomic model, like many scientific models, was a set of ideas—not an object. Dalton believed that matter was made of atoms that were too small to be seen by the human eye. He also thought that each type of matter was made of only one kind of atom. For example, gold atoms make up a gold nugget and give a gold ring its shininess, as well as its other properties.

Sizes of Atoms

Atoms are so small it would take about 1 million of them lined up in a row to equal the thickness of a human hair. To give you a better idea of how small atoms are, look at **Figure 25-4.** Imagine you are holding an orange in your hand. If you wanted to use only your eyes to see the individual atoms on the surface of the orange, the size of the orange would need to increase to the size of Earth. Then, imagine it is covered with billions and billions of marbles. Each marble would represent one of the atoms that make up the skin of the orange.

Figure 25-4 Imagining this orange is the size of Earth can help you visualize the size of an atom.

Figure 25-5 In this experiment, the magnet caused the cathode rays inside the tube to bend. **What do you think would happen to the cathode rays if the magnet were removed?**

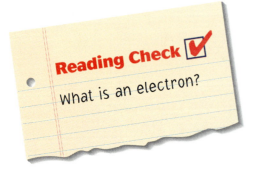

Reading Check ✓

What is an electron?

Discovering the Electron

One of the many pioneers in the development of today's atomic model was J.J. Thomson, an Englishman. He conducted experiments using a vacuum tube, which is a glass tube that has all the air pumped out of it and then is sealed at both ends. Thomson's tube had metal plates at both ends. The plates were connected to a high-voltage electrical source that gave one of the plates, the *anode*, a positive charge and the other, the *cathode*, a negative charge. During his experiments, Thomson observed rays that traveled from the cathode to the anode. Because the rays came from the cathode, Thomson called them cathode rays. The rays were bent by a magnet, as seen in **Figure 25-5,** showing that the rays were made up of particles that had mass. The rays were bent by charged plates, also. Thomson knew that unlike charges attract each other and like charges repel each other. When he saw that the rays bent toward a positively charged plate, he concluded that the cathode rays were made up of negative particles. These invisible, negatively charged particles, which came from the metal atoms that made up the cathode, are called **electrons.** ✓

Imagine Thomson's excitement at this discovery. He had shown that atoms are not too tiny to divide after all. Rather, they are made up of even smaller subatomic particles. Other scientists soon built on Thomson's results and found that the electron had a small mass—in fact, 1/1837 the mass of the lightest atom, the hydrogen atom. In 1906, Thomson received the Nobel Prize in Physics for his discovery of the electron.

Matter that has equal numbers of positive and negative charges, and therefore has no *net* charge, is said to be neutral. Because most matter is neutral, Thomson knew that atoms had to contain both positive and negative charges. He pictured the atom as being made up of electrons embedded in a ball of positive charge. You might compare his model, shown in **Figure 25-6,** to something like tiny chocolate chips spread around in a ball of cookie dough. But, Thomson's model did not provide all the answers to the questions that puzzled scientists about atoms.

Rutherford—The Nucleus

If electrons are the negatively charged particles in atoms, what are the positively charged particles that also must be present? Also, how are the parts of the atom arranged? In 1909, a team of scientists led by Ernest Rutherford in England began to work on the mystery of atomic structure. They bombarded materials with alpha particles. Alpha particles are high-energy, positively charged particles. When the scientists beamed alpha particles at an extremely thin piece of gold foil, they were amazed at the results. Most of the particles passed straight through the foil as if it were not there at all. Other particles changed direction or even bounced back. Rutherford thought the result so remarkable that he later said, "It was almost as incredible as if you had fired a 15-inch shell at a piece of tissue paper, and it came back and hit you."

Rutherford and his team soon concluded that because so many of the alpha particles passed straight through the gold foil, its atoms must be mostly empty space.

Visit the Glencoe Science Web Site at **www. glencoe.com/sec/ science/ca** for more information about electron energy levels in atoms.

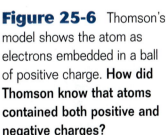

Figure 25-6 Thomson's model shows the atom as electrons embedded in a ball of positive charge. **How did Thomson know that atoms contained both positive and negative charges?**

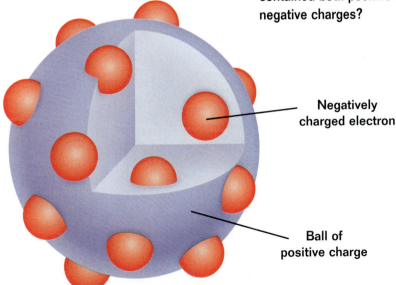

Negatively charged electron

Ball of positive charge

Figure 25-7 Rutherford concluded that the atom must be mostly empty space in which electrons are scattered. He also thought the nucleus of the atom must be small and positively charged. **Where is most of the mass of the atom concentrated?**

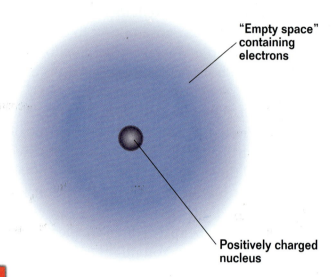

"Empty space" containing electrons

Positively charged nucleus

However, because some of the alpha particles bounced off something that they hit, the gold atoms must contain small, massive, positively charged objects. Rutherford called the positively charged, central part of the atom the **nucleus** (NEW klee us). He named the positively charged particles in the nucleus **protons.** He also suggested that electrons were scattered in the mostly empty space around the nucleus, as shown in **Figure 25-7.**

Discovering the Neutron

Rutherford had been puzzled by one part of his experiments with alpha particles. Alpha particles seemed to be heavier than they should be. What could possibly cause the extra mass? James Chadwick, a student of Rutherford's, answered the question. Chadwick experimented with particles given off by atoms that had been bombarded with alpha particles. He found that, unlike electrons, the paths of these new particles were not affected by an electric field. To explain his observations, he said that these particles came from the nucleus and had no charge. Chadwick called these uncharged particles **neutrons.** His proton-neutron model of the atomic nucleus is still accepted today.

Today's Model of the Atom

Scientists in the early part of the twentieth century uncovered evidence that electrons in atoms were arranged in energy levels. The lowest energy level is closest to the nucleus and can hold only two electrons. Higher energy levels are farther from the nucleus and can contain more electrons. To explain these energy levels, some scientists thought that the electrons might orbit an atom's nucleus—something like how Earth and the other planets of our solar system orbit the sun.

The Electron Cloud Model

As a result of research that continues today, scientists now realize that because electrons are so small and move so fast, their energy levels are not neat, planetlike orbits around the nucleus. Rather, it seems most likely that the electrons move in what is called the atom's *electron cloud*, as shown in **Figure 25-8**. The electron cloud model helps explain what atoms do and what they don't do.

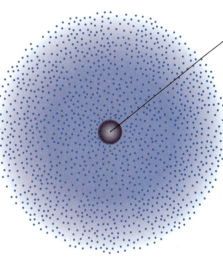

Nucleus

Figure 25-8 One model of the atom pictures the electrons moving around the nucleus in a region called an electron cloud. Dots represent places where electrons might be found. **What does the greater number of dots near the nucleus suggest?**

Section Assessment

1. List five things that are matter and five things that are not matter. Explain your answers.

2. Describe Dalton's contribution to today's understanding of matter.

3. Think of a rule that would help a fourth grader decide which things are matter and which things are not matter.

4. **Think Critically:** What made alpha particles heavier than Rutherford thought they should be?

5. **Skill Builder**
   Observing and Inferring Scientists inferred the structure of the atom based on their observations. Do the **Chapter 25 Skill Activity** on page 1018 and practice observing and inferring.

Science Journal Write a summary of what you learned about atoms. Include all of the vocabulary words listed in the Chapter Assessment in your summary.

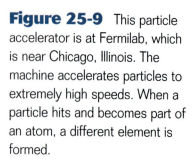

25•2 Elements

Organizing the Elements

Have you watched television today? TV sets are common, yet each one is a complex device. The outer case is made mostly of plastic, and the screen is made of glass. Many of the parts that conduct electricity are metals or combinations of metals called alloys. Other parts in the interior of the set contain materials that barely conduct electricity. These different materials have one thing in common. Each is made up of even simpler materials. In fact, if you had the proper equipment, you could separate the plastics, glass, and metals into these simpler materials.

Eventually, though, you would reach a point where you couldn't separate the materials any further. What you would have is a collection of elements. An **element** is a material that cannot be broken down to simpler materials by ordinary means. At this time, 112 elements are known and 90 of them occur naturally on Earth. These elements make up gases in the air, minerals in rocks, and liquids such as water. Examples include oxygen and nitrogen in the air you breathe and the metals gold, silver, aluminum, and iron. The other 22 are known as synthetic elements. Synthetic elements have important uses in medical testing and in smoke detectors and heart pacemaker batteries. These elements, which may be found in stars, have been made in laboratories by machines like the one shown in **Figure 25-9.**

What You'll Learn

► What an element is
► The meaning of atomic mass and atomic number
► What an isotope is
► What metals, metalloids, and nonmetals are

Vocabulary

element
atomic number
atomic mass
isotope
mass number
metal
nonmetal
metalloid

Why It's Important

► Everything on Earth is made of the elements found on the periodic table.

Figure 25-9 This particle accelerator is at Fermilab, which is near Chicago, Illinois. The machine accelerates particles to extremely high speeds. When a particle hits and becomes part of an atom, a different element is formed.

Figure 25-10 When you look for a certain book in the library, a system of organization called the Dewey Decimal System helps you find the book quickly and efficiently. **Describe a system of organization that can help you find a pair of matching, black socks quickly in the morning.**

EARTH SCIENCE
INTEGRATION

Elements in Minerals
The mineral fluorite contains fluoride, a form of the element fluorine. Fluorite is added to water and is used in making toothpastes. It makes tooth enamel harder and helps fight tooth decay.

Suppose that you go to a library to look up information for a school assignment. Or, maybe you want to find a book that a friend told you about. When you go to the library, do you look on shelves at random as you walk up and down the rows? Probably not, unless you have lots of time or are just browsing. More likely, you depend on the library's system of organization to find the book you want quickly and efficiently, as shown in **Figure 25-10.**

The Periodic Table

When scientists need to look up information about an element or select one to use in the laboratory, they want to be quick and efficient, too. Chemists have created a chart called the periodic table of the elements to help them organize and display the elements. When you walk into a laboratory or science classroom, you often see this chart on the wall. Each element is represented by a chemical symbol that contains one to three letters. The symbols are a form of chemical shorthand that chemists use to save time and space—both on the periodic table and in written formulas. The symbols are an important part of an international system that is understood by scientists everywhere.

Using Math

Your body is made up primarily of five elements. By mass, the elements are:

oxygen	65%
carbon	18%
hydrogen	10%
nitrogen	3%
calcium	2%
other	2%

Make a circle graph that represents the elements in your body.

Chlorine

17

Cl

35.453

Atomic Number and Atomic Mass

Look up the element chlorine on the periodic table found inside the back cover of your textbook. Cl is the symbol for chlorine, as shown in **Figure 25-11,** but what are the two numbers? The top number, called the element's atomic number, is always a whole number. The **atomic number** tells you the number of protons in the nucleus of each atom of that element. Every atom of chlorine, for example, has 17 protons in its nucleus.

The number beneath the element's symbol is its atomic mass. An element's **atomic mass** tells you how heavy its atoms are compared with atoms of other elements. The unit scientists use for atomic mass is called the atomic mass unit, which is given the symbol u.

Isotopes and Mass Number

All the atoms of an element don't have to have the same mass. Some atoms of an element can have different numbers of neutrons in their nuclei than other atoms. Every chlorine atom contains 17 protons in its nucleus; however, some chlorine nuclei have 18 neutrons and others have 20. These two naturally occurring types of chlorine atoms are called isotopes. **Isotopes** (I suh tohps) are atoms of the same element that have different numbers of neutrons. You can tell someone exactly what type of chlorine atom you are referring to by using its mass number. An atom's **mass number** is the sum of its protons and neutrons [Mass number = number of protons + number of neutrons].

The atoms of chlorine that contain 17 protons and 18 neutrons have a mass number of 35 and are called chlorine-35. Those atoms that contain 17 protons and 20 neutrons are called chlorine-37. These two isotopes of chlorine are shown in **Figure 25-12.**

Figure 25-12 Chlorine is found naturally as two isotopes, chlorine-37 and chlorine-35. Chlorine-37 atoms are heavier than chlorine-35 atoms. The average mass of all chlorine atoms found naturally is 35.453 u. **Which type of chlorine atom is more numerous in nature?**

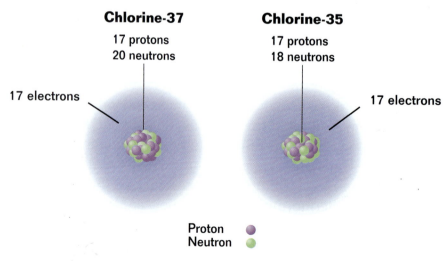

Chlorine-37
17 protons
20 neutrons
17 electrons

Chlorine-35
17 protons
18 neutrons
17 electrons

Proton
Neutron

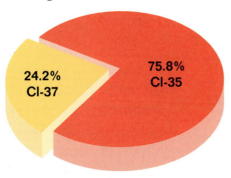
Average Atomic Mass = 35.453 u

24.2%
Cl-37

75.8%
Cl-35

Figure 25-13 Chlorine-35 atoms make up 75.8 percent of chlorine. The remaining 24.2 percent of chlorine atoms are chlorine-37. If you have 1000 atoms of chlorine, 758 of the atoms are chlorine-35. The remaining 242 atoms are chlorine-37. The total mass of the 1000 atoms is 35 453 u, so the average mass of one chlorine atom is 35.453 u. **If an element has only one isotope, how does the mass of the isotope compare with the atomic mass of the element?**

Look at the periodic table block for chlorine, **Figure 25-11.** The element's atomic mass of 35.453 u can be misleading because not one chlorine atom has that mass. About 75 percent of chlorine atoms are chlorine-35 and 25 percent are chlorine-37, as shown in **Figure 25-13.** Therefore, 35.453 u is simply the average mass of chlorine atoms.

Classification of Elements

Elements fall into three general groups: metals, metalloids (MET ul oydz), and nonmetals. You use metals every day because they have many useful physical properties.

Metals generally have a shiny or metallic luster. Metals are good conductors of heat and electricity. For example, copper is often used in electrical circuits and cookware because it conducts heat and electricity well. All metals except mercury are solids at room temperature. Metals are malleable (MAL yuh bul), which means they can be bent and pounded into various shapes. Metals are also ductile, which means they can be drawn into wires without breaking, like the ones shown in **Figure 25-14.** If you look at the periodic table in the back of

Figure 25-14 Metals can be drawn into wires, a property called ductility. A wire's gauge is related to its thickness. A small number means that the wire is thicker.

Figure 25-15 Chlorine, bromine, and iodine are often used as disinfectants. **What nonmetals make up most of the air you breathe?**

this textbook, you can see that most of the elements are metals.

Nonmetals are elements that are usually dull. They are poor conductors of heat and electricity. Many are gases at room temperature, as shown in **Figure 25-15.** The solid nonmetals are generally brittle, meaning they cannot change shape easily without breaking. You can see that, except for hydrogen, the nonmetals are found on the right side of the periodic table.

Metalloids are elements such as silicon and germanium, which have characteristics of both metals and nonmetals. Some are shiny and many are conductors, but they are not as good at conducting heat and electricity as metals. All metalloids are solids at room temperature. Metalloids are found between the metals and nonmetals on the periodic table. ✔

Reading Check ✔

What is a metalloid?

Section Assessment

1. What are isotopes?

2. Explain some of the uses of metals.

3. **Think Critically:** Hector is new to your class today. He missed the lesson on how to use the periodic table to find information about the elements. Describe how you would help Hector find the atomic number for the element oxygen. Explain what this information tells him about oxygen.

4. **Skill Builder**

    Interpreting Data Look up the atomic mass of the element boron in the periodic table inside the back cover of this book. The naturally occurring isotopes of boron are boron-10 and boron-11. Which of the two isotopes is more abundant? Explain your reasoning. If you need help, refer to Interpreting Data in the **Skill Handbook** on page 996.

Using Math

An atom of niobium has a mass number of 91. How many neutrons are in the nucleus of the atom?

An isotope of phosphorus has 15 protons and 15 neutrons in the nucleus of each of its atoms. What is the mass number of the isotope?

Elements and the Periodic Table

The periodic table organizes the elements. But, what do these elements look like, and what are they used for? In this activity, you'll examine some elements and share your findings with your classmates.

What You'll Investigate

What are some of the characteristics of the chemical elements, and what are they used for?

Goals

- **Classify** the chemical elements.
- **Make** your own periodic table that shows the classification of the elements.

Procedure

1. From the list provided by your teacher, select the number of elements you are assigned.
2. **Design** an index card for each of your selected elements. On each element's card, mark its atomic number in the upper left-hand corner and write its symbol and name in the upper right-hand corner.

Materials

- Large index cards
- Merck Index
- Encyclopedia
  other reference materials
- Large bulletin board
- Paper (8½ × 14)
- Thumbtacks
  pushpins

  Alternate Materials

3. Research each of the elements and write several sentences on the card about its appearance, its other properties, and its uses.
4. Based upon its properties, **decide** if each of your elements is likely a metal, a metalloid, or a nonmetal. Use the color of magic marker chosen by your teacher to write the appropriate word—*metal, metalloid,* or *nonmetal*—on each of your cards.
5. Work with your classmates to **make** a large periodic table. Use thumbtacks to attach your cards on a bulletin board in their proper positions on the table.
6. Draw your own periodic table on an 8½ × 14 sheet of paper. Put the elements' symbols and atomic numbers in the proper places on the table.

Conclude and Apply

1. **Interpret** the class data and **classify** the elements into the categories: metals, metalloids, and nonmetals. Highlight each of the three categories in a different color on your periodic table.
2. **Predict** the properties of a yet-undiscovered element located directly under francium on the periodic table.

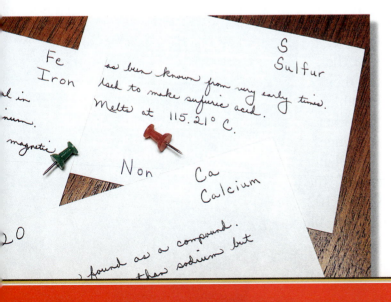

Development of the Periodic Table

Elements such as gold, silver, tin, copper, lead, and mercury have been known since ancient times. As more elements were discovered, people began to recognize patterns in their properties. Later, scientists used the patterns to develop ways of classifying the elements. For example, in 1817, Johann Döbereiner noticed that the atomic mass of strontium was halfway between the masses of calcium and barium, elements with similar chemical properties.

In the Cards

In the mid-nineteenth century, Dmitri Mendeleev published the first periodic table. Mendeleev recognized patterns in the properties and atomic masses of certain elements. In trying to extend the patterns, he created a card for each of the more than 60 elements known at the time. Each card contained the element's symbol, its atomic mass, and its characteristic chemical and physical properties. Mendeleev then arranged the cards on a table in order of increasing atomic mass, grouping elements of similar properties together. The resulting periodic table showed vertical, horizontal, and diagonal relationships. Mendeleev left blank spaces in his table for as-yet-undiscovered elements, and he predicted in detail what the chemical and physical properties of the missing elements would be when they were found.

New Discoveries

With the discovery of the atomic nucleus and isotopes in the early twentieth century, it became apparent that the properties of the elements vary periodically with their atomic numbers. Therefore, modern periodic tables arrange the elements according to atomic number rather than atomic mass. In the mid-1900s, the last major changes to the periodic table resulted from the work of Glenn Seaborg and his coworkers with the discovery of the transuranium elements from atomic number 94 to 102. Locate the element seaborgium on the periodic table. Scientists today continue to discover new elements.

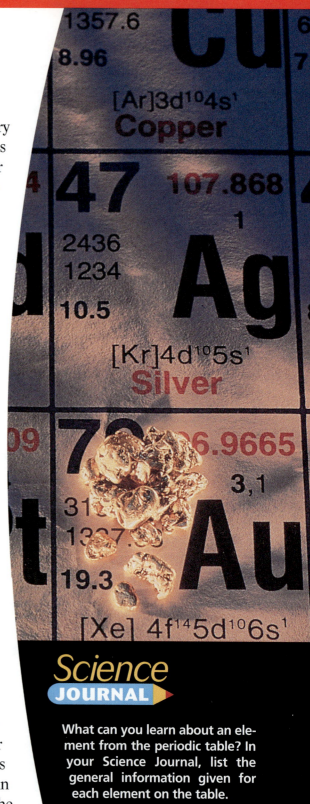

Science JOURNAL

What can you learn about an element from the periodic table? In your Science Journal, list the general information given for each element on the table.

Compounds and Mixtures

Substances

Scientists classify matter in several ways. For example, a sample of matter that has the same composition and properties throughout is called a **substance.** The chemical elements you learned about in Section 25-2 are pure substances. When elements combine with each other, different kinds of matter are formed.

Compounds

What do you call the colorless liquid that flows when you turn on the kitchen faucet? You probably call it water, but maybe you've seen it written H_2O and wondered what that meant. Hydrogen and oxygen occur both naturally as colorless gases, but H_2O tells you that these two elements can combine, as shown in **Figure 25-16,** to form a new, pure substance called a compound. A **compound** is a pure substance whose smallest unit is made up of atoms of more than one element. Millions of compounds can be made from combinations of elements, and the compounds almost always have properties that are different from the elements that make them up. Have you ever used hydrogen peroxide to disinfect a cut? Hydrogen peroxide is another compound made from the elements hydrogen and oxygen.

What You'll Learn

► What a compound is
► The difference between types of mixtures

Vocabulary
substance
compound
law of definite proportions
mixture

Why It's Important

► Compounds and mixtures are part of your everyday life.

Figure 25-16 A space shuttle is powered by the reaction between liquid hydrogen and liquid oxygen. The reaction produces a large amount of energy and a single compound, water. **Why would a car that burns hydrogen rather than gasoline be friendly to the environment?**

Compounds Need Formulas

What's the difference between water and hydrogen peroxide? H_2O is the chemical formula for water, and it tells you more than what elements make up the compound. Look at **Figure 25-17.** Water is made up of two atoms of hydrogen for every one atom of oxygen. H_2O_2 is the formula for hydrogen peroxide. The subscripts, numbers written below and to the right of the elements' symbols, mean that there are two atoms of hydrogen for every two atoms of oxygen in hydrogen peroxide. Carbon dioxide, CO_2, is another common compound. Carbon dioxide is made up of one atom of carbon for every two atoms of oxygen. Carbon and oxygen also can form the compound carbon monoxide, CO, a gas that is poisonous to all warm-blooded animals. As you can see, no subscript is used when one atom is present. The **law of definite proportions** states that a given compound is always made of the same elements in the same proportion by mass. For example, water always has two hydrogen atoms for every oxygen atom. ✔

Reading Check ✔

Propane has three atoms of carbon for every eight atoms of hydrogen. What is propane's chemical formula?

Figure 25-17 The elements hydrogen and oxygen can combine to form two compounds, water and hydrogen peroxide. Although both compounds are made up of the same elements, the ratios of hydrogen and oxygen atoms are different.

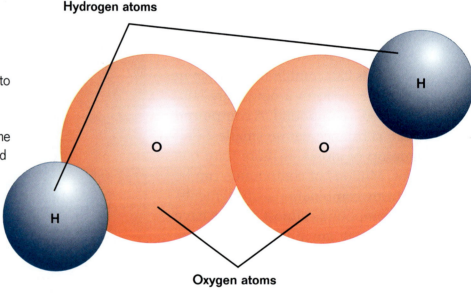

Hydrogen atoms

Oxygen atoms

A H_2O_2, the formula for hydrogen peroxide, shows that it contains two hydrogen atoms for every two oxygen atoms.

B H_2O, the formula for water, shows that it contains two hydrogen atoms for each oxygen atom. **What is the ratio of hydrogen atoms to carbon atoms in methane, which has the formula CH_4?**

Mixtures

When two or more substances (elements or compounds) come together but don't combine to make a new, pure substance, a **mixture** results. Unlike compounds, the proportions of the substances in a mixture can be changed. For example, if you put some sand into a bucket of water, you have a mixture of sand and water. If you add more sand or more water, it's still a mixture of sand and water. The makeup of air, a mixture of nitrogen, oxygen, and other gases, can vary somewhat from place to place and time to time. Look around your classroom, home, or neighborhood. What other mixtures do you see? Did you know that your blood is a mixture made up of elements and compounds? It contains white blood cells, red blood cells, water, and a number of dissolved elements. The blood parts can be separated easily and used by different parts of your body.

You can often use a liquid to separate the parts of a mixture of solids. For example, you could add water to a mixture of sugar and sand. Only the sugar would dissolve in the water. The sand could then be separated from the sugar and water by pouring the mixture through a filter. Then, heating would dry off the water, leaving the sugar behind.

Visit the Glencoe Science Web Site at **www. glencoe.com/sec/ science/ca** for more information about mixtures.

LIFE SCIENCE
◀ INTEGRATION

Problem Solving

Drinking Water from Salt Water

Suppose you are on a ship or live in a place that is near an ocean but does not have much freshwater for people to drink.

Can you use change in physical state to create a method for removing salt from ocean water? Distillation is the process of heating a mixture to separate its parts. Parts of the mixture boil at different temperatures. A more nearly pure substance results when the vapor from each part is cooled and condensed.

A liquid mixture placed in the flask on the left is heated to boiling. As the vapor passes through the tube in the condenser in the middle, it is surrounded by cold water

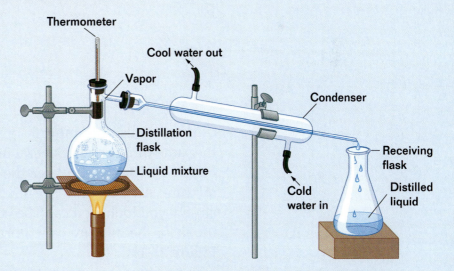

and condenses to a liquid. The liquid drips into the flask on the right.

Think Critically: Examine the distillation system in the photo. How could you use such a system to produce freshwater from ocean water?

Figure 25-18 Many commmom materials are uniform mixtures.

A Sterling silver dinnerware is 92.5 percent silver and 7.5 percent copper.

B The tea in this glass is a uniform mixture that is mostly water. **Is the mixture of ice and tea a uniform mixture?**

C The brass trombone is 50 to 80 percent copper and 20 to 50 percent zinc. **A uniform mixture of iron and carbon is used in making cars and many other products. What is this mixture called?**

Mixtures can be uniform or nonuniform. Uniform means the same throughout. Several uniform mixtures are shown in **Figure 25-18.** You can't see the different parts in this type of mixture. Air is a uniform mixture of gases. No matter how closely you look, you can't see the individual parts that make up air or the mixture called brass in the trombone shown in **Figure 25-18C.**

In a nonuniform mixture such as sand and water, you can see the different parts. A pepperoni and mushroom pizza is a tasty kind of nonuniform mixture. Other examples of this kind of mixture include tacos, a stew, a toy box full of toys, or your laundry basket at the end of the week. Several nonuniform mixtures are shown in **Figure 25-19.**

Figure 25-19 Nonuniform mixtures are part of your everyday life.

B Blood is a nonuniform mixture of many materials, including water, proteins, glucose, and fats. Some of these materials can be separated in the laboratory.

A You can see pieces of solid orange floating in liquid if you look at a glass of orange juice closely.

C Areas of different color in a rock show that it is made up of crystals of different materials. **A clear fruit drink is made up of many substances. Why is it a uniform mixture?**

Section Assessment

1. List three examples of compounds and three examples of mixtures.

2. The chemical formula for baking soda is $NaHCO_3$. Use the periodic table to write the names of the elements in baking soda. Which element's atoms are most numerous in baking soda?

3. How can you tell that a substance is a compound by looking at its formula?

4. **Think Critically:** Was your breakfast this morning a compound, a uniform mixture, or a nonuniform mixture? Review the definitions for a compound and a uniform mixture. Explain your answer based on these definitions.

5. **Skill Builder**
Comparing and Contrasting
Compare and contrast compounds and mixtures. If you need help, refer to Comparing and Contrasting in the **Skill Handbook** on page 992.

Using Computers

Database Use a computerized card catalog to find out about one element from the periodic table. Include information about the mixtures and/or compounds the element is found in. If you need help, refer to page 1005.

Mystery Mixture

Materials

- Test tubes (3)
- Cornstarch
- Sugar
- Baking soda
- Mystery mixture
- Small scoops (3)
- Dropper bottles (2)
- Iodine solution
- White vinegar
- Candle
- Test-tube holder
- Small pie pan
- Matches

Cornstarch, baking powder, and powdered sugar are compounds that look alike. To avoid mistaking one for another, you may need to learn how to identify each one. You can learn chemical tests that identify these different compounds. For example, some compounds react with certain liquids to produce gases. Other combinations produce distinctive colors. Some compounds have high melting points. Others have low melting points.

What You'll Investigate

How can the compounds in an unknown mixture be identified by experimentation?

Goals

- **Test** for the presence of certain compounds.
- **Decide** which of these compounds are present in an unknown mixture.

Safety Precautions

Use caution when handling hot objects. Substances could stain or burn clothing. Be sure to point the test tube away from your face and your classmates while heating.

Procedure

1. **Copy** the data table into your Science Journal. **Record** your results for each of the following steps.

2. Place a small scoopful, or the amount indicated by your teacher, of cornstarch on the pie pan. Do the same for sugar and baking soda. Add a drop of vinegar to each. Wash and dry the pan after you have recorded your observations.

3. Place a small scoopful, or the amount indicated by your teacher, of cornstarch, sugar, and baking soda on the pie pan. Add a drop of iodine solution to each.

4. Place a small scoopful, or the amount indicated by your teacher, of each compound in a separate test tube. Hold the test tube with the test-tube holder. Gently heat the bottom of each test tube with the candle.

5. Now, use steps 2 to 4 to **test** your mystery mixture and find out which of these compounds it contains.

Conclude and Apply

1. Use your observations to form a hypothesis as to which compounds are in your mystery mixture. Describe how you arrived at your conclusion.

2. How would you be able to tell if all three compounds were not in your mystery mixture sample?

3. What would you conclude if you tested baking powder from your kitchen and found that it fizzed with vinegar, turned blue with iodine, and did not melt when heated?

Results of Tests			
To be tested	Vinegar fizzes	Iodine turns blue	Compound melts
Cornstarch			
Sugar			
Baking soda			
Mystery mix			

Chapter 25 Reviewing Main Ideas

For a **preview** of this chapter, study this Reviewing Main Ideas before you read the chapter. After you have studied this chapter, you can use the Reviewing Main Ideas to **review** the chapter.

The Glencoe MindJogger, Audiocassettes, and CD-ROM provide additional opportunities for review.

Section
25-1 STRUCTURE OF MATTER

Matter is anything that occupies space and has mass. It includes all the things that you can see, touch, taste, or smell. Matter does not include light, sound, or heat. *Can you think of anything else that is not matter?*

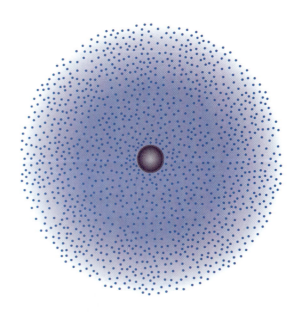

WHAT MAKES UP MATTER?

Matter is made up of atoms. **Atoms** are made of smaller parts called **protons, neutrons, and electrons.** Many models of atoms have been created as scientists try to discover and define the atom's internal structure. *What other models do you know about?*

Section
25-2 ELEMENTS

Elements are the basic building blocks of matter. Each element has a unique set of properties and is generally classified as a metal, metalloid, or nonmetal. The chemical symbol for each element is understood by scientists everywhere. An element's **atomic number** tells how many protons its atoms contain, and its **atomic mass** tells how heavy its atoms are. **Isotopes** are two or more atoms of the same element that have different numbers of neutrons. *What element has the symbol Co?*

Chlorine
17
Cl
35.453

Reading Check ✓
Create a timeline of the important discoveries about atoms. Include the names of the scientists. Check other reference sources for dates when necessary.

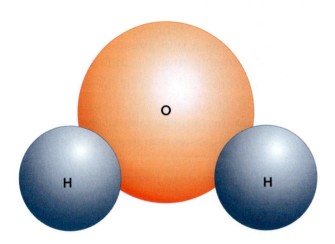

Section
25-3 COMPOUNDS

Compounds are pure substances produced when elements combine. Compounds contain specific proportions of the elements that make them up. A compound's properties are different from those of the elements from which it is formed. *Name five common compounds.*

MIXTURES

Mixtures are combinations of compounds and elements that have not formed new, pure substances. Uniform mixtures contain individual parts that cannot be seen. However, you can see the individual parts of nonuniform mixtures. *What are two mixtures of each type that you know about?*

Using Vocabulary

a. atom
b. atomic mass
c. atomic number
d. compound
e. electron
f. element
g. isotopes
h. law of conservation of matter
i. law of definite proportions
j. mass number
k. matter
l. metals
m. metalloids
n. mixtures
o. neutron
p. nonmetals
q. nucleus
r. proton
s. substance

Using the list above, replace the underlined words with the correct Vocabulary word.

1. The particle in the nucleus of the atom that carries a positive charge is the <u>neutron</u>.

2. The new substance formed when elements join is a <u>mixture</u>.

3. Anything that has mass and takes up space is <u>metal</u>.

4. The particles in the atom that account for most of the mass are protons and <u>electrons</u>.

5. Elements that are shiny, malleable, ductile, and good conductors of heat and electricity are <u>nonmetals</u>.

Checking Concepts

Choose the word or phrase that best answers the question.

6. What is a solution an example of?
   A) element
   B) nonuniform mixture
   C) compound
   D) uniform mixture

7. The nucleus of one atom contains 12 protons and 12 neutrons, while the nucleus of another atom contains 12 protons and 16 neutrons. What are the atoms?
   A) chromium atoms
   B) two different elements
   C) isotopes of magnesium
   D) negatively charged

8. What is a compound?
   A) a mixture of compounds and elements
   B) a combination of two or more elements
   C) anything that has mass and occupies space
   D) the building block of matter

9. What does the atom consist of?
   A) electrons, protons, and alpha particles
   B) neutrons and protons
   C) electrons, protons, and neutrons
   D) elements, protons, and electrons

10. In an atom, where is an electron located?
    A) in the nucleus with the proton
    B) on the periodic table of the elements
    C) with the neutron to create a positive charge
    D) in a cloudlike formation surrounding the nucleus

11. How is matter defined?
    A) the negative charge in an atom
    B) anything that has mass and occupies space
    C) the mass of the nucleus
    D) sound, light, and energy

12. What are two atoms that have the same number of protons?
    A) metals
    B) nonmetals
    C) isotopes
    D) metalloids

13. What are the majority of the elements on the periodic table?
    A) metals
    B) metalloids
    C) nonmetals
    D) compounds

14. Which element is a metalloid?
    A) bromine
    B) silicon
    C) potassium
    D) iron

15. What are nonuniform mixtures?
    A) two kinds of mixtures
    B) the same throughout—the parts can-not be seen
    C) made of several different parts that can be seen
    D) like a soft drink

Thinking Critically

16. A chemical formula is written to indicate the makeup of a compound. What is the ratio of sulfur atoms to oxygen atoms in SO_2?
17. An atom contains seven electrons and seven protons. What element is this atom? Explain your answer.
18. What happens to an element when it becomes part of a compound?
19. Cobalt-60 and cobalt-59 are isotopes. How can they be the same element but have different mass numbers?
20. What did Rutherford's gold foil experiment tell scientists about atomic structure?

Developing Skills

If you need help, refer to the Skill Handbook.

21. **Interpreting Scientific Illustrations:** Look at the drawings of the two atoms below. Explain whether or not the atoms are isotopes.

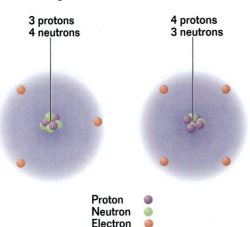

3 protons
4 neutrons

4 protons
3 neutrons

Proton
Neutron
Electron

THE PRINCETON REVIEW

Test-Taking Tip

What Does the Test Expect of Me? Find out what concepts, objectives, or standards are being tested well before the test. Keep these concepts in mind as you solve the questions.

Test Practice

Use these questions to test your Science Proficiency.

1. Which list of terms **BEST** describes the properties of metals?
   A) dull, brittle, nonconducting
   B) malleable, ductile, shiny, good conductors
   C) shiny, brittle, can conduct electricity
   D) gaseous, high density

2. Mixtures are divided into two categories. Which pair of examples **BEST** represents the two types of mixtures?
   A) a pizza and a tossed salad
   B) a baseball card collection and a CD collection
   C) a soft drink and a taco
   D) an iced soft drink and iced tea

3. What particles are found in the nucleus of a carbon-12 atom?
   A) 12 protons
   B) 12 neutrons and 12 protons
   C) 12 neutrons
   D) 6 protons and 6 neutrons

4. Which of these is **NOT** an element?
   A) water
   B) hydrogen
   C) chlorine
   D) oxygen

CHAPTER

26 Energy

Chapter Preview

Skills Preview

Skill Builders
- Make and Use a Graph
- Use Numbers

Activities
- Observe and Infer
- Interpret Data

MiniLabs
- Classify
- Compare and Contrast

Reading Check ✔

As you read this chapter about energy, list the cause-and-effect relationships you identify.

Explore Activity

Imagine yourself downhill skiing in the winter. You skillfully change the direction and speed of your skis by changing your body position. A surfboard rider feels the same sense of connection between his body position and the board's motion. So do a cyclist on a bike and a young child on a swing. All are aware of something changing—position, speed, or direction. Energy plays a part in all of these changes. Where else have you seen energy causing change?

Observe Energy

1. Obtain a new, wide rubber band.

2. As you hold the rubber band in both hands, touch it to your lower lip.

3. After moving it away from your face, quickly stretch the rubber band several times.

4. Touch the rubber band to your lip again. What differences do you observe?

5. Obtain additional materials from your teacher to observe more energy changes.

6. Throw away the rubber band after the activity.

Record your observations for each material in your Science Journal. Set up a table to help you compare your results.

What You'll Learn

▶ What energy is and the forms it takes
▶ The difference between potential energy and kinetic energy

Vocabulary
energy
kinetic energy
potential energy
law of conservation of energy

Why It's Important

▶ The more you know about energy, the more efficiently you will use it.

Energy

Energy is a term you probably use every day. You may say that eating a plate of spaghetti gives you energy or that a gymnast has a lot of energy. But, do you know that a burning fire, a bouncing ball, and a tank of gasoline also have energy? Exactly what is energy?

What is energy?

The ancient Greek word for energy was *energos*, which means "active." Until the 1900s, people thought that energy was stored inside objects. Now we say that **energy** is the ability to cause change. Energy can change the temperature, shape, speed, or direction of an object. Energy can change the shape of modeling clay or the temperature of a cup of water. As you can see in **Figure 26-1,** you can use the energy of your muscles to change the speed of a bicycle by pedaling faster or slower, or by putting on the brakes. The person on a skateboard in **Figure 26-1** uses energy to the change the direction the skateboard takes.

Figure 26-1 The riders of the skateboard and bike use energy to change their speed and direction.

Energy Transformations

If you ask your friends what comes to mind when they think of energy, you will get many different answers. Some may mention the energy in a flame. Others may say energy is needed to run a race. These answers suggest that energy comes in different forms from a variety of sources. Is that true? A flame gives off energy in the form of heat and light. Eating a good breakfast gives your body the energy to move, think, and grow. Your body stores most of its energy in the form of fat. Nuclear power plants use energy from the center of the atom. It seems that energy comes in many forms. What other examples of energy can you think of?

Change Can Cause Change

Push down a bicycle pedal and the gears in the back wheel turn. The chemical energy in your muscles has been changed to mechanical energy. In the natural world, energy often changes from one form to another. Any change of energy from one form to another is called an energy transformation. Energy transformations take place all around you. When a car sits in the sun all day, the energy of light waves changes to a form of energy that warms the inside of the car. The energy in the chemicals used to make the fireworks in **Figure 26-2** changes to light, sound, and motion. In the Explore Activity, the energy you used to stretch and move the rubber band changed into energy that raised the temperature of the band.

During these and other types of energy transformations, the total amount of energy stays the same. No energy is ever lost or gained. Only the form of energy changes.

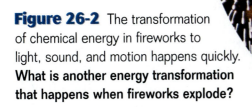

Figure 26-2 The transformation of chemical energy in fireworks to light, sound, and motion happens quickly. **What is another energy transformation that happens when fireworks explode?**

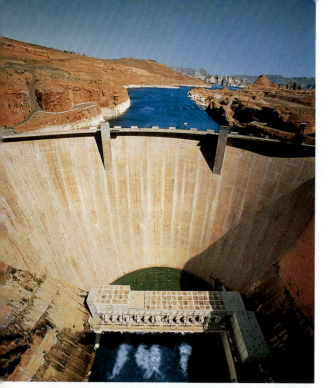

Figure 26-3 Glen Canyon Dam is located on the Colorado River in Arizona. Pipes lead water from the reservoir behind the dam to the hydroelectric generators in the power plant, which is located in front of the dam. The energy of the rushing water spins the generators' turbines, and kinetic energy is transformed into electricity. **What are some benefits of using water as a source of energy?**

Useful Changes

Since the earliest times, humans have experimented with different forms of energy. When early humans learned to make fires, they learned to use the chemical energy in wood to cook, stay warm, and light their way in the dark. Today, electrical energy is changed into thermal energy that warms your home. Also, electrical energy changes to light energy in a lightbulb when you flip on a switch. Chemical energy in fuel changes to the type of energy that runs the engine in the bus you take to school. The water heater in your home transforms energy in natural gas, or in electrical energy, to thermal energy that warms the water for a bath or shower. A hydroelectric plant, as shown in **Figure 26-3,** and a wind power plant transform the energy of moving water and wind into electrical energy.

Kinetic and Potential Energy

You've seen that energy can take many forms, such as light, heat, and motion. Two main types of energy are called kinetic energy and potential energy.

Kinetic Energy

If you were asked if a football thrown downfield has energy, you might say that it does because it is moving. Objects in motion have a type of energy called **kinetic** (kuh NET ihk) **energy.** A football thrown by a quarterback has kinetic energy. A skydiver falling toward Earth also has kinetic energy.

How much kinetic energy does it have?

Not all moving objects have the same amount of kinetic energy. Look at **Figure 26-4.** Which would have more kinetic energy, a train coming down the track or a girl in-line skating? The amount of kinetic energy an object has depends on the mass and speed of the object. If the train and the girl are traveling at the same speed, the train has more kinetic energy than the girl on skates because it has more mass. In this example, even if the train moves slowly and the girl skates as fast as she can, the train still has more kinetic energy because its mass is so much greater than the skater's mass. What would happen if two objects had the same mass? How would the kinetic energies of two trains heading toward the city compare if they had the same mass? The train that is traveling at the higher speed would have more kinetic energy than the slower one.

Figure 26-4 When comparing the kinetic energies of any objects, you must consider both the masses and the speeds of the objects.

A Suppose this train and skater are moving at the same speed. **Which of them has more kinetic energy? Explain.**

B The racehorse and empty luggage cart are about the same mass. The horse is running around the track while the luggage cart is at rest. **Which of them has more kinetic energy? Explain.**

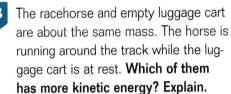

Potential Energy

Suppose the ski lift in **Figure 26-5** takes a skier to the top of a hill and lets her rest there. Do you think the skier still has energy? She does. An object does not have to be moving to have energy. The skier has potential energy. A teacher may say that you have potential—the ability to do more work than you are doing right now. **Potential** (puh TEN chul) **energy** is not energy that comes from motion. It is energy that comes from position or condition. A skier at the top of a hill has potential energy. Even though she is not moving, she has the ability to move.

In general, whenever you raise an object above its original position, you give it the ability to fall. The energy the ski lift uses in taking a skier up a hill is changed. This energy becomes stored as potential energy in the skier. When more energy is used to raise her higher, there is more energy that has been transformed and stored in the skier as potential energy. This idea is similar to pouring water into a bottle and storing it to be used later during a basketball game. You can store potential energy to be used later when you need it. ✔

Potential Energy and Kinetic Energy Are Related

One of the easiest ways to see the difference between potential and kinetic energy is to work with a pendulum, as in **Figure 26-6.** A pendulum is a weight that swings back and forth from a single point.

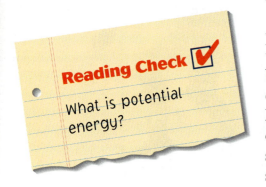

Reading Check
What is potential energy?

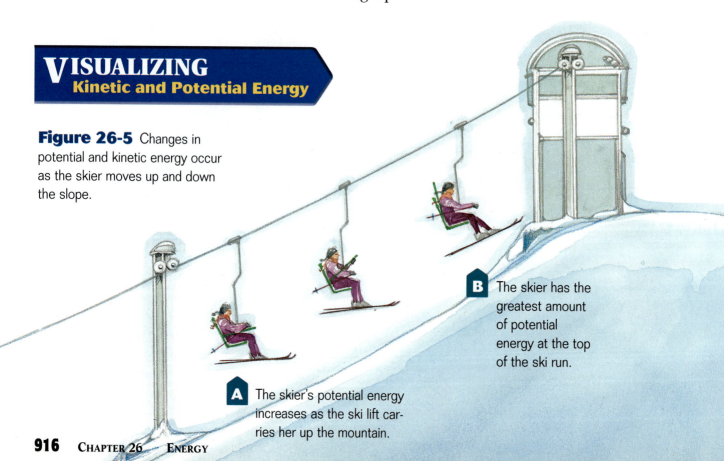

VISUALIZING
Kinetic and Potential Energy

Figure 26-5 Changes in potential and kinetic energy occur as the skier moves up and down the slope.

B The skier has the greatest amount of potential energy at the top of the ski run.

A The skier's potential energy increases as the ski lift carries her up the mountain.

A swing on a backyard swing set is a pendulum. The energy you use to pull back on a swing is changed and stored in the swing as potential energy. Similarly, potential energy can be stored in any pendulum by moving the weighted end to one side. When you let go of a pendulum, any stored potential energy in the pendulum is released. The pendulum swings down in a curved path, called an arc. The instant the pendulum moves, potential energy is transformed into kinetic energy.

There is a direct relationship between the amount of potential energy an object has and the amount of energy that can be transformed into kinetic energy. When a book is placed on a shelf, it has potential energy. That energy becomes kinetic energy if the book falls off the shelf. A book placed on a higher shelf has more potential energy—and more kinetic energy as it falls—than it would have on a lower shelf.

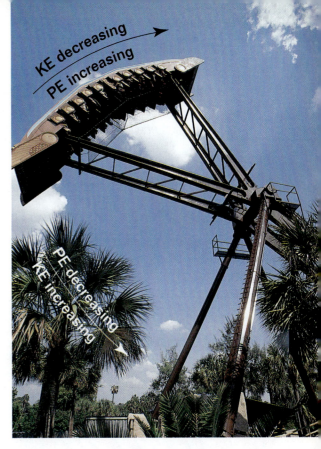

Transfer of Kinetic Energy

Kinetic energy can be transferred from one object to another when those objects collide. Think about the changes and transfer of energy during bowling. Success in bowling depends on the fact that energy can be transferred from one object to another. Even if the bowling ball does not touch all the pins, you can knock them all down with one roll of the ball. A transfer of kinetic energy also takes place when dominoes fall. You only need to give the first domino in the row a bit of kinetic energy by tapping it just enough to make it fall against the next

Figure 26-6 The people on this amusement park ride experience energy changes as the pendulum swings. **At what points would the potential energy be the greatest? The kinetic energy?**

C When the skier begins to ski down the slope, her potential energy starts to transform into kinetic energy.

D As the skier moves further down the mountain, more and more potential energy changes to kinetic energy. She has the least amount of potential energy just before reaching the bottom of the ski run.

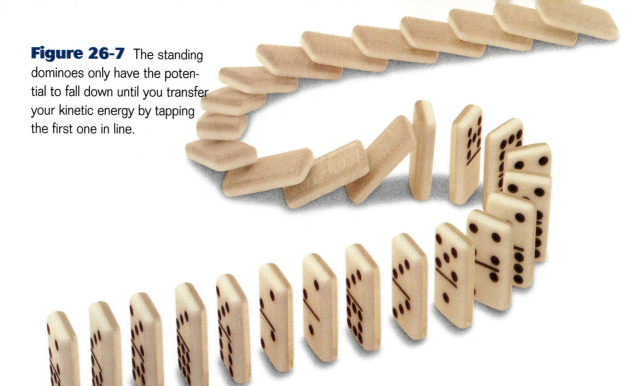

Figure 26-7 The standing dominoes only have the potential to fall down until you transfer your kinetic energy by tapping the first one in line.

Mini Lab

Classifying Types of Energy

Procedure

1. Examine the following list of activities.
2. Classify each activity as involving potential or kinetic energy. Hint: Ask yourself if the energy involved is stored (potential), moving (kinetic), or both.
   a. Eat an apple.
   b. Turn on a flashlight.
   c. Push a ball along the floor.
   d. Lift a weight.
   e. Burn a birthday candle.

Analysis

1. Make a table in your Science Journal with two columns.
2. Label the left column "potential" and the right column "kinetic."
3. List the type of activity you examined above in the correct column.
4. Compare your classifications with those of your lab partner.

domino. As the first domino falls into the next one, its kinetic energy is transferred to the second domino. This transfer of kinetic energy continues from domino to domino until the last one falls, as shown in **Figure 26-7.** It is important to know the difference between potential and kinetic energy. It is this difference that sometimes allows you to store energy for later use.

Conserving Energy

Following the trail of energy as it moves from source to source can be a challenge. In 1840, James Joule described the law of conservation of energy. According to the **law of conservation of energy,** energy cannot be created or destroyed. It only can be transformed from one form into another. This means the total amount of energy in the whole universe never changes. The universe doesn't make more energy. Energy doesn't just vanish into thin air either. The only change is the form in which energy may appear. Track the flow of energy in the case of a soccer ball. A soccer player has chemical energy in her muscles from the food she ate. The chemical energy is released as she swings her leg. Her leg now has kinetic energy.

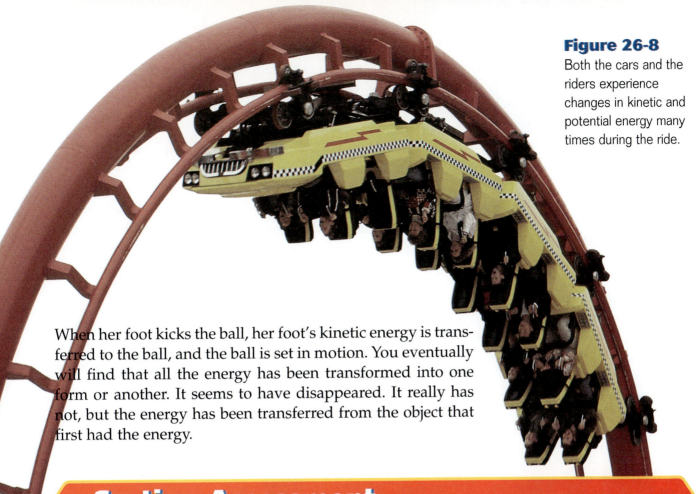

Figure 26-8
Both the cars and the riders experience changes in kinetic and potential energy many times during the ride.

When her foot kicks the ball, her foot's kinetic energy is transferred to the ball, and the ball is set in motion. You eventually will find that all the energy has been transformed into one form or another. It seems to have disappeared. It really has not, but the energy has been transferred from the object that first had the energy.

Section Assessment

1. If you are riding in a roller coaster as in **Figure 26-8,** how do you think your speed is related to your kinetic energy? Your potential energy?

2. As a roller coaster climbs to the top of the steepest hill on its track, when does the first car have the greatest potential energy? When does it have the greatest kinetic energy?

3. State the law of conservation of energy in your own words.

4. **Think Critically:** You get up in the morning, get dressed, eat breakfast, walk to the bus stop, and ride to school. List three different energy transformations that have taken place.

5.  **Skill Builder**
   Making and Using Graphs A pendulum swings seven times per minute. If the string were half as long, the pendulum would swing ten times per minute. If the original length were twice as long, the pendulum would swing five times per minute. Make a bar graph that shows these data. Draw a conclusion from the results. If you need help, refer to Making and Using Graphs in the **Skill Handbook** on page 989.

Science Journal
   In your Science Journal, write a short paragraph about what energy transformations took place when last night's dinner was prepared.

Materials

- A desk
  *table
- Sugar (30 g)
- Whole milk (120 mL)
  *half & half (120 mL)
- Small, self-sealing freezer bag (1-quart or less)
- Ice
- Coffee can (large with lid)
- Rock salt (230 g)
- Thermometer
  *Alternate Materials

Where's the energy?

Did you know that several energy transfers occur during the process of making ice cream? At the beginning of this activity, you will transfer energy to the container of ingredients by rolling it back and forth across the desk. This will help the ingredients mix together. As the ingredients form small crystals, you also will observe another type of energy transfer as you make the ice cream.

What You'll Investigate

What are the various energy transfers that occur during the process of making ice cream?

Goals

- **Observe** a transfer of energy.
- **Measure** a temperature change.

Safety Precautions

Do not taste, eat, or drink any materials used in the lab.

Procedure

1. **Put** the milk and sugar into the freezer bag.
2. **Take** the temperature of the mix and record it.
3. **Seal** the bag well and place the freezer bag inside the large coffee can.
4. **Pack** ice around and over the freezer bag.
5. **Pour** rock salt over the ice. Put the lid on the coffee can.
6. **Roll** the can across the desk at least 15 times.
7. **Let** the can stand for 15 minutes.
8. **Check** to see if the ice cream has frozen. If not, repeat steps 6 and 7.
9. **Take** the temperature of the ice cream and record it.

Conclude and Apply

1. What different types of energy can you **conclude** were involved in making the ice cream?
2. **Infer** what type of energy transferred out of the liquid mixture so it could become ice cream. How do you know?

Temperature and Thermal Energy

Temperature

What's today's temperature? If you looked at a thermometer, listened to a weather report on the radio, or saw a weather map on the news similar to the map in **Figure 26-9,** you probably used the air temperature to help you decide what to wear. Some days are so hot you don't need a jacket. Others are so cold you want to bundle up.

Hot and cold are terms that are used in everyday language to indicate temperature. They are not scientific words because they mean different things to different people. A summer day that seems hot to one person may seem just right to another. If you usually live in Florida but go swimming in the ocean off the coast of Maine while on vacation, you might find the water unbearably cold. Have you ever complained that a classroom was too cold when other students insisted that it was too warm?

Temperature Is an Average

What is temperature? Any material or object is made up of particles that are invisible to the naked eye. The particles that make up any object are constantly moving, even if the object appears to be perfectly still. Everything you can think of—your hand, the pencil on your desk, or even the desktop—is made up of moving particles. You learned that moving objects have kinetic energy. Because the particles that make up an object are in constant motion, they have kinetic energy. Faster-moving particles have more kinetic energy.

What You'll Learn

▶ The differences among temperature, thermal energy, and heat
▶ Important uses of thermal energy
▶ How thermal energy moves

Vocabulary

temperature
thermal energy
heat
radiation
conduction
convection

Why It's Important

▶ The transfer of thermal energy is involved in warming Earth, producing weather, cooking your food, and warming and cooling your home.

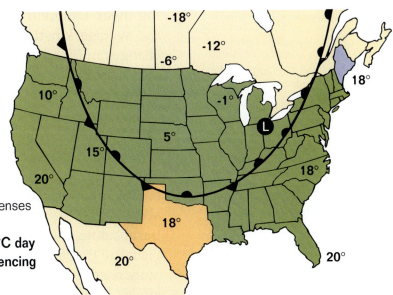

Figure 26-9 Each person senses temperature differently. **Would a person in Texas describe an 18°C day differently from a person experiencing an 18°C day in Maine? Why?**

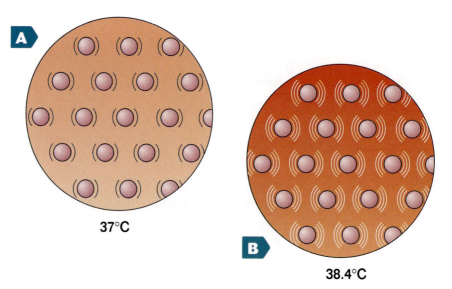

Figure 26-10 The temperature of the particles in B is higher than the temperature of the particles in A. **How does the motion of the particles differ in A and B? Why?**

37°C

38.4°C

If you could measure the kinetic energy of each particle in an object and average them, you would find the average kinetic energy of the particles. **Temperature** is a measure of the average kinetic energy of the particles in any object. The greater the average kinetic energy is, the higher an object's temperature is. For example, **Figure 26-10** shows particles at the normal human body temperature of 37°C. If a person has a body temperature of 38.4°C, the particles in the person's body have more kinetic energy than usual.

Temperature Scales

Because everyone experiences temperature differently, you cannot accurately measure temperature by how it feels to you. Recall that temperature is the average kinetic energy of all the particles. But, there is no easy method to measure the kinetic energy of each particle and then calculate an average. That is because the particles are extremely small. Even scientists using sensitive instruments have a difficult time observing them. Different temperature scales are used to measure the average kinetic energy of particles. These scales divide changes in kinetic energy of the particles into regular intervals. That is, the units are spaced apart evenly.

One scale you may use is the Fahrenheit (FAYR un hit) scale. On the Fahrenheit scale, water freezes at 32°F and boils at 212°F. A second temperature scale you will use in science class is the Celsius (SEL see us) scale. On the Celsius temperature scale, the freezing point of water is 0°C and water's boiling point is 100°C. Scientists often use the Kelvin, or absolute, temperature scale. It has this name because 0 K is the absolute lowest temperature an object can have. One can visualize that all particle motion stops at 0 K. As the temperature rises above 0 K, the particles begin to move with greater kinetic energy.

Thermal Energy

Hot soup will warm you because it has a large amount of thermal energy. **Thermal energy** is the total kinetic energy of the particles in a material. Because temperature is a measure of the average kinetic energy of an object's particles, it is also a measure of thermal energy. The amount of thermal energy in a bowl of soup is determined by the amount of soup in the bowl and the total amount of energy in the particles that make it up. Thermal energy flows from a warmer object to a cooler one. Thermal energy in the bowl of soup will transfer to your body and you will become warmer. ☑

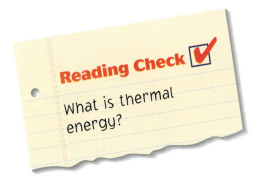

Reading Check ✔

What is thermal energy?

Heat and Thermal Energy

Thermal energy is what you may have been calling heat. It is important to note that heat and thermal energy are not the same. Look at **Figure 26-11.** Suppose you pick up a tall glass of iced tea. If you hold the glass for a long time, the drink warms up. Thermal energy from your hand transfers to the drink. A transfer of thermal energy from one object to another because of a difference in temperature is **heat.** Heat flows from warmer objects to cooler ones. Heat flows out of your hand and into the glass of iced tea. The thermal energy of the drink increases so it's temperature increases.

Heat also flows from warmer to cooler objects in a refrigerator. Your food is kept cold because thermal energy of the food is decreased by the flow of heat to the cold air inside the refrigerator. Refrigerators are designed to remove heat from the space inside where the food is stored.

How much heat?

When the same amount of heat is transferred to different materials, those materials may not experience the same increase in temperature. This difference is based on the chemical makeup and the amount of the material.

For example, water must absorb a large amount of heat before its temperature rises one degree. That is why water often is used as a coolant. The water in a car's radiator carries thermal energy away from the engine. How does the temperature of the water in a swimming pool compare to the air on a hot summer day? How do they compare at night when the air has cooled? The water is slower than its surroundings to change temperature. It takes longer for a large body of water to warm up or cool down

Figure 26-11 Heat flows from your hand to the glass of iced tea, making your hand feel cold. **Why do people wear gloves in cold weather?**

than it takes an equally large area of land or the surrounding air. As a result, air temperatures near a large lake or ocean remain fairly moderate year-round.

How do you feel heat?

Think about getting into a car that has been closed up on a sunny day. Do you prefer a car that has fabric-covered or vinyl-covered seats? Even though the masses of the seats are similar and the temperatures of the surroundings are the same, the vinyl material feels hotter on your skin than the fabric does. Your sense of touch responds to heat not to the actual temperature. Heat flows to your skin more easily from the vinyl than from the fabric. The greater the heat flow, the hotter the object feels to your skin. ✔

Transfer of Thermal Energy

A transfer of thermal energy into a material may cause a rise in the temperature of the material. The amount of thermal energy absorbed depends on the type of material. It also depends on the amount of material. The greater the amount of material there is, the more thermal energy it absorbs before its temperature rise can be measured. Suppose you transferred enough thermal energy to cause a small pot of water to boil. If you put the same amount of energy into a bathtub full of water, the temperature rise would be small, as shown in **Figure 26-12.** The heat absorbed must be shared by more particles of water in the bathtub. The average increase of thermal energy in each particle is quite small.

Reading Check ✔

Why do some materials feel hotter on your skin than others?

Figure 26-12 Applying an equal amount of thermal energy to the pan of water and the bathtub of water would not increase the water temperature the same number of degrees.

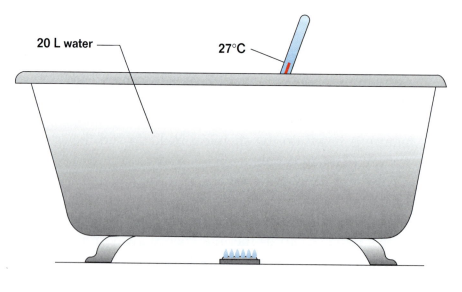

20 L water — 27°C

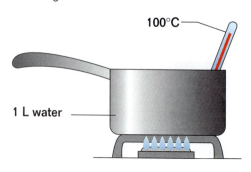

100°C

1 L water

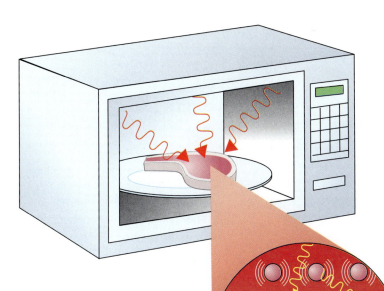

Figure 26-13
A microwave oven uses microwave radiation to transfer thermal energy to a food item. Microwaves increase the motion of the particles of water in the food. As the particles move faster, the food becomes warmer and cooks.

Thermal Energy on the Move

An overall transfer of energy occurs if there is a temperature difference between two areas or objects. Heat flows from warm places to cooler ones. Remember that temperature is a measure of thermal energy in an object. Heat flows from an area having greater thermal energy to an area that has less thermal energy. Thermal energy is transferred three ways: radiation, conduction, and convection. Conduction and convection transfer thermal energy through solids, liquids, or gases. Radiation however transfers thermal energy when little or no matter is present.

Radiation

Radiation is energy that travels by waves in all directions from its source. These waves may be visible light waves or types of energy waves that you cannot see. When these strike an object, their energy can be absorbed and the object's temperature rises. Radiation can travel through air and even through space where there is almost no material. The sun transfers energy to Earth through radiation. If you are out walking on a cool but sunny day, bend down to touch the sidewalk that is exposed to the sunlight. Perhaps you will notice that it feels warm. The pavement absorbs energy transferred from the sun by radiation. You take advantage of radiation when you warm yourself by a fire. The fire transfers its thermal energy to you. You become warmer. You also can use radiation to cook food. The microwave oven in your kitchen, such as the one shown in **Figure 26-13,** cooks food because of a transfer of energy by radiation.

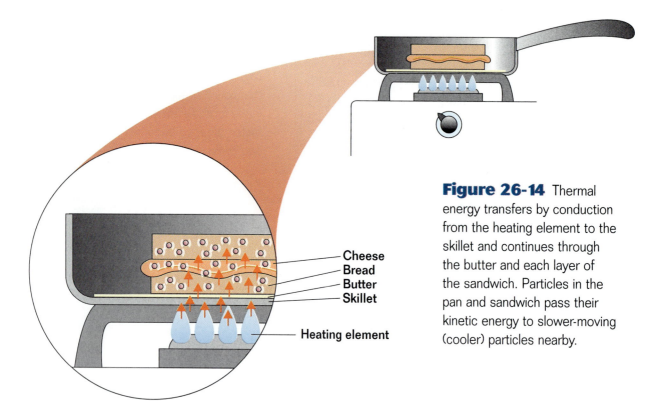

Figure 26-14 Thermal energy transfers by conduction from the heating element to the skillet and continues through the butter and each layer of the sandwich. Particles in the pan and sandwich pass their kinetic energy to slower-moving (cooler) particles nearby.

Cheese
Bread
Butter
Skillet

Heating element

Conduction

Have you ever picked up a silver spoon that was in a pot of boiling water and discovered that the spoon was now hotter than it was when you placed it there? Yeow! Quick! Where is the pot holder? The spoon handle became hot because of conduction. **Conduction** is the transfer of thermal energy from particle to particle through a material when there is a temperature difference. Conduction occurs because of the exchange of kinetic energy between the particles in a material, much the same way kinetic energy is transferred from a bowling ball to the pins. In the example of the spoon, kinetic energy continues to be transferred from the hotter end of the spoon to the cooler end because of the temperature difference.

Look at **Figure 26-14.** When you put a pan on the stove to make a grilled-cheese sandwich, the thermal energy from the stove transfers to the pan, making the particles within the pan move faster. Some of these particles bump into the particles in the bread and butter that are on the surface of the pan. Energy is transferred to the sandwich. This transferred energy causes the bread to toast and the cheese to melt. Even though conduction is a transfer of kinetic energy from particle to particle, the particles involved don't travel from one place to another. They simply move in place, bumping into each other and transferring energy from faster-moving particles to slower-moving ones. ☑

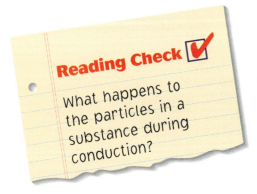

Reading Check ☑

What happens to the particles in a substance during conduction?

Conductors

Sometimes you want thermal energy to transfer rapidly, for example, as when you thaw frozen food. You could put a frozen hamburger on a metal tray to speed up the thawing process. Materials through which it is easy to transfer thermal energy are conductors. Most metals are good conductors of thermal energy. Metals such as gold, silver, and copper are superior conductors. That is why the silver spoon became so hot in the boiling water. Copper is widely available and less expensive than gold or silver. Copper can be attached to another metal, such as steel, to make a cooking pan. Many steel cooking pans have copper bottoms. A copper bottom conducts thermal energy more evenly. It helps spread heat across the bottom surface of the pan to prevent hot spots from forming. This allows food to cook evenly. ☑

Reading Check ☑

What materials make good conductors?

Insulators

Materials that don't allow thermal energy to be conducted easily are insulators. You usually want your pizza to stay warm, so the best pizza places deliver it in an insulated box, as shown in **Figure 26-15.** The material used is one that will not transfer thermal energy. If you put a plastic spoon in boiling water, it's easy to hold it for a long time without burning your fingers because plastic transfers thermal energy poorly. Many cooking pans have plastic handles that won't melt instead of metal ones. These handles remain at a comfortable temperature while the pans are used for cooking. Other examples of insulators include wood and rubber. Ceramic tiles or several layers of cloth often are used as insulators.

Using Math

The yearly copper production average is 8 million metric tons. Most copper ores contain less than two percent copper. How many metric tons of copper ore are mined each year?

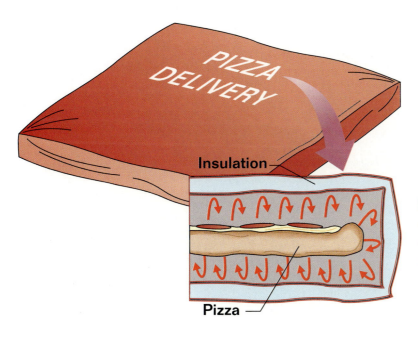

Figure 26-15 The material inside an insulated pizza carrier keeps the thermal energy from transferring out of the box and the carrier so your pizza stays warm.

Mini Lab

Comparing Energy Content

Procedure

1. Pour equal amounts of hot, cold, and room-temperature water into each of three transparent, labeled containers.
2. Measure and record the temperature of the water in each container.
3. Use a dropper to gently put a drop of food coloring in the center of each container.
4. After two minutes, observe each container.

Analysis

1. How are kinetic energy and temperature related?
2. In which container do the water particles have the most kinetic energy?
3. Based on the speed at which the food coloring spreads through the water, rank the containers from fastest to slowest. What can you infer about how water temperature affected the movement of the food coloring?

They protect a table surface from the hot bottoms of pans because these materials do not transfer thermal energy easily.

Convection

Some energy transfers involve particles that do not stay in place but move from one place to another. **Convection** transfers thermal energy when particles move from one place to another where there is a difference in temperature. This is most common in gases and liquids. Cool air sinks because it is more dense than warm air. Your home is heated by using the idea of convection. Look at **Figure 26-16.** Air is warmed in the furnace. The warm, less-dense air is then forced up through the air duct by the furnace's fan. The warm air circulates and rises through the room. As the air cools, it becomes more dense. The cool air sinks toward the floor, and it is then pulled through the air duct by the furnace's fan to be warmed again and recirculated. In the case of water, the warmer, less-dense water is forced up as the cooler, more-dense water sinks. Have you ever seen noodles cooking? The noodles are carried upward and downward as the hot water moves to the top, cools at the surface,

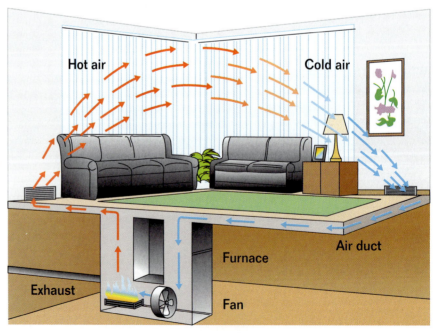

Figure 26-16 The furnace's fan helps circulate thermal energy through your home. Warmer air particles move upward while cooler air particles move downward.

and then sinks. Convection causes warm and cool currents in the atmosphere, which produce Earth's weather.

The effects of warm and cool air currents are especially important to understanding how hurricanes and tornadoes form. Convection currents also are formed in oceans by cold water flowing from the poles and warm water flowing from tropical regions.

Have you ever seen an eagle or a hawk coasting high in the air? Look at the seagull in **Figure 26-17.** A bird can stay in the air without flapping its wings because it is held up by a thermal. A thermal is a column of warm air that is forced up as cold air around it sinks. It is a convection current in the air. A thermal is the same type of current used by people who are hang gliding. It helps keep them in the air as long as possible. You can see that thermal energy and its transfer affect you daily. How many uses of thermal energy can you see around you right now?

Figure 26-17 Moving air caused by convection helps lift this seagull so it does not need to flap its wings constantly.

Section Assessment

1. How is thermal energy transferred? List three ways and give an example for each from nature.

2. Popcorn can be cooked in a hot-air popper, in a microwave oven, or in a pan on the stove. Identify each method as convection, conduction, or radiation.

3. What condition must exist for transfer of thermal energy to occur?

4. **Think Critically:** How are temperature, thermal energy, and heat different?

5. 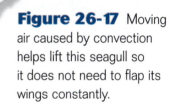 **Skill Builder**

   Using Numbers When selecting an energy source for heating a home, consumers try to think about cost. Do the **Chapter 26 Skill Activity** on page 1019 and use proportions to determine the area of the solar collector needed to heat a home.

Using Math

To change a temperature from the Fahrenheit scale to the Celsius scale, you subtract 32 from the Fahrenheit temperature and multiply the difference by 5/9. If the temperature is 77°F, what is the Celsius temperature?

Can you observe a temperature change?

Materials

- Thermometers (−10°C to 110°C) (4)
- Self-sealing freezer bags (2)
- Water (100 mL)
- Ice cubes (2 to 3)
- Pancake syrup (100 mL)
  *corn syrup
- Beakers (4 large)
  *heat-safe glass containers
- Spoon
  *stirring rod
  *Alternate Materials

Different substances absorb thermal energy differently. You will heat two different materials. Then, by comparing the temperature of each material, you will infer which substance can absorb the most thermal energy before rising in temperature.

What You'll Investigate

Which material can absorb more thermal energy?

Goals

- **Measure** a temperature change.
- **Infer** a material's ability to absorb thermal energy.

Safety Precautions

- Use care when handling the heated bags and hot water.
- Do not taste, eat, or drink any materials used in the lab.

Procedure

1. **Design** two data tables in which to record your data of the temperature measurements of the hot- and cold-water beakers. Use the sample table to help you.

2. **Pour** 200 mL of hot tap water (about 90°C) into each of two large beakers.

3. **Pour** 200 mL of cool, tap water into each of two large beakers. Add two or three ice cubes and stir until the ice melts.

4. **Pour** 100 mL of room-temperature water into one bag and 100 mL of syrup into the other bag. Tightly seal both bags.

5. **Record** the starting water temperature of each hot beaker.

Place each bag into its own beaker of hot water.

6. **Record** the water temperature in each of the hot-water beakers every two minutes until the temperature does not change.

7. **Record** the starting water temperature of each cold beaker. If any ice cubes remain, **remove** them from the cold water.

8. Carefully **remove** the bags from the hot water and **put** each into its own beaker of cold water.

9. **Record** the water temperature in each of the cold-water beakers every two minutes until there is no change in temperature.

Water Temperatures—Hot Beaker			
Water–filled bag		Syrup–filled bag	
Time (min)	Temperature (°C)	Time (min)	Temperature (°C)
0		0	
2		2	
4		4	
6		6	
8		8	

Conclude and Apply

1. **Look** at your data. Which beaker of hot water reached a lower temperature—the beaker with the water-filled or syrup-filled bag?

2. In which beaker of cold water did you observe the greater temperature change after adding the bags?

3. Which material absorbed more heat? Which released more heat?

4. **Infer** which material conducts thermal energy better. Would either material make a good insulator? Explain.

Chemical Energy

Observing Chemical Energy

At dusk on a hot summer day, you may have seen fireflies glowing. Did you ever wonder how they make their eerie light? If you have seen light sticks at Halloween that glow for a short period of time, you have observed the same principle as behind the fireflies' glow. Energy in the form of light is released when a chemical reaction takes place inside the light stick. A campfire or a fire in an outdoor grill, such as the one in **Figure 26-18**, releases thermal energy and light energy because of a chemical reaction taking place. Whether or not you realize it, you experience and observe chemical energy in many reactions every day.

What is a chemical reaction?

In a chemical reaction, substances are either made or broken down. When particles of substances combine, bonds form between them. These bonds hold the particles together and a new product is formed. When a substance is broken down, the bonds between the particles are broken. This causes the particles to split apart.

Figure 26-18 The chemical energy stored in these charcoal briquettes is released and transformed into thermal energy and light energy.

Figure 26-19 The oxygen and hydrogen gases will not react unless energy is added.

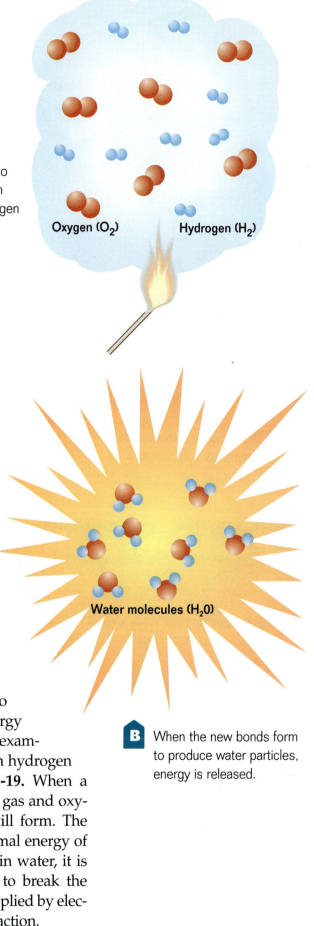

A The added energy from the flame causes the bonds to break in the oxygen particles and hydrogen particles.

Oxygen (O₂)   Hydrogen (H₂)

Water molecules (H₂O)

B When the new bonds form to produce water particles, energy is released.

Energy is stored in the bonds between particles in a substance. This stored (potential) energy within chemical bonds is called **chemical energy.** The potential energy stored in oil, gas, and coal is an important source of chemical energy. Food provides a source of chemical energy for our bodies. The muscles in our bodies transform some of this chemical energy into mechanical energy when they move. A weight lifter stores chemical energy in muscles in order to be able to lift heavier weights. Can you think of other examples of chemical reactions you participated in today?

Energy in Reactions

Changes in energy are a part of every chemical reaction. To break bonds, energy must be added. The reverse is also true. When bonds form, energy is released. Most reactions do not take place on their own. In some reactions, energy must be added before the reaction can begin. For example, energy is needed to start the reaction between hydrogen and oxygen to form water. Look at **Figure 26-19.** When a lighted match is placed in a mixture of hydrogen gas and oxygen gas, the mixture will explode and water will form. The energy to begin the reaction comes from the thermal energy of the flame. Once particles are bound together, as in water, it is difficult to split them apart. It requires energy to break the bonds. Energy to break chemical bonds can be supplied by electricity, heat, light, or motion, depending on the reaction.

Figure 26-20 Many processes take place in the preparation of food. The ingredients in moist, soft cookie dough use energy to change and become crispy, airy cookies.

Energy-Absorbing Reactions

Some chemical reactions need energy to keep going. A reaction that absorbs energy is called an endothermic (en duh THUR mihk) reaction. Endothermic chemical reactions take place in the preparation of food as shown in **Figure 26-20.** Thermal energy is absorbed by the food as it cooks. For example, an endothermic reaction takes place in some kinds of cookie dough. The baking soda absorbs energy and produces a gas that puffs up the cookies.

A process in nature that absorbs a lot of energy is photosynthesis. During photosynthesis, some cells in the leaves of green plants transform the energy from sunlight into chemical energy in the form of sugar. Once the plant is deprived of sunlight, the reaction stops. Photosynthesis is probably the most important endothermic process on Earth. Because of photosynthesis, plants provide us, and almost all other living things, with food and oxygen.

Problem Solving

Chemical Energy in Action

Lashawna twisted her ankle at track practice. To help ease the pain until she could have it checked, her coach suggested that she soak her ankle in a solution of Epsom salts.

Lashawna filled a small tub with lukewarm water. She then added half a box of Epsom salts to the water. As she was stirring the solution with her hand, the water became cool.

Lashawna didn't understand why the temperature of the water changed. Was she imagining things? How can you explain why the water became cold?

Think Critically: What kind of process takes place in the solution of Epsom salts, endothermic or exothermic? Explain.

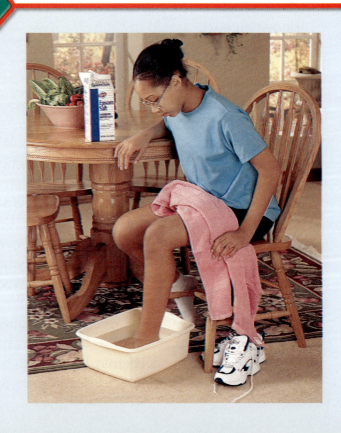

Figure 26-21 Demolition experts use the energy released by the reaction that causes the dynamite explosion to destroy this building in Hartford, Connecticut.

Energy-Releasing Reactions

Some chemical reactions are important because of their products. Other reactions are important because of the energy that is released. Exothermic (ek soh THUR mihk) reactions are reactions that give off energy. If you have used a chemical hand warmer on a cold day, then you felt the thermal energy released by the exothermic reaction taking place inside the hand warmer. The energy released from a dynamite explosion will demolish an old building as in **Figure 26-21.** Charcoal briquettes release a lot of energy as they react with oxygen, causing them to burn at a high temperature. Combustion, the burning of material in the presence of oxygen, is a familiar exothermic reaction. What are other exothermic reactions?

Rate of Reaction

The rate of a chemical reaction can be sped up or slowed down by changing the temperature, stirring the mixture, or adding a catalyst. For example, will a spoonful of sugar dissolve faster in a glass of iced tea or in a cup of hot tea? If you have ever watched closely, you might have noticed that sugar dissolves faster in the hot tea. Dissolving sugar is a process that can be sped up by increasing the temperature.

What if you added sugar to your iced tea only to watch it sink and sit at the bottom of the glass? How would you get the sugar to dissolve? You would probably stir the iced tea to make the sugar dissolve faster. Even though the sugar dissolves on its own at the bottom of the glass, stirring it makes the dissolving process go more quickly.

A catalyst is a substance that changes the rate of a chemical reaction without any change to its own structure. Many cell processes in your body are sped up by the presence of catalysts. Catalysts in your body are substances called enzymes.

LIFE SCIENCE ◀ INTEGRATION

Figure 26-22
Salivary glands release saliva as you chew. The enzyme in saliva speeds up the chemical reaction that breaks down food as it travels to the stomach.

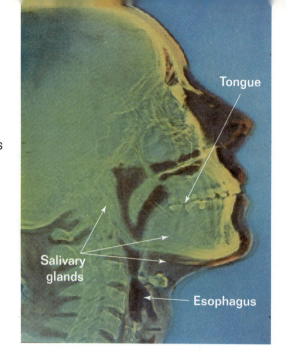

Tongue

Salivary glands

Esophagus

Visit the Glencoe Science Web Site at **www. glencoe.com/sec/ science/ca** for more information about enzymes.

For example, when you chew a piece of bread, glands in your mouth, as shown in **Figure 26-22,** produce saliva that contains an enzyme. The enzyme in saliva acts as a catalyst to help break down starches more quickly into smaller molecules.

Many other chemical reactions depend on catalysts to help them work better. For example, the production of vegetable shortening, synthetic rubber, and high-octane gasoline are all chemical processes that succeed with the help of catalysts.

Section Assessment

1. Where is chemical energy found?

2. What happens to bonds when new products are made?

3. Name three ways to speed up a reaction.

4. **Think Critically:** How are exothermic and endothermic reactions different? How are they similar?

5. **Skill Builder**
Classifying Divide the following list of reactions into two groups by classifying each reaction as endothermic or exothermic: burning wood, striking a match to light it, baking bread, and exploding dynamite. Explain why you placed each reaction into one group. If you need help, refer to Classifying in the **Skill Handbook** on page 985.

Using Computers

Word Processing Write one sentence that states, in your own words, the main idea of each major paragraph in this section about chemical energy. Use a word processor to type your summary of these important concepts. If you need help, refer to page 1004.

Hot-Vent Inhabitants

Some Like It Hot

Deep below the ocean surface, where no sunlight can reach, Earth's crust moves apart and forms cracks in the seafloor called hydrothermal vents. Superheated, mineral-rich fluid as hot as 350°C flows out of the vents. In spite of the extreme temperatures, more than 300 species of organisms live in and around hydrothermal vents. Fish and giant tube worms (seen at left), giant clams, mussels, crabs, shrimp, microorganisms such as bacteria, and other life-forms live in this harsh, deep-ocean environment.

Extreme Environments

Microorganisms that live at these high temperatures are called thermophiles. Thermophiles living around hydrothermal vents have remarkable adaptations for surviving in such an environment. For example, some of these microorganisms use sulfur-containing compounds—rather than sunlight—as an energy source. Scientists once thought that life could not exist under extreme environmental conditions. Because life was discovered around hydrothermal vents, however, scientists theorize that microorganisms similar to those in hot-vent communities exist in other places long thought to be lifeless.

Europa, Jupiter's fourth-largest moon, is one place scientists are looking for signs of life. Although Europa's surface is solid ice, there may be a warm layer of liquid water underneath. If water and a geothermal energy source exist on Europa, life-forms also might be there and would give clues to early life-forms on Earth.

Future Uses

Research has shown that thermophilic bacteria have unique enzymes that help them survive brutal heat. Unlike more common enzymes, those of thermophiles do not stop functioning when exposed to high temperatures. Such enzymes may be useful in medicine and industry. For instance, medical researchers are investigating the use of these enzymes as anticancer and anti-AIDS agents.

interNET CONNECTION

Visit the Glencoe Science Web Site at **www.glencoe.com/sec/science/ca** to find more information about deep-sea vents.

For a **preview** of this chapter, study this Reviewing Main Ideas before you read the chapter. After you have studied this chapter, you can use the Reviewing Main Ideas to **review** the chapter.

GLENCOE TECHNOLOGY

The Glencoe MindJogger, Audiocassettes, and CD-ROM provide additional opportunities for review.

Section

26-1 ENERGY CHANGES

Energy has the ability to cause change. It can change the temperature, shape, speed, or direction of an object. Some common types of energy forms are mechanical, chemical, thermal, light, nuclear, and electrical. *What are some examples of how energy changes form?*

KINETIC AND POTENTIAL ENERGY

Moving objects have **kinetic energy.** An object's mass and speed affect how much kinetic energy it has. Objects at rest can have stored energy in the form of **potential energy.** This energy comes from an object's position or condition—not from motion. *How are potential and kinetic energy related?*

CONSERVING ENERGY

Kinetic energy, as well as other forms of energy, can be transferred from one object to another. When energy is transferred or changes form, the total amount of energy stays the same. Energy cannot be created or destroyed. *After the last domino in the row falls, what happens to all the kinetic energy from the first domino?*

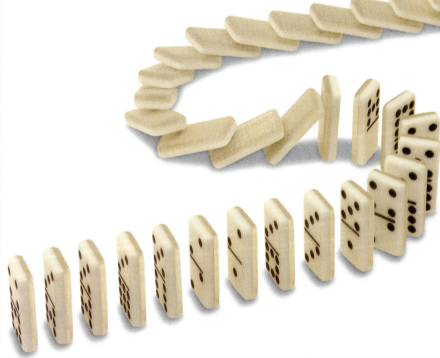

Section 26-2 TEMPERATURE

Temperature measures the average kinetic energy of the particles in a material. Particles having more kinetic energy have higher temperatures than particles with less kinetic energy. The Fahrenheit, Celsius, and Kelvin scales are used to measure temperature. *Which would have more kinetic energy—the particles in an ice cube or a glass of water?*

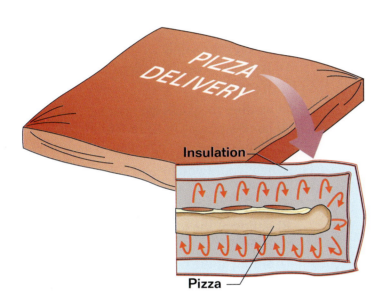

PIZZA DELIVERY

Insulation

Pizza

THERMAL ENERGY

Thermal energy is the total amount of kinetic energy of the particles in a material. The movement of thermal energy from a warmer object to a cooler one is called **heat.** The ability to absorb heat depends on the type of material and its quantity. Thermal energy moving by **radiation** travels by waves in all directions.

Conduction is the transfer of kinetic energy from particle to particle as they bump into each other.

Convection transfers energy by the movement of particles from one place to another. *What kind of energy transfer is involved in cooking a meal in a pan on the stove?*

Section 26-3 CHEMICAL ENERGY

The energy stored in chemical bonds is **chemical energy.** The energy stored in food and oil is an important source of chemical energy. Chemical reactions that release energy are exothermic reactions. Reactions that absorb energy are endothermic reactions. Raising the temperature, stirring, and adding catalysts can speed up chemical reactions. Reactions taking place in your body every day use enzymes as catalysts. Catalysts are used in making a number of commercial products. *How do catalysts affect chemical reactions?*

Chapter 26 Assessment

Using Vocabulary

a. chemical energy
b. conduction
c. convection
d. energy
e. heat
f. kinetic energy
g. law of conserva-
   tion of energy
h. potential energy
i. radiation
j. temperature
k. thermal energy

Each of the following sentences is false. Make the sentence true by replacing the italicized word with a word from the above list.

1. Transfer of energy by direct contact is *radiation*.
2. Energy of motion is *potential energy*.
3. The movement of thermal energy from warm to cool objects is *temperature*.
4. A measure of the average kinetic energy of the molecules in a substance is called *heat*.
5. *Kinetic energy* is energy that is stored.

Checking Concepts

Choose the word or phrase that best answers each question.

6. Which of the following correctly describes energy?
   A) It can be created.
   B) It can be destroyed.
   C) It cannot change form.
   D) It can cause change.

7. What does a thermometer measure?
   A) heat
   B) total energy
   C) average kinetic energy
   D) chemical energy

8. What happens if two objects at different temperatures are touching?
   A) Thermal energy transfers from the warmer object.
   B) Thermal energy transfers from the cooler object.
   C) Thermal energy transfers to the warmer object.
   D) No thermal energy transfer takes place.

9. During an energy transfer, what happens to the total amount of energy?
   A) It increases.
   B) It decreases.
   C) It stays the same.
   D) It depends on the energy form being transferred.

10. How does the sun's energy reach us?
    A) conduction
    B) convection
    C) radiation
    D) insulation

11. When would you have the most potential energy?
    A) walking up the hill
    B) sitting at the top of the hill
    C) running up the hill
    D) sitting at the bottom of the hill

12. Which is **NOT** the name of a temperature scale?
    A) Joule
    B) Kelvin
    C) Celsius
    D) Fahrenheit

13. What is the name given to any material that transfers thermal energy easily?
    A) thermal
    B) insulator
    C) metal
    D) conductor

14. What also will increase as the speed of an object increases?
    A) kinetic energy
    B) mass
    C) weight
    D) potential energy

15. What type of energy transfer produces weather?
    A) radiation
    B) conduction
    C) convection
    D) atmospheric

Thinking Critically

16. Much discussion has focused on the need to drive more efficient cars and use less electricity. If the law of conservation of energy is true, why are people concerned about energy usage?

17. If heat flows in only one direction, how can both hot and cold liquids reach room temperature as they sit on a table?

18. Think about what happens to Jack and Jill in the nursery rhyme. What kinds of energy are used? How was each energy form used?

19. Compare the three temperature scales you learned about. How are they different? How are they similar?

20. Use what you know about the movement of thermal energy to explain why you would place a minor burn on your arm under cool, running water.

Developing Skills

If you need help, refer to the **Skill Handbook.**

21. **Concept Mapping:** Below is a concept map of the energy changes of a gymnast bouncing on a trampoline. Complete the map by indicating the type of energy—kinetic, potential, or both—the gymnast has at each of the following stages:
a) halfway up, b) the highest point,
c) halfway down, d) the lowest point, just before hitting the trampoline.

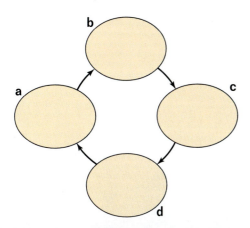

THE PRINCETON REVIEW

Test-Taking Tip

Make Yourself Comfortable When you take a test, try to make yourself as comfortable as possible. You will then be able to focus all your attention on the test.

Test Practice

Use these questions to test your Science Proficiency.

1. The sun is a source of thermal energy. Which description below **BEST** illustrates a change from thermal energy to potential chemical energy when solar energy strikes Earth?
   A) ocean water warms
   B) atmosphere cools
   C) leaves of plants make food
   D) icebergs melt

2. As you ski down a mountain, what type of energy transformation occurs?
   A) Kinetic energy changes to potential energy.
   B) Potential energy changes to kinetic energy.
   C) Chemical energy changes to potential energy.
   D) Mechanical energy changes to potential energy.

3. In an endothermic reaction, what happens to the energy?
   A) Energy is released.
   B) Energy is absorbed.
   C) Energy is made.
   D) There is no energy transfer.

CHAPTER
27
Waves

Chapter Preview

Skills Preview

Skill Builders
• Map Concepts
• Compare and Contrast

Activities
• Classify
• Measure in SI

MiniLabs
• Compare and Contrast
• Observe

Reading Check ✔

As you read, jot down ways your life would change if there were no waves. What would your life be like? Could you live at all?

Explore Activity

Think about a beautiful autumn day. You are sitting by a lake in a park. You hear music coming from a nearby school band practicing for a big game. A fish jumps out of the water and falls back making a splash. You see a circle of waves that move away from the fish's entry point. The circular waves pass by a floating leaf that fell from a tree nearby. How does the leaf move in response to the waves?

Observe Wave Behavior

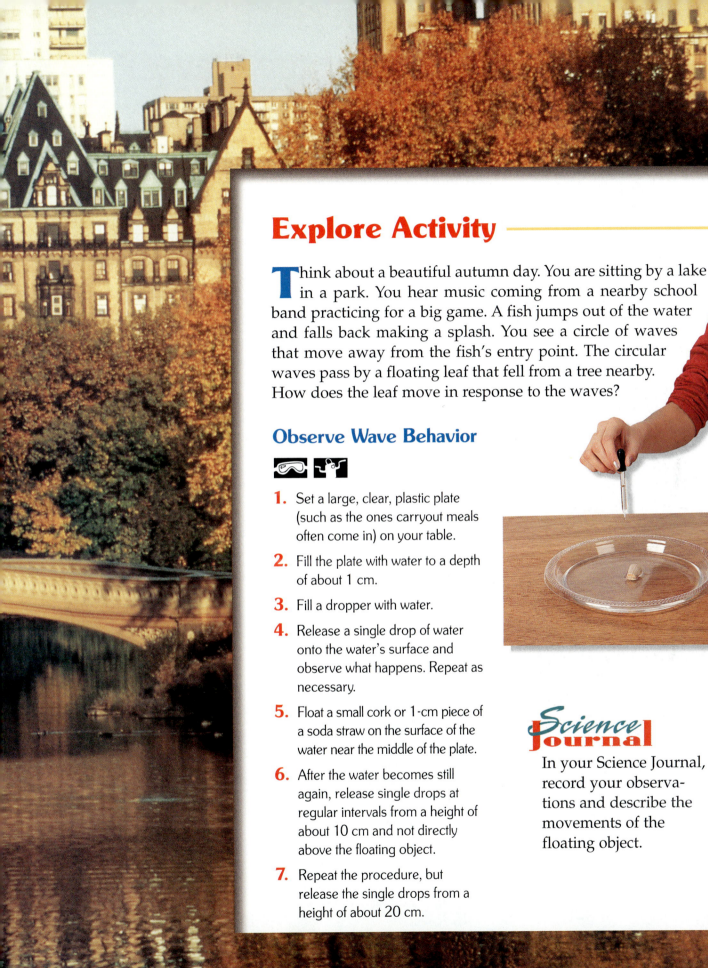

1. Set a large, clear, plastic plate (such as the ones carryout meals often come in) on your table.

2. Fill the plate with water to a depth of about 1 cm.

3. Fill a dropper with water.

4. Release a single drop of water onto the water's surface and observe what happens. Repeat as necessary.

5. Float a small cork or 1-cm piece of a soda straw on the surface of the water near the middle of the plate.

6. After the water becomes still again, release single drops at regular intervals from a height of about 10 cm and not directly above the floating object.

7. Repeat the procedure, but release the single drops from a height of about 20 cm.

Science **Journal**

In your Science Journal, record your observations and describe the movements of the floating object.

What are waves?

What You'll Learn

▶ Waves carry energy, not matter
▶ The difference between transverse waves and compressional waves

Vocabulary

wave
mechanical wave
electromagnetic wave
transverse wave
compressional wave

Why It's Important

▶ You can hear music because of waves.

Waves Carry Energy

In the Explore Activity, you saw that falling drops of water can move a floating object. You know that you can make something move by giving it a push or pull. But, the drops didn't hit the floating object. How did the energy from the falling drops travel through the water and move the object? Did you also notice that the ripples that moved in circles from the drop's entry point had peaks and valleys? These peaks and valleys make up water waves.

Waves are regular disturbances that carry energy through matter or space without carrying matter, as shown in **Figure 27-1A.** You also transfer energy when you throw a basketball or baseball to a friend. But, there is an important difference between a moving ball and a moving wave. As shown in **Figure 27-1B,** throwing a ball involves the transport of matter as well as energy.

Mechanical Waves

How does a wave carry energy but not matter? Here is one example you already know about. Sound travels as one type of wave motion. The sounds from a CD player reach your ears when the speakers vibrate back and forth and make sound waves.

Figure 27-1 The wave and the ball both carry energy.

A Waves on the water's surface carry energy from place to place, but the water itself moves mostly up and down.

B When you throw a ball to a friend, the ball carries both energy and matter. **What is another example of a moving object carrying both energy and matter?**

The sound waves transfer energy to anything in their path. When the waves reach your ears, they make your eardrums vibrate, as in **Figure 27-2.** If you've ever felt your house shake after a clap of thunder, you know that sound waves can carry large amounts of energy.

Waves that require matter to carry energy are called **mechanical waves.** The matter through which a mechanical wave travels is called a medium. A mechanical wave travels as energy is transferred from particle to particle in the medium. For example, a sound wave travels through the air because energy is transferred from gas molecule to gas molecule. Without a medium, you would not hear sounds. For example, sound waves can't travel in outer space. Imagine that you're standing on the moon. A person standing near you is telling you what she sees. But because there is no air on the moon to carry the sound, you won't hear a word she says—even if she yells at the top of her lungs.

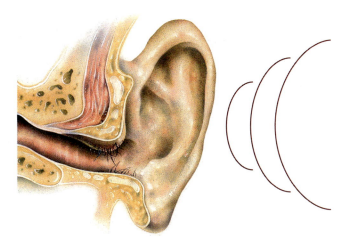

Figure 27-2 When you hear a sound, it's because sound waves traveling through the air make your eardrums vibrate.

Water Waves

Water waves—like the ones you made in the Explore Activity—are also mechanical waves. Each falling water drop touched water molecules when it hit the water's surface. Thus, the droplet's energy was carried from molecule to molecule through the water. Remember that the molecules of water do not move forward along with the wave. Rather, the water's surface moves up and down. In this same way, the wave transfers energy to a boat or other floating object, as shown in **Figure 27-3.** Absorbing some of the energy, the object bobs up and down and moves slowly away from the source of the wave.

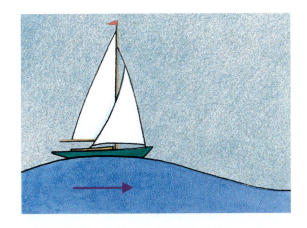

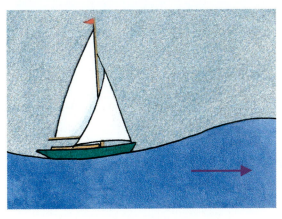

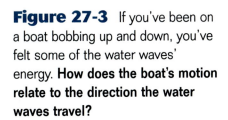

Figure 27-3 If you've been on a boat bobbing up and down, you've felt some of the water waves' energy. **How does the boat's motion relate to the direction the water waves travel?**

Electromagnetic Waves

When you listen to the radio, watch TV, or use a microwave oven to cook, you use a different kind of wave—one that doesn't need matter as a medium.

Waves that do not require matter to carry energy are called **electromagnetic waves.** Electromagnetic waves can travel through air. They can even travel through the solid walls of your home. These are the kind of waves that bring you radio and TV programs. Electromagnetic waves also can travel through space to carry information to and from spacecraft. The X rays a doctor uses to see if you broke a bone and the light that carries the sun's energy to Earth are also electromagnetic waves.

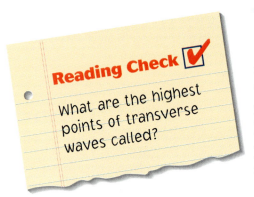

Reading Check ✔

What are the highest points of transverse waves called?

Transverse Waves

In a mechanical **transverse wave,** matter moves back and forth at right angles to the direction the wave travels. All electromagnetic waves are transverse waves. You can make a model of a transverse wave. Tie one end of a rope to a doorknob. Hold the other end in your hand. Now, shake the end in your hand up and down. By adjusting the way you shake the rope, you can create a wave that seems to vibrate in place.

Does the rope appear to move toward the doorknob? It doesn't really move toward the door, because if it did, you also would be pulled in that direction. What you see is energy moving along the "rope" wave. You can see that the wave has peaks and valleys at regular intervals. As shown in **Figure 27-4,** the high points of transverse waves are called crests. The low points are called troughs. ✔

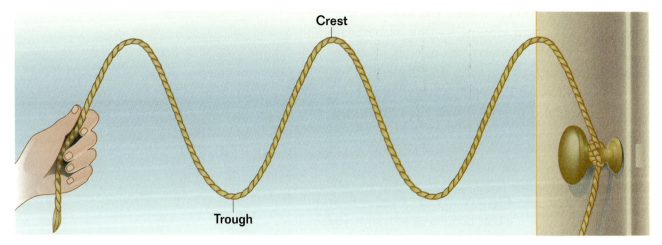

Crest

Trough

Figure 27-4 What does the vibrating rope carry from the hand to the door?

Figure 27-5 Sound waves are compressional waves.

 A This compressional wave carries energy along the spring, while the spring itself vibrates forward and backward.

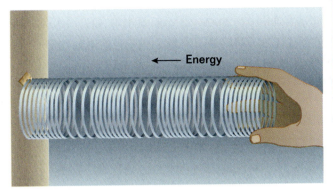

 **B** Vibrating strings make compressional waves that carry the harp's music to your ears. **What do you think vibrates to make compressional waves when a musician plays a trumpet?**

Compressional Waves

Mechanical waves can be either transverse or compressional. In a **compressional wave,** matter in the medium moves forward and backward in the same direction the wave travels. You can make a compressional wave by squeezing together and releasing several coils of a coiled spring toy, as shown in **Figure 27-5A.** When a compressional wave travels along a coiled spring, does the whole spring move along with the wave? If you tied a string around a single coil, you could watch that coil's movement as the wave passes. You would see that the coil moves forward and backward as the wave passes. So, like transverse waves, compressional waves carry only energy forward along the spring. The matter of the spring does not move along with the wave.

Sound Waves

Sound waves are compressional waves. How do you make sound waves when you talk or sing? If you hold your fingers against your throat while you hum, you can feel vibrations. These vibrations are actually the movements of your vocal cords. If you touch a stereo speaker while it's playing, you can feel the vibrations of the speaker, too. The sounds produced by the harp shown in **Figure 27-5B** are made when the strings of the instrument are made to vibrate.

Mini Lab

Comparing Sounds

Procedure

1. Hold a wooden ruler firmly on the edge of your desk so that most of it extends off the edge of the desk.
2. Pluck the free end of the ruler so that it vibrates up and down. Pluck it easily at first, then with more energy.
3. Repeat step 2, moving the ruler about 1 cm further onto the desk. Continue until only about 5 cm extend off the edge.

Analysis

1. Compare the loudness of the sounds produced by using little energy with those using more energy.
2. Compare the pitches produced by the longer and shorter lengths of the object.

Making Sound Waves

How do vibrating vocal cords, strings, and other objects make sound waves? To find out, look at the drumhead stretched over the open end of the drum shown in **Figure 27-6.** When the drumhead moves upward, it touches some of the invisible particles that make up the air. When everything is quiet, the air particles are spaced about the same distance apart. But when the drumhead moves up, it pushes the air particles together. These groups of particles that are squeezed together are called a compressional. When the drumhead moves downward, the air particles have more room and move away from each other. A place where particles are spaced far apart is called a rarefaction (rar uh FAK shun).

Figure 27-6 A vibrating drumhead makes compressions and rarefactions in the air. **How do your vocal cords make compressions and rarefactions in air?**

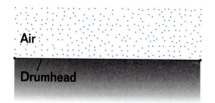
Air
Drumhead

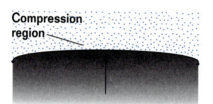
Compression region

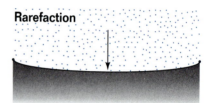
Rarefaction

Section Assessment

1. Give one example of a transverse wave and one example of a compressional wave.

2. Why can't a sound wave travel from a satellite to Earth?

3. Is light a mechanical wave or an electromagnetic wave? A transverse wave or a compressional wave?

4. **Think Critically:** How is it possible for a sound wave to transmit energy, but not matter?

5. **Skill Builder**
   Concept Mapping Create a concept map that shows the relationships between the following: *waves, mechanical waves, electromagnetic waves, compressional waves,* and *transverse waves.* If you need help, refer to Concept Mapping in the **Skill Handbook** on page 986.

Using Computers

Word Processing Use word-processing software to write short descriptions of the waves you encounter during a typical day. If you need help, refer to page 1004.

Wave Properties

Amplitude

Waves have characteristics that you can see and measure. For example, you can describe a wave in a lake or ocean by how high it rises above, or falls below, the normal water level. This is called the wave's amplitude. The **amplitude** of a transverse wave is one-half the distance between a crest and a trough, as shown in **Figure 27-7A.** In a compressional wave, the amplitude is greater when the particles of the medium are squeezed closer together in each compression and spread farther apart in each rarefaction.

Amplitude and Energy

A wave's amplitude is important. It is a measure of the energy the wave carries. For example, the waves that make up bright light have greater amplitudes than the waves that make up dim light. Waves of bright light carry more energy than the waves that make up dim light. In a similar way, loud sound waves have greater amplitudes than soft sound waves. Loud sounds carry more energy than soft sounds.

If you've seen pictures of a hurricane that strikes a coastal area, you know that the waves caused by the hurricane can damage anything that stands in their path. Waves with large amplitudes carry more energy than waves with smaller amplitudes. The waves caused by the hurricane have much more energy than the small waves or ripples on a pond, as you can see in **Figure 27-7B.**

What You'll Learn

► What wave frequency and wavelength are
► Waves travel at different speeds

Vocabulary
amplitude
wavelength
frequency

Why It's Important

► A wave's energy depends on its amplitude.

Figure 27-7 A wave's amplitude is a measure of how much energy it carries.

A The higher the crests (and the lower the troughs) of a wave, the greater the wave's amplitude is.

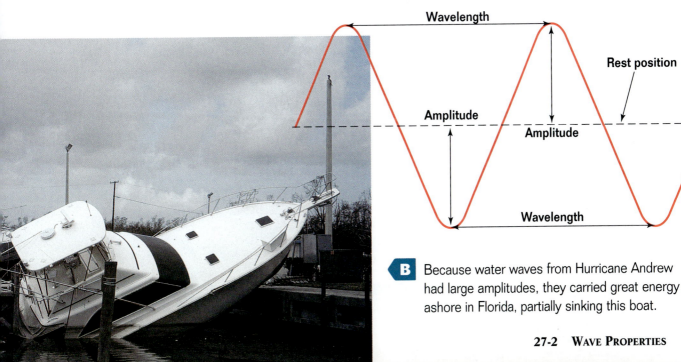

B Because water waves from Hurricane Andrew had large amplitudes, they carried great energy ashore in Florida, partially sinking this boat.

Tsunamis are huge sea waves that are caused by underwater earthquakes or volcanic eruptions. Because of their large amplitudes, tsunamis carry tremendous amounts of energy. They cause great damage when they move ashore.

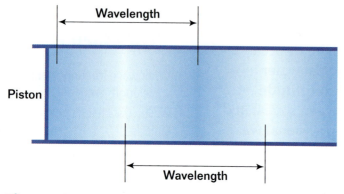

Figure 27-8 The wavelength of a compressional wave is measured from one compression or rarefaction to the next. **When the piston moves to the right, does it make a compression or a rarefaction?**

Figure 27-9 The wavelengths and frequencies of electromagnetic waves vary greatly. **Which waves have longer wavelengths, radio waves or visible light waves?**

Wavelength

Another way to describe a wave is by its wavelength. **Wavelength** is the distance between a point on one wave and an identical point on the next wave—from a crest to a crest or from a trough to a trough, as shown in **Figure 27-7A.** For a compressional wave, the wavelength is the distance between adjacent compressions or rarefactions, as shown in **Figure 27-8.**

Wavelength is an important characteristic of a wave. For example, the difference between red light and green light is that they have different wavelengths. Like all electromagnetic waves, light is a transverse wave. The wavelength of visible light determines its color. In this example, the wavelength of red light is longer than the wavelength of green light. Some electromagnetic waves, like X rays, have short wavelengths. Others, like microwaves in an oven, have longer wavelengths. The range of wavelengths of electromagnetic waves is shown in **Figure 27-9.**

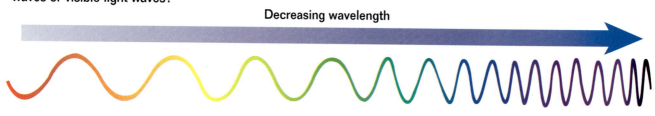

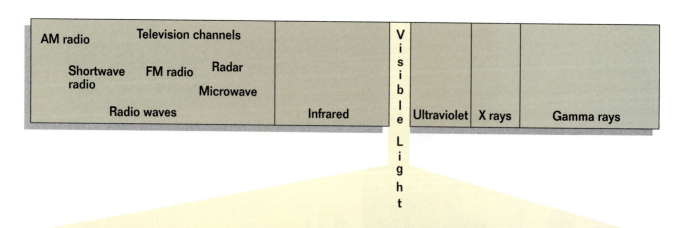

Frequency

The **frequency** of a wave is the number of waves that pass a given point in 1 s. Frequency is measured in waves per second, or hertz (Hz). For a given speed, waves with longer wavelengths have lower frequencies. Fewer long waves pass a given point in 1 s. Waves with shorter wavelengths have higher frequencies because more waves pass a given point in 1 s. Frequency is illustrated in **Figure 27-10A** and **B.**

The wavelength of an electromagnetic light wave determines the color of the light. In a sound wave, the frequency (associated with its wavelength) determines the pitch. Pitch is the highness or lowness of a sound. A flute makes musical notes with a high pitch. A tuba produces notes with a low pitch. When you sing "do re mi fa so la ti do," both the pitch and frequency increase from note to note. In other words, high-pitched sound waves have high frequencies. Low-pitched sound waves have low frequencies. ☑

PHYSICS INTEGRATION

Global Positioning Systems
Maybe you've used a global positioning system (GPS) receiver to determine your location while driving, boating, or hiking. Earth-orbiting satellites send out electromagnetic radio waves that give the satellites' exact locations and times of transmission. The GPS receiver calculates the distance to each satellite and displays your location to within about 16 m.

Wave Speed

You've probably watched a distant thunderstorm approach on a hot summer day. You see a bolt of lightning flash between a dark cloud and the ground. Do the sound waves, or thunder, produced by the lightning bolt reach your ears at the same instant you see the lightning? If the thunderstorm is many kilometers away, several seconds may pass between the time you see the lightning and you hear the thunder. This happens because light travels much faster in air than sound does. Light is an electromagnetic wave that travels through air at about 300 million m/s. Sound is a mechanical wave that travels through air at about 340 m/s.

Reading Check ☑

What determines the pitch of a sound?

Figure 27-10 Wave A has a longer wavelength and a lower frequency than wave B. **Why does a wave with a long wavelength have a low frequency?**

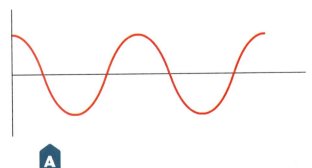

A

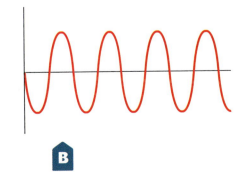

B

Determining Wave Speed

You can calculate the speed of a wave by multiplying its frequency by its wavelength. For example, suppose you know that a sound wave has a frequency of 266 Hz and a wavelength of 1.29 m. (Remember that 266 Hz means that 266 sound waves pass a given point in 1 s.) The wave's speed is given by the following calculation.

$$\text{wave frequency} \times \text{wavelength} = \text{wave speed}$$
$$266 \text{ Hz} \times 1.29 \text{ m} = 343 \text{ m/s}$$

The speed of the wave is 343 m/s.

Light waves don't always travel at the same speed. For example, the speed of light waves is slightly higher in empty space than in air. And, light waves travel only about 200 million m/s in glass. You can see that this is much slower than the speed light travels in air. The speed of sound waves varies, too. Have you ever heard sounds while swimming underwater? Have you ever put your ear against a wall or on the ground to hear something more clearly? If you have, you may have noticed something interesting. Sound travels faster in liquids and solids than in gases like air.

Using Math

You can calculate the speed of a wave in meters per second (m/s) by multiplying the wave's frequency in hertz (Hz) by its wavelength in meters (m). This calculation is possible because 1 Hz = 1/s. For example, 266 Hz × 1.29 m = 266 1/s × 1.29 m = 343 m/s.

Section Assessment

1. Why is the statement "The speed of light is 300 million m/s" not always correct?

2. How does the frequency of a wave change as its wavelength changes?

3. In what part of a compressional wave are the particles spaced farthest apart?

4. Why is a sound wave with a large amplitude more likely to damage your hearing than one with a small amplitude?

5. **Think Critically:** Explain the differences between the waves that make up bright green light and dim red light.

6. **Skill Builder**
   Interpreting Scientific Diagrams
   Scientific diagrams can help you understand wave properties. Do the **Chapter 27 Skill Activity** on page 1020 to learn about a compressional wave, its parts, and its wavelength.

Using Math

If a sound wave traveling through water has a speed of 1470 m/s and a frequency of 2340 Hz, what is its wavelength?

Waves on a Spring

Waves are rhythmic disturbances that carry energy through matter or space. Studying waves can help you understand how the sun's energy reaches Earth and sounds travel through the air.

Materials
- Long, coiled spring toy
- Meterstick
- Stopwatch
- Piece of colored yarn (5 cm)

What You'll Investigate

In this activity, you will create transverse and compressional waves on a coiled spring and investigate some of their properties.

Goals

- **Create** transverse and compressional waves on a coiled spring.
- **Investigate** wave properties such as speed and amplitude.

Procedure

1. **Prepare a data table** such as the one shown.

2. Work in pairs or groups and clear a place on an uncarpeted floor about 6 m long and 2 m wide.

3. While one team member grasps one end of the coiled spring toy with one hand, another team member should stretch it to the length suggested by the teacher. **Measure** the length of the coiled spring toy. **CAUTION:** *Coiled springs can be damaged permanently by overstretching or tangling. Be careful to follow the teacher's instructions.*

4. **Create** a wave by having one team member make a quick sideways snap of the wrist. Time several waves as they travel from one end of the coiled spring toy to the other. Record the average time in your data table.

5. Repeat step 4 using waves that have slightly larger amplitudes.

6. Use one hand to squeeze together about 20 of the coils near you. **Observe** what happens to the unsqueezed coils. Release the coils and **observe** what happens.

7. Quickly push one end of the coiled spring toward your partner, then pull it back to its original position.

8. Tie the piece of colored yarn to a coil near the middle of the coiled spring toy. Repeat step 7, **observing** what happens to the string.

Wave Data	
Length of stretched spring toy	
Average time for a wave to travel from end to end—step 4	
Average time for a wave to travel from end to end—step 5	

Conclude and Apply

1. **Classify** the wave pulses you created in steps 4 and 5 and those you created in steps 6 to 8 as compressional or transverse.

2. **Calculate** and **compare** the speeds of the waves in steps 4 and 5.

3. **Classify** the unsqueezed coils in step 6 as a compression or a rarefaction.

4. **Compare and contrast** the motion of the yarn in step 8 with the motion of the wave. Did the coil that had the yarn attached to it move along the coiled spring toy or did the wave's energy pass through that coil?

Wave Behavior

Reflection

What You'll Learn

▶ Waves can reflect from some surfaces

▶ How waves usually change direction when they move from one material into another

▶ Waves are able to bend around barriers

Vocabulary

reflection   diffraction
refraction   interference

Why It's Important

▶ Without wave reflection, you couldn't read the words on this page.

You've probably yelled to a friend across a gymnasium or down a long hallway. When you did this, you might have heard an echo of your voice. What property of sound caused the echo?

When you look in a mirror, what property of light lets you see your face? Both the echo of your voice and the face you see in the mirror are caused by wave reflection. **Reflection** occurs when a wave strikes an object or surface and bounces off. An echo is reflected sound. Sound reflects from all surfaces. Your echo bounced off the walls, floor, ceiling, furniture, and people. In old western movies, light reflected off a mirror was often used to send a message over long distances. When you see your face in a mirror, as shown in **Figure 27-11A,** reflection occurs. Light from your face hits the mirror and reflects back to your eyes.

A mirror is smooth and even. However, when light reflects from an uneven or rough surface, you can't see an image because the reflected light scatters in many different directions, as shown in **Figure 27-11B.**

Figure 27-11

A If light didn't reflect from you and the mirror, you wouldn't be able to see yourself in the mirror.

B The building at the far left has a rough surface that scatters light in different directions. Its surface is not smooth and shiny like the building on the right, which is mirror-like. **Why should a mirror's reflective surface be made as smooth as possible?**

Refraction

You've already seen that a wave changes direction when it reflects from a surface. Can a wave change its direction at other times? Perhaps you've used a magnifying glass to examine your skin, an insect, a coin, or a stamp. An object appears larger when viewed through a magnifying glass. This happens because the light rays from the object change direction when they pass from the air into the glass. They change direction again when they pass from the glass into the air. The bending of a wave as it moves from one medium into another is called **refraction.**

Refraction and Wave Speed

The speed of a wave is different in different substances. For example, light waves move slower in water than in air. Refraction occurs when the speed of a wave changes as it passes from one substance to another. As shown in **Figure 27-12A** and **B,** a line has been drawn perpendicular to the water's surface. This line is called the normal.

Try at Home
Mini Lab

Observing How Light Refracts

Procedure

1. Fill a large, opaque drinking glass or cup nearly to the brim with water.

2. Place a white soda straw in the water at an angle, with approximately one-third of its length extending out of the water.

3. Looking directly down into the cup from above, observe the straw where it meets the water.

4. Placing yourself so that the straw angles to your left or right, slowly back away about 1 m. If necessary, lower your head until you eliminate any unwanted glare from the water's surface. Observe the straw as it appears above, at, and below the surface of the water.

Analysis

1. Describe the straw's appearance as you looked directly down on it.

2. Compare the straw's appearance above and below the water's surface when you looked at it from the side. Draw a diagram and explain the apparent effect.

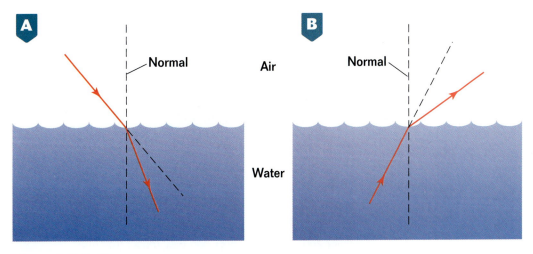

Figure 27-12 As the light ray in A passes from air into water, it refracts toward the normal. As the light ray in B passes from water into air, it refracts away from the normal.

When a light ray passes from air into water, it slows down and bends toward the normal. The more the light ray slows, the more its direction changes. When the ray passes from water into air, it speeds up and bends away from the normal.

You notice refraction when you look at an angle into a lake or pond and spot a fish near the bottom. Refraction makes the fish appear to be closer to the surface and farther away from you than it really is, as shown in **Figure 27-13.** Refraction also gives diamonds and other gems their wonderful sparkle. **Figure 27-14** illustrates how refraction and reflection produce a rainbow when light waves from the sun pass into and out of water droplets in the air.

Reading Check

What produces a rainbow?

Diffraction

It's time for lunch. You're walking down the hallway to the cafeteria. As you near the open door, you can hear people talking and the clink and clank of tableware. But how do the sound waves reach your ears before you get to the door? The sound waves must be able to bend around the corners of the door, as shown in **Figure 27-15A. Diffraction** is the bending of waves around a barrier.

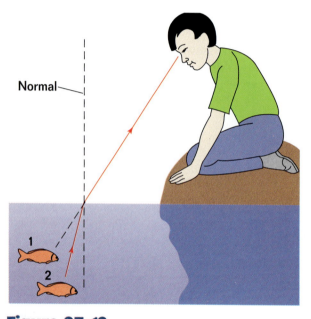

Figure 27-13
Refraction makes the fish at location 2 appear to be at location 1.

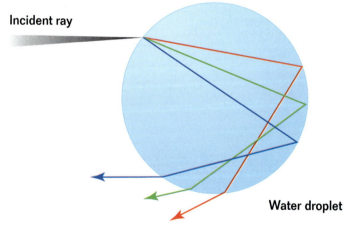

Figure 27-14 Light rays refract when they enter and leave a raindrop, and they reflect from the far side of the drop. Because different colors refract at different angles, they leave the drop separated into the colors of the spectrum. (Ray angles have been shown larger than they actually are for clarity.) **Which color of light shown on the diagram refracts most?**

VISUALIZING Diffraction

Figure 27-15 Sound waves and light waves diffract differently through an open door.

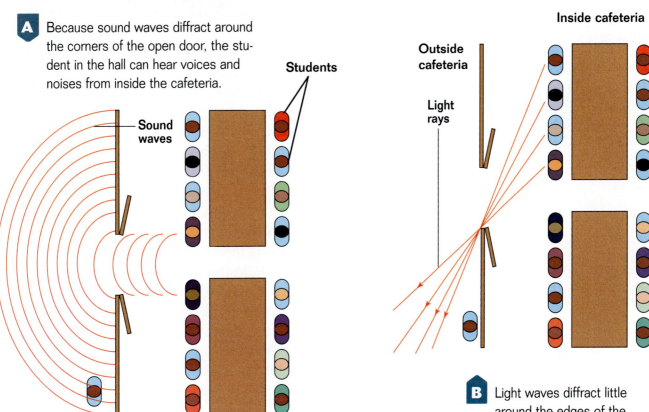

A Because sound waves diffract around the corners of the open door, the student in the hall can hear voices and noises from inside the cafeteria.

Students

Sound waves

Outside cafeteria

Inside cafeteria

Inside cafeteria

Outside cafeteria

Light rays

B Light waves diffract little around the edges of the open door. So, persons inside the cafeteria can be seen only when the student in the hall meets light rays streaming through the door. **How does diffraction explain why a boat inside a harbor rocks slightly from water waves outside the harbor?**

Diffraction of Light

Can light waves diffract, too? You can't see your friends in the cafeteria until you reach the open door, so the light waves must not diffract as much as the sound waves, as shown in **Figure 27-15.**

Are light waves able to diffract at all? As a matter of fact, light waves do bend around the edges of an open door. You can see some effects of light diffraction when you view a bright light through a small slit such as the one between two pencils held close together. However, the amount the light bends is extremely small. As a result, the diffraction of light is far too small to allow you to see around the corner into the cafeteria. The reason that light waves don't diffract much when they pass through an open door is that the wavelengths of visible light are much smaller than the width of the door. Sound waves that you can hear have much longer wavelengths. They bend more readily around the corners of an open door. Waves diffract best when the wavelength of the wave is similar in size to the barrier or opening.

Interference

Imagine a marching band that has only one of each kind of instrument. When this band performs on a football field, will it fill the stadium with sound? Having several of each instrument play the same notes at the same times produces much louder and more spectacular music. For example, the sound waves of many trumpets combine to make sound waves with larger amplitudes. The sound produced by many trumpets is therefore louder than the sound from a single trumpet. The ability of two or more waves to combine and form a new wave when they overlap is called **interference** (ihn tur FEER uns).

Constructive interference occurs when waves meet, for example, crest to crest and trough to trough. The amplitudes of these combining waves add together to make a larger wave, as shown in **Figure 27-16A, B,** and **C.** Destructive interference occurs, for example, when the crest of one wave meets the trough of another wave. In destructive interference, the amplitudes of the combining waves make a smaller wave. Sometimes, they produce no wave at all, as shown in **Figure 27-16D, E,** and **F** on the next page.

Reflected light waves sometimes produce interesting interference patterns. The colorful interference patterns that result from the microscopic pits in compact discs are one example.

*inter***NET**
CONNECTION

Visit the Glencoe Science Web Site at **www. glencoe.com/sec/ science/ca** for more information about wave interference.

Problem Solving

Scattering Light

Why is the sky blue and the sunset red? Surprisingly, both effects have the same cause. Sunlight contains all colors of the visible spectrum. When sunlight passes through Earth's atmosphere, particles in the air scatter some colors more than others. Shorter-wavelength violet and blue light waves are scattered most, green and yellow waves a little, and longer-wavelength orange and red light waves even less.

The sky appears blue during the day because the scattered blue light waves reflect to your eyes from dust particles and water droplets in the air. However, at sunrise and sunset, the sky appears red because light waves from the sun pass through more of the atmosphere before reaching Earth's surface. With so much of the blue and violet light scattered away, only the orange and red waves reach your eyes.

Think Critically: You've seen the beautiful array of colors in a rainbow on a day that has both sunshine and water droplets in the air. You've viewed the colorful light pattern from a compact disc. What do the blue color of the daytime sky, the red color of a sunset, a multicolored rainbow, and the light pattern from a compact disc have in common? How are they different?

Figure 27-16

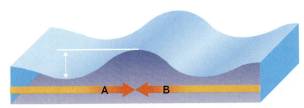

A **Constructive Wave Interference**
Crests of waves A and B approach each other from different directions. The waves have equal amplitudes.

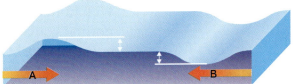
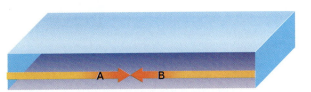

D **Destructive Wave Interference**
A crest of wave A and trough of wave B approach each other from different directions. The amplitude of A equals the amplitude of B.

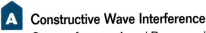

B When crests A and B meet, they briefly form a new wave, A + B, which has an amplitude equal to the sum of the amplitudes of the two waves.

E When the waves meet, they briefly form a new wave, A + B, which has an amplitude of zero for an instant.

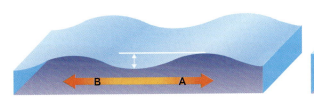
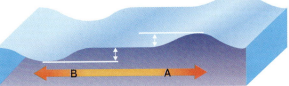

C The waves have passed through each other unchanged.

F The waves have passed through each other unchanged. **Compare and contrast constructive and destructive interference.**

Useful Interference

You may have seen someone cut grass with a power lawn mower or cut wood with a chain saw. In the past, many people who've performed these tasks have damaged their hearing because of the loud noises produced by these machines. Today, ear protectors can reflect and absorb some of the noise from lawn mowers and chain saws. The ear protectors lower the amplitudes of the harmful waves. The smaller-amplitude waves that reach the ears no longer damage eardrums.

Pilots of small planes have had an interesting problem. They couldn't shut out all the noise of the plane's motor. If they did, they wouldn't be able to hear instructions from air-traffic controllers. Engineers invented special earphones that contain electronic circuits. These circuits produce sound frequencies that destructively interfere with engine noise that might be harmful.

However, the sound frequencies produced do not interfere with human voices, allowing the pilot to hear and understand normal conversation. In these examples, destructive interference can be a benefit, as shown in **Figure 27-17.**

Figure 27-17 Some airplane pilots use ear protectors that muffle engine noise but don't block human voices. People who operate chain saws need ear protectors that greatly reduce the engine noise that could be harmful.

Section Assessment

1. White objects reflect light. Why don't you see your reflection when you look at a building made of rough, white stone?

2. If you're standing on one side of a building, how are you able to hear the siren of an ambulance on the other side of the building?

3. What behavior of light enables magnifying glasses and contact lenses to bend light rays and help people see more clearly?

4. **Think Critically:** Why don't light rays that stream through an open window into a darkened room spread evenly through the entire room?

5.  **Skill Builder**
Comparing and Contrasting When light rays pass from water into a certain type of glass, the rays refract toward the normal. Compare and contrast the speed of light in water and in the glass. If you need help, refer to Comparing and Contrasting in the **Skill Handbook** on page 992.

Science **Journal**
Look and listen carefully as you travel home from school or walk down the street where you live. What examples of wave reflection and refraction do you notice? Describe each of these in your Science Journal, and explain whether it's an example of reflection or refraction.

Science & Math

Graphing Waves

Constructive and Destructive Interference

Waves have special characteristics. The wavelength is the horizontal distance between a point on one wave and an identical point on the next wave. The amplitude is the vertical distance from the crest (or trough) of a wave to a position halfway between crest and trough.

When two waves meet in such a way that a new wave with greater amplitude is formed, it is called constructive interference. If the new wave formed has a smaller amplitude than either original wave or an amplitude of zero, it is called destructive interference.

Problem

Draw a graph for the new wave formed by combining Waves A and B.

Solution

Notice that nine points on each wave are labeled with red dots and numbers. These points will be used to graph the new wave.

To graph the new wave formed by combining Waves A and B, find nine points for the new graph by adding the "height" of Waves A and B at each labeled point.

Point 1 (new): height of Wave A point 1 + height of Wave B point 1 = 0 + 0 = 0.

Point 2 (new): height of Wave A point 2 + height of Wave B point 2 = 2 + 4 = 6.

Point 3 (new): height of Wave A point 3 + height of Wave B point 3 = 4 + 8 = 12.

Continuing the process, you'll find that the remaining points have heights 6, 0, 6, 12, 6, and 0. A graph for the new wave looks like this:

To find a wave's amplitude, count the vertical units between the lowest and highest points on the graph and divide by 2. Because the new wave has greater amplitude (6) than either Wave A (2) or B (4), this problem is an example of constructive interference.

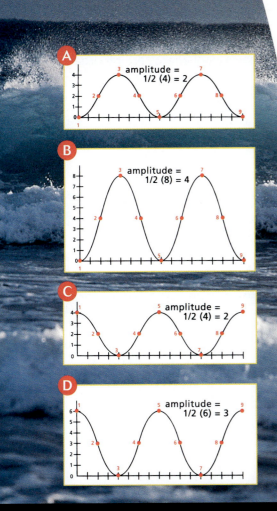

Practice
PROBLEMS

In the following problems, draw the graph and determine whether each is a case of constructive or destructive interference.

1. Draw a graph for the new wave formed by combining Waves B and D.

2. Draw a graph representing the combination of Waves C and D.

3. Draw a graph representing the combination of Waves A and C.

4. Draw graphs for two waves of your choice. Show the new wave formed by combining the two.

Activity 27•2

Doing the Wave

Materials

- Coiled spring toy
- Stopwatch
  *clock with a second hand
- Meterstick
- Tape

  *Alternate Materials

When an earthquake occurs, the waves of energy are recorded at points all over the world by instruments called seismographs. By comparing the data that they collected from their seismographs, scientists discovered that the interior of Earth must be made of layers of different materials. How did the seismographs tell them that Earth is not the same medium all the way through?

Recognize the Problem

Can the speed of a wave be used to identify the medium through which it travels?

Form a Hypothesis

Think about what you know about the relationship between the frequency, wavelength, and speed of a wave in a medium. **Make a hypothesis** about how you can measure the speed of a wave within a medium and use that information to identify an unknown medium.

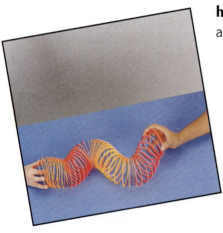

Goals

- **Measure** the speed of a wave within a coiled spring toy.
- **Predict** whether the speed you measured will be different in other types of coiled spring toys.

Data Sources

Go to the Glencoe Science Web Site at **www.glencoe.com/sec/ science/ca** for more information, hints, and data collected by other students.

	Wave Data					
Trial	Length spring was stretched (m)	Number of crests	Wavelength (m)	Number of vibrations timed	Number of seconds vibrations were timed (s)	Wave speed (m/s)
1						
2						
3						

Test Your Hypothesis

Plan

1. **Make a data table** in your Science Journal like the one shown.

2. **Write** a detailed description of the coiled spring toy you are going to use. Be sure to include its mass and diameter, the width of a coil, and what it is made of.

3. Decide as a group how you will **measure** the frequency and length of waves in the spring toy. What are your variables? Which variables must be controlled? What variable do you want to measure?

4. Repeat your experiment three times.

Do

1. Make sure your teacher approves your plan before you begin.

2. Carry out the experiment as you have planned.

3. While you are doing the experiment, **record** your observations and measurements in your data table.

Analyze Your Data

1. **Calculate** the frequency of the waves by dividing the number of vibrations you timed by the number of seconds you timed them. Record your results in your data table.

2. Use the following formula to **calculate** the speed of a wave in each trial.

   wavelength $\times$ wave frequency = wave speed

3. **Average** the wave speeds from your trials to determine the speed of a wave in your coiled spring toy.

Draw Conclusions

1. **Post** the description of your coiled spring toy and your results on the Glencoe Science Web Site.

2. **Compare and contrast** your results with the results of other students.

3. How does the type of coiled spring toy and the length it was stretched affect the wave speed? Was your hypothesis supported?

4. Would it make a difference if an earthquake wave were transmitted through Earth's solid mantle or the molten outer core?

For a **preview** of this chapter, study this Reviewing Main Ideas before you read the chapter. After you have studied this chapter, you can use the Reviewing Main Ideas to **review** the chapter.

The Glencoe MindJogger, Audiocassettes, and CD-ROM provide additional opportunities for review.

Section
27-1 WAVES CARRY ENERGY

Waves are rhythmic disturbances that carry energy but not matter. **Mechanical waves** can travel only through matter. Other waves, called **electromagnetic waves,** can travel through space. *What kind of waves carry the sun's energy to Earth? An earthquake's energy through Earth?*

TRANSVERSE AND COMPRESSIONAL WAVES

In a mechanical **transverse wave,** matter in the medium the wave travels through moves back and forth at right angles to the direction the wave travels. In a **compressional wave,** matter in the medium moves forward and backward in the same direction as the wave. *Why doesn't a sound wave travel through space?*

Section
27-2 AMPLITUDE, FREQUENCY, AND WAVELENGTH

Waves can be described by their characteristics. The **amplitude** of a transverse wave is one half the distance between a crest and a trough. **Wavelength** is the distance between a point on one wave and an identical point on the next wave. The **frequency** of a wave is the number of waves that pass a given point in 1 s. *How is the amplitude of a wave related to the amount of energy it carries?*

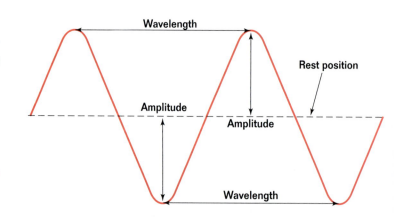

Wavelength

Rest position

Amplitude

Amplitude

Wavelength

Reading Check

- Construct a chart that compares and contrasts reflection, refraction, diffraction, and interference.

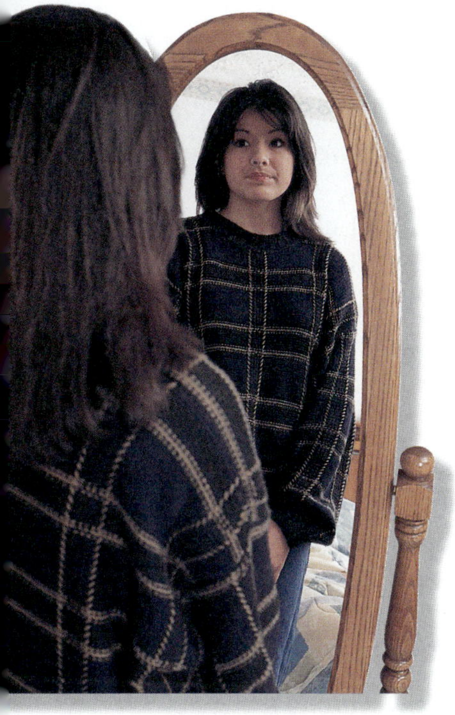

Section 27-3 REFLECTION

Reflection occurs when a wave strikes an object or surface and bounces off. You can see your image in a mirror because of reflection. ***How does wave reflection explain echoes in a large canyon?***

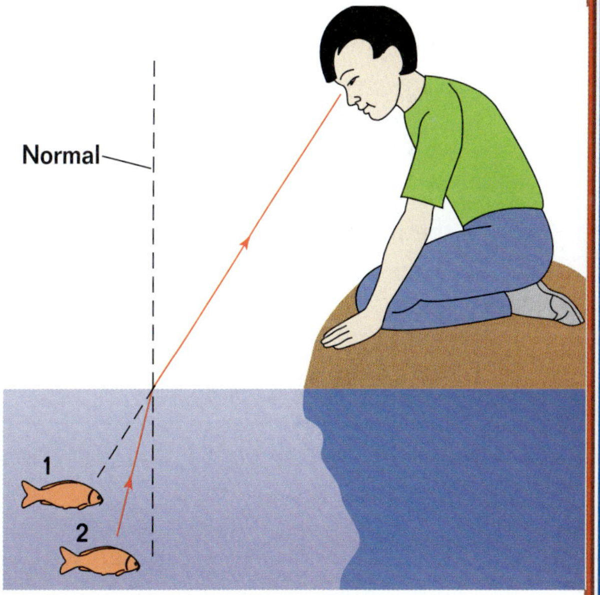

REFRACTION

The bending of a wave as it moves from one medium into another is called **refraction.** A wave changes direction, or refracts, when its speed changes. ***In what situation does a wave not change its direction when it passes from one medium into another?***

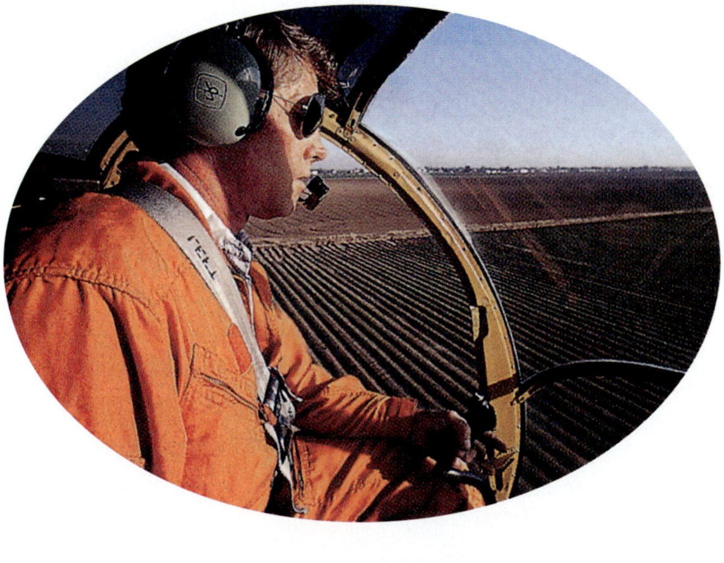

DIFFRACTION AND INTERFERENCE

The bending of waves around a barrier is called **diffraction.** The ability of two or more waves to combine and form a new wave when they overlap is called **interference.** ***What kind of interference produces waves with the largest amplitudes?***

Chapter 27 Assessment

Using Vocabulary

a. amplitude
b. compressional wave
c. diffraction
d. electromagnetic wave
e. frequency
f. interference
g. mechanical wave
h. reflection
i. refraction
j. transverse wave
k. wave
l. wavelength

Using the list above, replace the underlined words with the correct Vocabulary words.

1. <u>Diffraction</u> is the change in direction of a wave.
2. The type of wave that has rarefactions is a <u>transverse wave</u>.
3. The distance between two adjacent crests of a transverse wave is the <u>frequency</u>.
4. The greater the <u>wavelength</u> of a wave, the more energy the wave carries.
5. A <u>mechanical wave</u> can travel through space.

Checking Concepts

Choose the word or phrase that best answers the question.

6. What is the material through which mechanical waves travel?
   A) charged particles
   B) space
   C) a vacuum
   D) a medium

7. What is carried from particle to particle in a water wave?
   A) speed   C) energy
   B) amplitude   D) matter

8. What are the lowest points on a transverse wave called?
   A) crests   C) compressions
   B) troughs   D) rarefactions

9. What determines the pitch of a sound wave?
   A) amplitude   C) speed
   B) frequency   D) refraction

10. What is the distance between adjacent wave compressions?
    A) one wavelength   C) 1 m/s
    B) 1 km   D) 1 Hz

11. What occurs when a wave strikes an object or surface and bounces off?
    A) diffraction   C) a change in speed
    B) refraction   D) reflection

12. What is the name for a change in the direction of a wave when it passes from one medium into another?
    A) refraction   C) reflection
    B) interference   D) diffraction

13. What type of wave is a sound wave?
    A) transverse
    B) electromagnetic
    C) compressional
    D) refracted

14. When two waves overlap and interfere destructively, what does the resulting wave have?
    A) a greater amplitude
    B) more energy
    C) a change in frequency
    D) a lower amplitude

15. What is the difference between blue light and green light?
    A) They have different wavelengths.
    B) One is a transverse wave and the other is not.
    C) They travel at different speeds.
    D) One is mechanical and the other is not.

Thinking Critically

16. Explain what kind of wave, transverse or compressional, is produced when an engine bumps into a string of coupled railroad cars on a track.

17. Is it possible for an electromagnetic wave to travel through a vacuum? Through matter? Explain your answers.

18. Why does the frequency of a wave decrease as the wavelength increases?

19. Why don't you see your reflected image when you look at a white, rough surface?

20. If a cannon fires at a great distance from you, why do you see the flash before you hear the sound?

Developing Skills

If you need help, refer to the **Skill Handbook**.

21. **Using Numbers:** A microwave travels at the speed of light and has a wavelength of 0.022 m. What is its frequency?

22. **Forming a Hypothesis:** Form a hypothesis that can explain this observation. Waves A and B travel away from Earth through Earth's atmosphere. Wave A continues on into space, but wave B does not.

23. **Recognizing Cause and Effect:** Explain how the object shown below causes compressions and rarefactions as it vibrates in air.

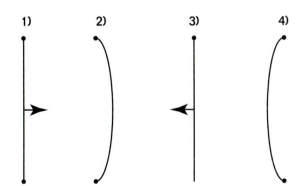

24. **Comparing and Contrasting:** AM radio waves have wavelengths between about 200 m and 600 m, while FM radio waves have wavelengths of about 3 m. Why can AM radio signals often be heard behind buildings and mountains while FM radio signals cannot?

THE PRINCETON REVIEW

Test-Taking Tip

Don't Cram If you don't know the material by the week before the test, you're less likely to do well. Set up a time line for your practice and preparation so that you're not rushed. Then, you will have time to deal with any problem areas.

Test Practice

Use these questions to test your Science Proficiency.

1. Two sounds have the same pitch, but one is louder than the other. What is different about the two sounds?
   A) their amplitudes
   B) their frequencies
   C) their wavelengths
   D) their speeds

2. What produces the colors seen when light reflects from CDs?
   A) wavelength
   B) interference
   C) refraction
   D) compression

3. The speed of a light ray increases as it passes at an angle from one medium into another. What happens to the ray?
   A) Its direction does not change.
   B) It travels along the normal.
   C) It bends toward the normal.
   D) It bends away from the normal.

4. What kind of waves requires a medium?
   A) all transverse waves
   B) only some compressional waves
   C) all electromagnetic waves
   D) all mechanical waves

Appendices

Appendix A

Safety in the Science Classroom

1. Always obtain your teacher's permission to begin an investigation.

2. Study the procedure. If you have questions, ask your teacher. Be sure you understand any safety symbols shown on the page.

3. Use the safety equipment provided for you. Goggles and a safety apron should be worn during an investigation.

4. Always slant test tubes away from yourself and others when heating them.

5. Never eat or drink in the lab, and never use lab glassware as food or drink containers. Never inhale chemicals. Do not taste any substances or draw any material into a tube with your mouth.

6. If you spill any chemical, wash it off immediately with water. Report the spill immediately to your teacher.

7. Know the location and proper use of the fire extinguisher, safety shower, fire blanket, first aid kit, and fire alarm.

8. Keep all materials away from open flames. Tie back long hair and loose clothing.

9. If a fire should break out in the classroom, or if your clothing should catch fire, smother it with the fire blanket or a coat, or get under a safety shower. NEVER RUN.

10. Report any accident or injury, no matter how small, to your teacher.

Follow these procedures as you clean up your work area.

1. Turn off the water and gas. Disconnect electrical devices.

2. Return all materials to their proper places.

3. Dispose of chemicals and other materials as directed by your teacher. Place broken glass and solid substances in the proper containers. Never discard materials in the sink.

4. Clean your work area.

5. Wash your hands thoroughly after working in the laboratory.

Table A-1

First Aid	
Injury	**Safe Response**
Burns	Apply cold water. Call your teacher immediately.
Cuts and bruises	Stop any bleeding by applying direct pressure. Cover cuts with a clean dressing. Apply cold compresses to bruises. Call your teacher immediately.
Fainting	Leave the person lying down. Loosen any tight clothing and keep crowds away. Call your teacher immediately.
Foreign matter in eye	Flush with plenty of water. Use eyewash bottle or fountain.
Poisoning	Note the suspected poisoning agent and call your teacher immediately.
Any spills on skin	Flush with large amounts of water or use safety shower. Call your teacher immediately.

Appendix
B

SI/Metric to English Conversions

	When you want to convert:	To:	Multiply by:
Length	inches	centimeters	2.54
	centimeters	inches	0.39
	feet	meters	0.30
	meters	feet	3.28
	yards	meters	0.91
	meters	yards	1.09
	miles	kilometers	1.61
	kilometers	miles	0.62
Mass and Weight*	ounces	grams	28.35
	grams	ounces	0.04
	pounds	kilograms	0.45
	kilograms	pounds	2.2
	tons (short)	tonnes (metric tons)	0.91
	tonnes (metric tons)	tons (short)	1.10
	pounds	newtons	4.45
	newtons	pounds	0.23
Volume	cubic inches	cubic centimeters	16.39
	cubic centimeters	cubic inches	0.06
	cubic feet	cubic meters	0.03
	cubic meters	cubic feet	35.30
	liters	quarts	1.06
	liters	gallons	0.26
	gallons	liters	3.78
Area	square inches	square centimeters	6.45
	square centimeters	square inches	0.16
	square feet	square meters	0.09
	square meters	square feet	10.76
	square miles	square kilometers	2.59
	square kilometers	square miles	0.39
	hectares	acres	2.47
	acres	hectares	0.40
Temperature	Fahrenheit	$5/9 \, (°F - 32)$ =	Celsius
	Celsius	$9/5 \, (°C) + 32$ =	Fahrenheit

*Weight as measured in standard Earth gravity

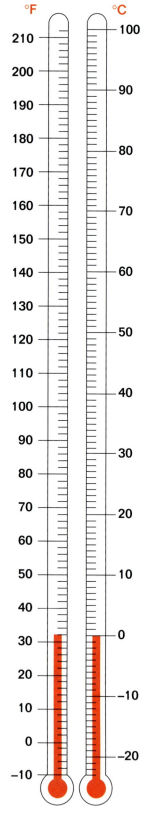

Appendix
C

SI Units of Measurement

Table C-1

SI Base Units					
Measurement	**Unit**	**Symbol**	**Measurement**	**Unit**	**Symbol**
length	meter	m	temperature	kelvin	K
mass	kilogram	kg	amount of substance	mole	mol
time	second	s			

Table C-2

Units Derived from SI Base Units		
Measurement	**Unit**	**Symbol**
energy	joule	J
force	newton	N
frequency	hertz	Hz
potential difference	volt	V
power	watt	W
pressure	pascal	Pa

Table C-3

Common SI Prefixes					
Prefix	**Symbol**	**Multiplier**	**Prefix**	**Symbol**	**Multiplier**
Greater than 1			Less than 1		
mega-	M	1 000 000	*deci-*	d	0.1
kilo-	k	1 000	*centi-*	c	0.01
hecto-	h	100	*milli-*	m	0.001
deca-	da	10	*micro-*	μ	0.000 001

Appendix

D

Care and Use of a Microscope

Eyepiece Contains a magnifying lens you look through

Body tube Connects the eyepiece to the revolving nosepiece

Arm Supports the body tube

Revolving nosepiece Holds and turns the objectives into viewing position

Low-power objective Contains the lens with low-power magnification

High-power objective Contains the lens with the highest magnification

Stage clips Hold the microscope slide in place

Stage Supports the microscope slide

Coarse adjustment Focuses the image under low power

Light source Allows light to reflect upward through the diaphragm, the specimen, and the lenses

Fine adjustment Sharpens the image under high and low magnification

Base Provides support for the microscope

Care of a Microscope

1. Always carry the microscope holding the arm with one hand and supporting the base with the other hand.

2. Don't touch the lenses with your fingers.

3. Never lower the coarse adjustment knob when looking through the eyepiece lens.

4. Always focus first with the low-power objective.

5. Don't use the coarse adjustment knob when the high-power objective is in place.

6. Store the microscope covered.

Using a Microscope

1. Place the microscope on a flat surface that is clear of objects. The arm should be toward you.

2. Look through the eyepiece. Adjust the diaphragm so that light comes through the opening in the stage.

3. Place a slide on the stage so that the specimen is in the field of view. Hold it firmly in place by using the stage clips.

4. Always focus first with the coarse adjustment and the low-power objective lens. Once the object is in focus on low power, turn the nosepiece until the high-power objective is in place. Use ONLY the fine adjustment to focus with the high-power objective lens.

Making a Wet-Mount Slide

1. Carefully place the item you want to look at in the center of a clean, glass slide. Make sure the sample is thin enough for light to pass through.

2. Use a dropper to place one or two drops of water on the sample.

3. Hold a clean coverslip by the edges and place it at one edge of the drop of water. Slowly lower the coverslip onto the drop of water until it lies flat.

4. If you have too much water or a lot of air bubbles, touch the edge of a paper towel to the edge of the coverslip to draw off extra water and force out air.

Diversity of Life: Classification of Living Organisms

Scientists use a six-kingdom system of classification of organisms. In this system, there are two kingdoms of organisms, Kingdoms Archaebacteria and Eubacteria, which contain organisms that do not have a nucleus and lack membrane-bound structures in the cytoplasm of their cells. The members of the other four kingdoms have cells which contain a nucleus and structures in the cytoplasm that are surrounded by membranes. These kingdoms are Kingdom Protista, Kingdom Fungi, the Kingdom Plantae, and the Kingdom Animalia.

Kingdom Archaebacteria

One-celled prokaryotes; absorb food from surroundings or make their own food by chemosynthesis; found in extremely harsh environments including salt ponds, hot springs, swamps, and deep-sea hydrothermal vents.

Kingdom Eubacteria

Cyanobacteria one-celled prokaryotes; make their own food; contain chlorophyll; some species form colonies; most are blue-green

Bacteria one-celled prokaryotes; most absorb food from their surroundings; some are photosynthetic; many are parasites; round, spiral, or rod-shaped

Kingdom Protista

Phylum Euglenophyta one-celled; can photosynthesize or take in food; most have one flagellum; euglenoids

Phylum Bacillariophyta one-celled; make their own food through photosynthesis; have unique double shells made of silica; diatoms

Phylum Dinoflagellata one-celled; make their own food through photosynthesis; contain red pigments; have two flagella; dinoflagellates

Phylum Chlorophyta one-celled, many-celled, or colonies; contain chlorophyll; make their own food; live on land, in fresh water, or salt water; green algae

Phylum Rhodophyta most are many-celled; photosynthetic; contain red pigments; most live in deep saltwater environments; red algae

Phylum Phaeophyta most are many-celled; photosynthetic; contain brown pigments; most live in saltwater environments; brown algae

Phylum Foraminifera many-celled; take in food; primarily marine; shells constructed of calcium carbonate, or made from grains of sand; forams

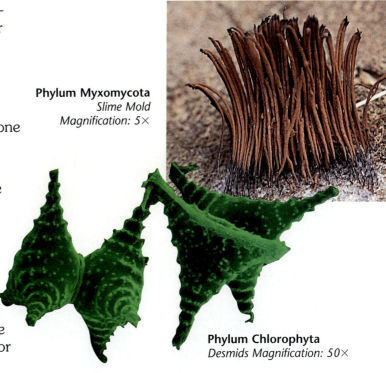

Phylum Myxomycota
Slime Mold
Magnification: 5×

Phylum Chlorophyta
Desmids Magnification: 50×

Phylum Rhizopoda one-celled; take in food; move by means of pseudopods; free-living or parasitic; amoebas

Phylum Zoomastigina one-celled; take in food; have one or more flagella; free-living or parasitic; zoomastigotes

Phylum Ciliophora one-celled; take in food; have large numbers of cilia; ciliates

Phylum Sporozoa one-celled; take in food; no means of movement; parasites in animals; sporozoans

Phylum Myxomycota and Acrasiomycota: one- or many-celled; absorb food; change form during life cycle; cellular and plasmodial slime molds

Phylum Oomycota many-celled; live in fresh or salt water; are either parasites or decomposers; water molds, rusts and downy mildews

Kingdom Fungi

Phylum Zygomycota many-celled; absorb food; spores are produced in sporangia; zygote fungi; bread mold

Phylum Ascomycota one- and many-celled; absorb food; spores produced in asci; sac fungi; yeast

Phylum Basidiomycota many-celled; absorb food; spores produced in basidia; club fungi; mushrooms

Phylum Deuteromycota: members with unknown reproductive structures; imperfect fungi; penicillin

Lichens organisms formed by symbiotic relationship between an ascomycote or a basidiomycote and green alga or cyanobacterium

Kingdom Plantae
Non-seed Plants

Division Bryophyta nonvascular plants; reproduce by spores produced in capsules; many-celled; green; grow in moist land environments; mosses and liverworts

Division Lycophyta many-celled vascular plants; spores produced in conelike structures; live on land; are photosynthetic; club mosses

Division Sphenophyta vascular plants; ribbed and jointed stems; scalelike leaves; spores produced in conelike structures; horsetails

Division Pterophyta vascular plants; leaves called fronds; spores produced in clusters of sporangia called sori; live on land or in water; ferns

Division Bryophyta
Liverwort

Lichens
British soldier lichen × 3

Seed Plants

Division Ginkgophyta: deciduous gymnosperms; only one living species; fan-shaped leaves with branching veins; reproduces with seeds; ginkgos

Division Cycadophyta: palmlike gymnosperms; large featherlike leaves; produce seeds in cones; cycads

Division Coniferophyta: deciduous or evergreen gymnosperms; trees or shrubs; needlelike or scalelike leaves; seeds produced in cones; conifers

Division Gnetophyta: shrubs or woody vines; seeds produced in cones; division contains only three genera; gnetum

Division Anthophyta: dominant group of plants; ovules protected in an ovary; sperm carried to ovules by pollen tube; produce flowers and seeds in fruits; flowering plants

Kingdom Animalia

Phylum Porifera: aquatic organisms that lack true tissues and organs; they are asymmetrical and sessile; sponges

Phylum Cnidaria: radially symmetrical organisms; have a digestive cavity with one opening; most have tentacles armed with stinging cells; live in aquatic environments singly or in colonies; includes jellyfish, corals, hydra, and sea anemones

Phylum Platyhelminthes: bilaterally symmetrical worms; have flattened bodies; digestive system has one opening; parasitic and free-living species; flatworms

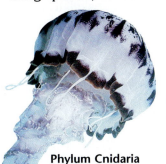

Phylum Cnidaria
Jellyfish

Phylum Arthopoda
Orb Weaver Spider

Phylum Arthropoda
Hermit Crab

Division Coniferophyta
Pine cone

Division Anthophyta
Strawberry Blossoms

Phylum Mollusca
Florida Fighting Conch

Phylum Annelida
Sabellid Worms Feather Duster

Division Anthophyta
Strawberries

Phylum Nematoda: round, bilaterally symmetrical body; digestive system with two openings; many parasite forms but mostly free-living; roundworms

Phylum Mollusca: soft-bodied animals, many with a hard shell; a mantle covers the soft body; aquatic and terrestrial species; includes clams, snails, squid, and octopuses

Phylum Annelida: bilaterally symmetrical worms; have round, segmented bodies; terrestrial and aquatic species; includes earthworms, leeches, and marine polychaetes

Phylum Arthropoda: largest phylum of organisms; have segmented bodies; pairs of jointed appendages; have hard exoskeletons; terrestrial and aquatic species; includes insects, crustaceans, spiders, and horseshoe crabs

Phylum Echinodermata: marine organisms; have spiny or leathery skin; water-vascular system with tube feet; radial symmetry; includes sea stars, sand dollars, and sea urchins

Phylum Chordata: organisms with internal skeletons; specialized body systems; paired appendages; all at some time have a notochord, dorsal nerve cord, gill slits, and a tail; include fish, amphibians, reptiles, birds, and mammals

Phylum Arthropoda
Giant Swallowtail Butterfly

Phylum Echinodermata
Blood Sea Star and Red Sea Urchin

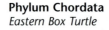

Phylum Chordata
Eastern Box Turtle

Phylum Chordata
Lemon Butterfly fish

Phylum Chordata
Great Horned Owl

Appendix

F

Minerals

Mineral (formula)	Color	Streak	Hardness	Breakage pattern	Uses and other properties
graphite (C)	black to gray	black to gray	1–1.5	basal cleavage (scales)	pencil lead, lubricants for locks, rods to control some small nuclear reactions, battery poles
galena (PbS)	gray	gray to black	2.5	cubic cleavage perfect	source of lead, used in pipes, shields for X rays, fishing equipment sinkers
hematite (Fe_2O_3)	black or reddish brown	reddish brown	5.27–6.5	irregular fracture	source of iron; converted to "pig" iron, made into steel
magnetite (Fe_3O_4)	black	black	6	conchoidal fracture	source of iron, naturally magnetic, called lodestone
pyrite (FeS_2)	light, brassy, yellow	greenish black	6–6.5	uneven fracture	source of iron, "fool's gold"
talc $(Mg_3Si_4O_{10}(OH)_2)$	white greenish	white	1	cleavage in one direction	used for talcum powder, sculptures, paper, and tabletops
gypsum $(CaSO_4 \cdot 2H_2O)$	colorless, gray, white brown	white	2	basal cleavage	used in plaster of paris and dry wall for building construction
sphalerite (ZnS)	brown, reddish brown, greenish	light to dark brown	3.27–4	cleavage in six directions	main ore of zinc; used in paints, dyes and medicine
muscovite $(KAl_3Si_3O_{10}(OH)_2)$	white, light gray, yellow, rose, green	colorless	2–2.5	basal cleavage	occurs in large flexible plates; used as an insulator in electrical equipment, lubricant
biotite $(K(Mg, Fe)_3(AlSi_3O_{10})(OH)_2)$	black to dark brown	colorless	2.27–3	basal cleavage	occurs in large flexible plates
halite $(NaCl)$	colorless, red, white, blue	colorless	2.5	cubic cleavage	salt; soluble in water; a preservative

Appendix

F

Minerals

Mineral (formula)	Color	Streak	Hardness	Breakage pattern	Uses and other properties
calcite ($CaCO_3$)	colorless, white, pale blue	colorless, white	3	cleavage in three directions	fizzes when HCl is added; used in cements and other building materials
dolomite ($CaMg(CO_3)_2$)	colorless, white, pink green, gray black	white	3.27–4	cleavage in three directions	concrete and cement; used as an ornamental building stone
fluorite (CaF_2)	colorless, white, blue green, red yellow, purple	colorless	4	cleavage in four directions	used in the manufacture of optical equipment; glows under ultraviolet light
hornblende ($(CaNa)_{2-3}(Mg, Al,Fe)_5(Al,Si)_2 Si_6O_{22}(OH)_2$)	green to black	gray to white	27–6	cleavage in two directions	will transmit light on thin edges; 6-sided cross section
feldspar ($KAlSi_3O_8$) ($NaAlSi_3O_8$) ($CaAl_2Si_2O_8$)	colorless, white to gray, green	colorless	6	two cleavage planes meet at ~90° angle	used in the manufacture of ceramics
augite ($(Ca, Na)(Mg, Fe, Al)(Al, Si)_2O_6$)	black	colorless	6	cleavage in two directions	square or 8-sided cross section
olivine ($(Mg, Fe)_2 SiO_4$)	olive, green	none	6.27–7	conchoidal fracture	gemstones, refractory sand
quartz (SiO_2)	colorless, various colors	none	7	conchoidal fracture	used in glass manufacture, electronic equipment, radios, computers, watches, gemstones

Appendix
G

Rocks

Rock Type	Rock Name	Characteristics
Igneous (intrusive)	Granite	Large mineral grains of quartz, feldspar, hornblende, and mica. Usually light in color.
	Diorite	Large mineral grains of feldspar, hornblende, mica. Less quartz than granite. Intermediate in color.
	Gabbro	Large mineral grains of feldspar, hornblende, augite, olivine, and mica. No quartz. Dark in color.
Igneous (extrusive)	Rhyolite	Small mineral grains of quartz, feldspar, hornblende, and mica or no visible grains. Light in color.
	Andesite	Small mineral grains of feldspar, hornblende, mica or no visible grains. Less quartz than rhyolite. Intermediate in color.
	Basalt	Small mineral grains of feldspar, hornblende, augite, olivine, mica or no visible grains. No quartz. Dark in color.
	Obsidian	Glassy texture. No visible grains. Volcanic glass. Fracture looks like broken glass.
	Pumice	Frothy texture. Floats. Usually light in color.
Sedimentary (detrital)	Conglomerate	Coarse-grained. Gravel or pebble-sized grains.
	Sandstone	Sand-sized grains 1/16 to 2 mm in size.
	Siltstone	Grains are smaller than sand but larger than clay.
	Shale	Smallest grains. Usually dark in color.
Sedimentary (chemical or biochemical)	Limestone	Major mineral is calcite. Usually forms in oceans, lakes, rivers, and caves. Often contains fossils.
	Coal	Occurs in swampy, low-lying areas. Compacted layers of organic material, mainly plant remains.
Sedimentary (chemical)	Rock Salt	Commonly forms by the evaporation of seawater.
Metamorphic (foliated)	Gneiss	Well-developed banding because of alternating layers of different minerals, usually of different colors. Common parent rock is granite.
	Schist	Well-defined parallel arrangement of flat, sheet-like minerals, mainly micas. Common parent rocks are shale, phyllite.
	Phyllite	Shiny or silky appearance. May look wrinkled. Common parent rocks are shale, slate.
	Slate	Harder, denser, and shinier than shale. Common parent rock is shale.
Metamorphic (non-foliated)	Marble	Interlocking calcite or dolomite crystals. Common parent rock is limestone.
	Soapstone	Composed mainly of the mineral talc. Soft with a greasy feel.
	Quartzite	Hard and well cemented with interlocking quartz crystals. Common parent rock is sandstone.

Topographic Map Symbols

Primary highway, hard surface	
Secondary highway, hard surface	
Light-duty road, hard or Improved surface	
Unimproved road	
Railroad: single track and multiple track	
Railroads in juxtaposition	

Buildings

Schools, church, and cemetery

Buildings (barn, warehouse, etc)

Wells other than water (labeled as to type)

Tanks: oil, water, etc. (labeled only if water)

Located or landmark object; windmill

Open pit, mine, or quarry; prospect

Marsh (swamp)

Wooded marsh

Woods or brushwood

Vineyard

Land subject to controlled inundation

Submerged marsh

Mangrove

Orchard

Scrub

Urban area

Spot elevation	×7369
Water elevation	670

Index contour

Supplementary contour

Intermediate contour

Depression contours

Boundaries: National

State

County, parish, municipal

Civil township, precinct, town, barrio

Incorporated city, village, town, hamlet

Reservation, National or State

Small park, cemetery, airport, etc.

Land grant

Township or range line, United States land survey

Township or range line, approximate location

Perennial streams

Elevated aqueduct

Water well and spring

Small rapids

Large rapids

Intermittent lake

Intermittent streams

Aqueduct tunnel

Glacier

Small falls

Large falls

Dry lake bed

Appendix
I

Weather Map Symbols

Sample Plotted Report at Each Station

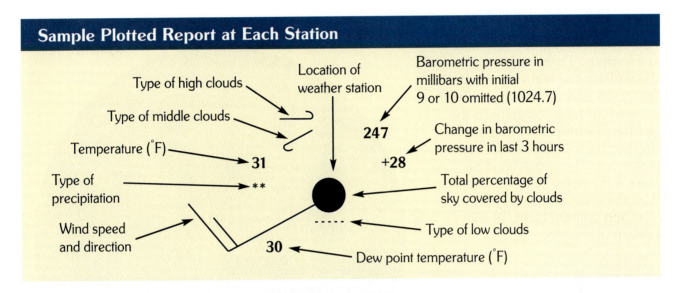

Type of high clouds

Type of middle clouds

Temperature (°F) — 31

Type of precipitation — **

Wind speed and direction

Location of weather station

Barometric pressure in millibars with initial 9 or 10 omitted (1024.7)

247

Change in barometric pressure in last 3 hours

+28

Total percentage of sky covered by clouds

- - - - - Type of low clouds

30 — Dew point temperature (°F)

Sample Plotted Report at Each Station

Precipitation		Wind Speed and direction		Sky coverage		Some types of high clouds	
≡	Fog	○	0 knots; calm	○	No cover		Scattered cirrus
★	Snow	/	1-2 knots	◍	1/10 or less		Dense cirrus in patches
●	Rain	∨	25-7 knots	◑	2/10 to 3/10		Veil of cirrus covering entire sky
↖	Thunder-storm	∨	8-12 knots	◕	4/10		
		∨	13-17 knots	◐	1/2		Cirrus not covering entire sky
,	Drizzle	∨	22-22 knots	◓	6/10		
		∨	23-27 knots	◒	7/10		
▽	Showers	∨	48-52 knots	◍	Overcast with openings		
		1 knot = 1.852 km/h		●	Complete overcast		

Some types of middle clouds		Some types of low clouds		Fronts and pressure systems	
∕	Thin altostratus layer	⌒	Cumulus of fair weather	(H) or High	Center of high-or
∕∕	Thick altostratus layer	⌣	Stratocumulus	(L) or Low	low-pressure system
⌒	Thin altostratus in patches	- - - - -	Fractocumulus of bad weather	▲▲▲▲	Cold front
⌢	Thin altostratus in bands	—	Stratus of fair weather	●●●●	Warm Front
				▲●▲●	Occluded front
				●▽●▽	Stationary front

Star Charts

Shown here are star charts for viewing stars in the northern hemisphere during the four different seasons. These charts are drawn from the night sky at about 35° north latitude, but they can be used for most locations in the northern hemisphere. The lines on the charts outline major constellations. The dense band of stars is the Milky Way. To use, hold the chart vertically, with the direction you are facing at the bottom of the map.

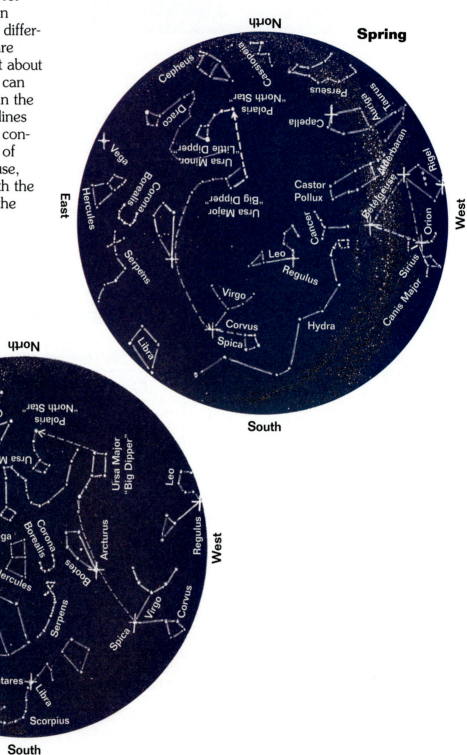

Appendix

J

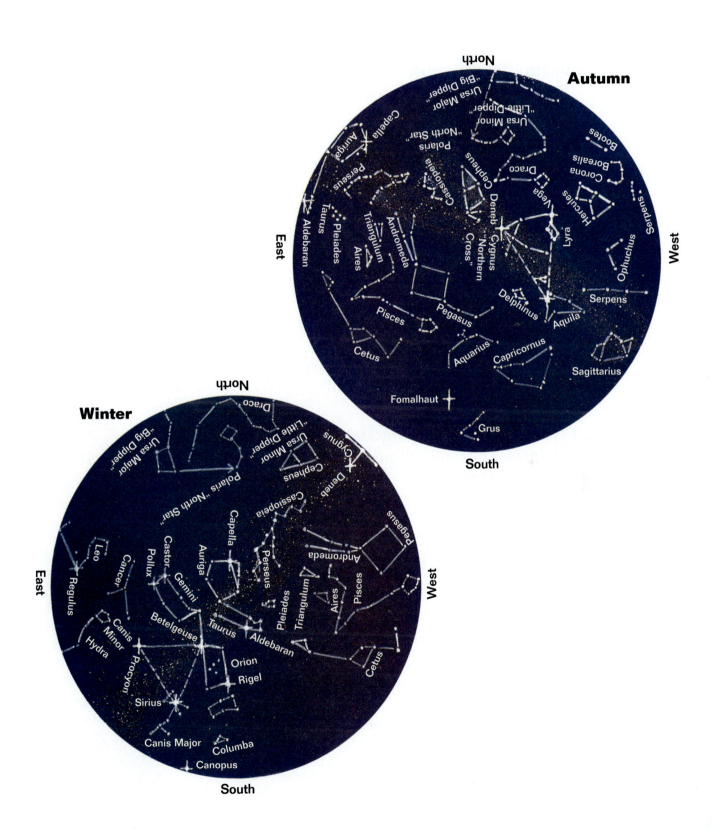

Skill Handbook

Table of Contents

Organizing Information

Communicating

The communication of ideas is an important part of our everyday lives. Whether reading a book, writing a letter, or watching a television program, people everywhere are expressing opinions and sharing information with one another. Writing in your Science Journal allows you to express your opinions and demonstrate your knowledge of the information presented on a subject. When writing, keep in mind the purpose of the assignment and the audience with which you are communicating.

Examples Science Journal assignments vary greatly. They may ask you to take a viewpoint other than your own; perhaps you will be a scientist, a TV reporter, or a committee member of a local environmental group. Maybe you will be expressing your opinions to a member of Congress, a doctor, or to the editor of your local newspaper, as shown in **Figure 1.** Sometimes, Science Journal writing may allow you to summarize information in the form of an outline, a letter, or in a paragraph.

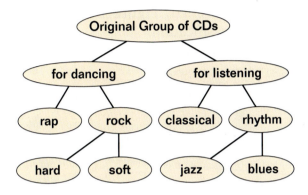

Figure 2 Classifying CDs

Classifying

You may not realize it, but you make things orderly in the world around you. If you hang your shirts together in the closet or if your favorite CDs are stacked together, you have used the skill of classifying.

Classifying is the process of sorting objects or events into groups based on common features. When classifying, first observe the objects or events to be classified. Then, select one feature that is shared by some members in the group, but not by all. Place those members that share that feature into a subgroup. You can classify members into smaller and smaller subgroups based on characteristics.

Remember, when you classify, you are grouping objects or events for a purpose. Keep your purpose in mind as you select the features to form groups and subgroups.

Example How would you classify a collection of CDs? As shown in **Figure 2,** you might classify those you like to dance to in one subgroup and CDs you like to listen to in the next subgroup. The CDs you like to dance to could be subdivided

Figure 1 A Science Journal entry

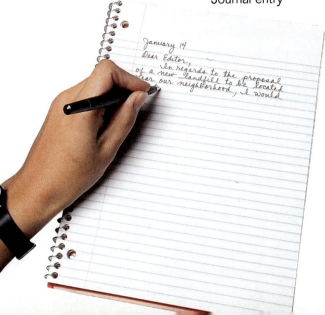

into a rap subgroup and a rock subgroup. Note that for each feature selected, each CD fits into only one subgroup. You would keep selecting features until all the CDs are classified. **Figure 2** shows one possible classification.

Figure 3 A recipe for bread contains sequenced instructions

Sequencing

A sequence is an arrangement of things or events in a particular order. When you are asked to sequence objects or events within a group, figure out what comes first, then think about what should come second. Continue to choose objects or events until all of the objects you started out with are in order. Then, go back over the sequence to make sure each thing or event in your sequence logically leads to the next.

Example A sequence with which you are most familiar is the use of alphabetical order. Another example of sequence would be the steps in a recipe, as shown in **Figure 3.** Think about baking bread. Steps in the recipe have to be followed in order for the bread to turn out right.

Concept Mapping

If you were taking an automobile trip, you would probably take along a road map. The road map shows your location, your destination, and other places along the way. By looking at the map and finding where you are, you can begin to understand where you are in relation to other locations on the map.

A concept map is similar to a road map. But, a concept map shows relationships among ideas (or concepts) rather than places. A concept map is a diagram that visually shows how concepts are related. Because the concept map shows relationships among ideas, it can make the meanings of ideas and terms clear, and help you understand better what you are studying.

There is usually not one correct way to create a concept map. As you construct one type of map, you may discover other ways to construct the map that show the

Figure 4 Network tree describing U.S. currency

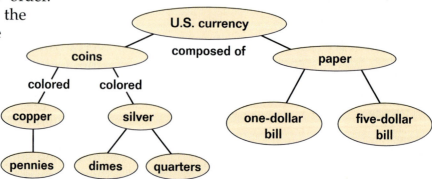

relationships between concepts in a better way. If you do discover what you think is a better way to create a concept map, go ahead and use the new one. Overall, concept maps are useful for breaking a big concept down into smaller parts, making learning easier.

Examples

Network Tree Look at the concept map about U.S. currency in **Figure 4.** This is called a network tree. Notice how some words are in ovals while others are written across connecting lines. The words inside the ovals are science concepts. The lines in the map show related concepts. The words written on the lines describe the relationships between concepts.

When you are asked to construct a network tree, write down the topic and list the major concepts related to that topic on a piece of paper. Then look at your list and begin to put them in order from general to specific. Branch the related concepts from the major concept and describe the relationships on the lines. Continue to write the more specific concepts. Write the relationships between the concepts on the lines until all concepts are mapped. Examine the concept map for relationships that cross branches, and add them to the concept map.

Events Chain An events chain is another type of concept map. An events chain map, such as the one describing a typical morning routine in **Figure 5,** is used to describe ideas in order. In science, an events chain can be used to describe a sequence of events, the steps in a procedure, or the stages of a process.

When making an events chain, first find the one event that starts the chain. This

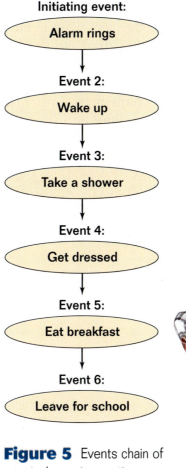

Initiating event:

Alarm rings

Event 2:

Wake up

Event 3:

Take a shower

Event 4:

Get dressed

Event 5:

Eat breakfast

Event 6:

Leave for school

Figure 5 Events chain of a typical morning routine

event is called the initiating event. Then, find the next event in the chain and continue until you reach an outcome. Suppose you are asked to describe what happens when your alarm rings. An events chain map describing the steps might look like **Figure 5.** Notice that connecting words are not necessary in an events chain.

Cycle Map A cycle concept map is a special type of events chain map. In a cycle concept map, the series of events does not produce a final outcome. Instead, the last event in the chain relates back to the initiating event.

As in the events chain map, you first decide on an initiating event and then list each event in order. Because there is no outcome and the last event relates back to the initiating event, the cycle repeats itself. Look at the cycle map describing the relationship between day and night in **Figure 6.**

Figure 6 Cycle map of day and night.

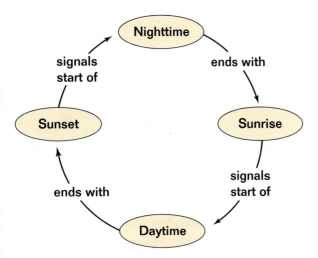

Spider Map A fourth type of concept map is the spider map. This is a map that you can use for brainstorming. Once you have a central idea, you may find you have a jumble of ideas that relate to it, but are not necessarily clearly related to each other. As illustrated by the homework spider map in **Figure 7,** by writing these ideas outside the main concept, you may begin to separate and group unrelated terms so that they become more useful.

Figure 7 Spider map about homework.

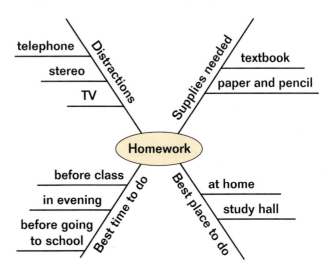

Making and Using Tables

Browse through your textbook and you will notice tables in the text and in the activities. In a table, data or information is arranged in a way that makes it easier for you to understand. Activity tables help organize the data you collect during an activity so that results can be interpreted.

Examples Most tables have a title. At a glance, the title tells you what the table is about. A table is divided into columns and rows. The first column lists items to be compared. In **Figure 8,** the collection of recyclable materials is being compared in a table. The row across the top lists the specific characteristics being compared. Within the grid of the table, the collected data are recorded.

What is the title of the table in **Figure 8?** The title is "Recycled Materials." What is being compared? The different materials being recycled and on which days they are recycled.

Making Tables To make a table, list the items to be compared down in columns and the characteristics to be compared across in rows. The table in

Figure 8 Table of recycled materials

Recycled Materials			
Day of Week	Paper (kg)	Aluminum (kg)	Plastic (kg)
Mon.	4.0	2.0	0.5
Wed.	3.5	1.5	0.5
Fri.	3.0	1.0	1.5

Figure 8 compares the mass of recycled materials collected by a class. On Monday, students turned in 4.0 kg of paper, 2.0 kg of aluminum, and 0.5 kg of plastic. On Wednesday, they turned in 3.5 kg of paper, 1.5 kg of aluminum, and 0.5 kg of plastic. On Friday, the totals were 3.0 kg of paper, 1.0 kg of aluminum, and 1.5 kg of plastic.

Using Tables How much plastic, in kilograms, is being recycled on Wednesday? Locate the column labeled "Plastic (kg)" and the row "Wed." The data in the box where the column and row intersect is the answer. Did you answer "0.5"? How much aluminum, in kilograms, is being recycled on Friday? If you answered "1.0," you understand how to use the parts of the table.

Making and Using Graphs

After scientists organize data in tables, they may display the data in a graph. A graph is a diagram that shows the relationship of one variable to another. A graph makes interpretation and analysis of data easier. There are three basic types of graphs used in science—the line graph, the bar graph, and the circle graph.

Examples

Line Graphs A line graph is used to show the relationship between two variables. The variables being compared go on two axes of the graph. The independent variable always goes on the horizontal axis, called the x-axis. The dependent variable always goes on the vertical axis, called the y-axis.

Suppose your class started to record the amount of materials they collected in one week for their school to recycle. The collected information is shown in **Figure 9.**

You could make a graph of the materials collected over the three days of the school week. The three weekdays are the independent variables and are placed on the x-axis of your graph. The amount of materials collected is the dependent variable and would go on the y-axis.

After drawing your axes, label each with a scale. The x-axis lists the three weekdays. To make a scale of the amount of materials collected on the y-axis, look at the data values. Because the lowest amount collected was 1.0 and the highest was 5.0, you will have to start numbering at least at 1.0 and go through 5.0. You decide to start numbering at 0 and number by ones through 6.0, as shown in **Figure 10.**

Next, plot the data points for collected paper. The first pair of data you want to plot is Monday and 5.0 kg of paper.

Figure 9 Amount of recyclable materials collected during one week

Materials Collected During Week		
Day of Week	Paper (kg)	Aluminum (kg)
Mon.	5.0	4.0
Wed.	4.0	1.0
Fri.	2.5	2.0

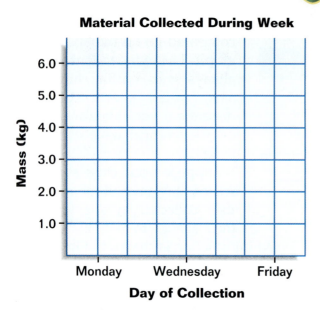

Figure 10 Graph outline for material collected during week

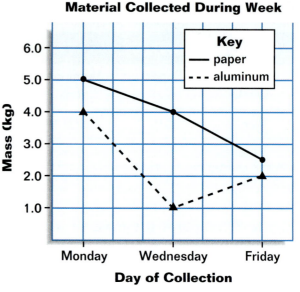

Figure 11 Line graph of materials collected during week

Locate "Monday" on the *x*-axis and locate "5.0" on the *y*-axis. Where an imaginary vertical line from the *x*-axis and an imaginary horizontal line from the *y*-axis would meet, place the first data point. Place the other data points the same way. After all the points are plotted, connect them with the best smooth curve. Repeat this procedure for the data points for aluminum. Use continuous and dashed lines to distinguish the two line graphs. The resulting graph should look like **Figure 11.**

Bar Graphs Bar graphs are similar to line graphs. They compare data that do not continuously change. In a bar graph, vertical bars show the relationships among data.

To make a bar graph, set up the *x*-axis and *y*-axis as you did for the line graph. The data is plotted by drawing vertical bars from the *x*-axis up to a point where the *y*-axis would meet the bar if it were extended.

Look at the bar graph in **Figure 12** comparing the mass of aluminum collected over three weekdays. The *x*-axis is the days on which the aluminum was collected. The *y*-axis is the mass of aluminum collected, in kilograms.

Circle Graphs A circle graph uses a circle divided into sections to display data. Each section represents part of the whole. All the sections together equal 100 percent.

Suppose you wanted to make a circle graph to show the number of seeds that germinated in a package. You would count the total number of seeds. You find that there are 143 seeds in the package. This represents 100 percent, the whole circle.

You plant the seeds, and 129 seeds germinate. The seeds that germinated will make up one section of the circle graph, and the seeds that did not germinate will make up the remaining section.

To find out how much of the circle each section should take, divide the number of seeds in each section by the total number of seeds. Then, multiply your answer by 360, the number of degrees in a circle, and round to the nearest whole number. The

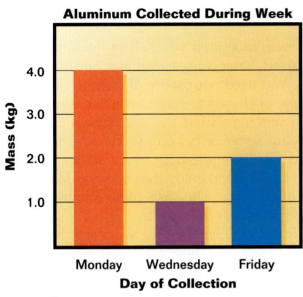

Aluminum Collected During Week

Mass (kg): 4.0, 3.0, 2.0, 1.0

Monday   Wednesday   Friday

Day of Collection

Figure 12 Bar graph of aluminum collected during week

section of the circle graph in degrees that represents the seeds germinated is figured below.

$$\frac{129}{143} \times 360 = 324.75 \text{ or } 325 \text{ degrees (or } 325°)$$

Plot this group on the circle graph using a compass and a protractor. Use the compass to draw a circle. It will be easier to

measure the part of the circle representing the non-germinating seeds, so subtract 325° from 360° to get 35°. Draw a straight line from the center to the edge of the circle. Place your protractor on this line and use it to mark a point at 325°. Use this point to draw a straight line from the center of the circle to the edge. This is the section for the group of seeds that did not germinate. The other section represents the group of 129 seeds that did germinate. Label the sections of your graph and title the graph as shown in **Figure 13**.

Figure 13 Circle graph of germinated seeds

Seeds Germinated

Not germinating (35°)

Germinating (325°)

Science Skill Handbook

Thinking Critically

Observing and Inferring

Observing Scientists try to make careful and accurate observations. When possible, they use instruments such as microscopes, thermometers, and balances to make observations. Measurements with a balance or thermometer provide numerical data that can be checked and repeated.

When you make observations in science, you'll find it helpful to examine the entire object or situation first. Then, look carefully for details. Write down everything you observe.

Example Imagine that you have just finished a volleyball game. At home, you open the refrigerator and see a jug of orange juice on the back of the top shelf. The jug, shown in **Figure 14,** feels cold as you grasp it. Then, you drink the juice, smell the oranges, and enjoy the tart taste in your mouth.

Figure 14 Why is this jug of orange juice cold?

As you imagined yourself in the story, you used your senses to make observations. You used your sense of sight to find the jug in the refrigerator, your sense of touch when you felt the coldness of the jug, your sense of hearing to listen as the liquid filled the glass, and your senses of smell and taste to enjoy the odor and tartness of the juice. The basis of all scientific investigation is observation.

Inferring Scientists often make inferences based on their observations. An inference is an attempt to explain or interpret observations or to say what caused what you observed.

When making an inference, be certain to use accurate data and observations. Analyze all of the data that you've collected. Then, based on everything you know, explain or interpret what you've observed.

Example When you drank a glass of orange juice after the volleyball game, you observed that the orange juice was cold as well as refreshing. You might infer that the juice was cold because it had been made much earlier in the day and had been kept in the refrigerator, or you might infer that it had just been made, using both cold water and ice. The only way to be sure which inference is correct is to investigate further.

Comparing and Contrasting

Observations can be analyzed by noting the similarities and differences between two or more objects or events that you observe. When you look at objects or events to see how they are similar, you are comparing them. Contrasting is looking for differences in similar objects or events.

Figure 15 Table comparing the nutritional value of *Cereal A* and *Cereal B*

Nutritional Value		
	Cereal A	**Cereal B**
Serving size	103 g	105 g
Calories	220	160
Total Fat	10 g	10 g
Protein	2.5 g	2.6 g
Total Carbohydrate	30 g	15 g

Example Suppose you were asked to compare and contrast the nutritional value of two kinds of cereal, *Cereal A* and *Cereal B.* You would start by looking at what is known about these cereals. Arrange this information in a table, like the one in **Figure 15.**

Similarities you might point out are that both cereals have similar serving sizes, amounts of total fat, and protein. Differences include *Cereal A* having a higher calorie value and containing more total carbohydrates than *Cereal B.*

Recognizing Cause and Effect

Have you ever watched something happen and then made suggestions about why it happened? If so, you have observed an effect and inferred a cause. The event is an effect, and the reason for the event is the cause.

Example Suppose that every time your teacher fed the fish in a classroom aquarium, she or he tapped the food container on the edge of the aquarium. Then, one day your teacher just happened to tap the edge of the aquarium with a pencil while making a point. You observed the fish swim to the surface of the aquarium to feed, as shown in **Figure 16.** What is the effect, and what would you infer to be the cause? The effect is the fish swimming to the surface of the aquarium. You might infer the cause to be the teacher tapping on the edge of the aquarium. In determining cause and effect, you have made a logical inference based on your observations.

Perhaps the fish swam to the surface because they reacted to the teacher's waving hand or for some other reason. When scientists are unsure of the cause of a certain event, they design controlled experiments to determine what causes the event. Although you have made a logical conclusion about the behavior of the fish, you would have to perform an experiment to be certain that it was the tapping that caused the effect you observed.

Figure 16 What cause-and-effect situations are occurring in this aquarium?

Practicing Scientific Processes

You might say that the work of a scientist is to solve problems. But when you decide how to dress on a particular day, you are doing problem solving, too. You may observe what the weather looks like through a window. You may go outside and see whether what you are wearing is heavy or light enough.

Scientists use an orderly approach to learn new information and to solve problems. The methods scientists may use include observing to form a hypothesis, designing an experiment to test a hypothesis, separating and controlling variables, and interpreting data.

Forming Operational Definitions

Operational definitions define an object by showing how it functions, works, or behaves. Such definitions are written in terms of how an object works or how it can be used; that is, what is its job or purpose?

Figure 17 What observations can be made about this dog?

Example Some operational definitions explain how an object can be used.

• A ruler is a tool that measures the size of an object.
• An automobile can move things from one place to another.

Or such a definition may explain how an object works.

• A ruler contains a series of marks that can be used as a standard when measuring.
• An automobile is a vehicle that can move from place to place.

Forming a Hypothesis

Observations You observe all the time. Scientists try to observe as much as possible about the things and events they study so they know that what they say about their observations is reliable.

Some observations describe something using only words. These observations are called qualitative observations. Other observations describe how much of something there is. These are quantitative observations and use numbers, as well as words, in the description. Tools or equipment are used to measure the characteristic being described.

Example If you were making qualitative observations of the dog in **Figure 17,** you might use words such as *furry, yellow,* and *short-haired.* Quantitative observations of this dog might include a mass of 14 kg, a height of 46 cm, ear length of 10 cm, and an age of 150 days.

Hypotheses Hypotheses are tested to help explain observations that have been made. They are often stated as *if* and *then* statements.

Examples Suppose you want to make a perfect score on a spelling test. Begin by thinking of several ways to accomplish this. Base these possibilities on past observations. If you put each of these possibilities into sentence form, using the words *if* and *then,* you can form a hypothesis. All of the following are hypotheses you might consider to explain how you could score 100 percent on your test:

If the test is easy, then I will get a perfect score.

If I am intelligent, then I will get a perfect score.

If I study hard, then I will get a perfect score.

Perhaps a scientist has observed that plants that receive fertilizer grow taller than plants that do not. A scientist may form a hypothesis that says: If plants are fertilized, then their growth will increase.

Designing an Experiment to Test a Hypothesis

In order to test a hypothesis, it's best to write out a procedure. A procedure is the plan that you follow in your experiment. A procedure tells you what materials to use and how to use them. After following the procedure, data are generated. From this generated data, you can then draw a conclusion and make a statement about your results.

If the conclusion you draw from the data supports your hypothesis, then you can say that your hypothesis is reliable. *Reliable* means that you can trust your conclusion. If it did not support your hypothesis, then you would have to make new observations and state a new hypothesis—just make sure that it is one that you can test.

Example Super premium gasoline costs more than regular gasoline. Does super premium gasoline increase the efficiency or fuel mileage of your family car? Let's figure out how to conduct an experiment to test the hypothesis, *"if* premium gas is more efficient, *then* it should increase the fuel mileage of our family car." Then a procedure similar to **Figure 18** must be written to generate data presented in **Figure 19** on the next page.

These data show that premium gasoline is less efficient than regular gasoline. It took more gasoline to travel one mile (0.064) using premium gasoline than it does to travel one mile using regular gasoline (0.059). This conclusion does not support the original hypothesis made.

PROCEDURE

1. Use regular gasoline for two weeks.

2. Record the number of miles between fill-ups and the amount of gasoline used.

3. Switch to premium gasoline for two weeks.

4. Record the number of miles between fill-ups and the amount of gasoline used.

Figure 18 Possible procedural steps

Figure 19 Data generated from procedure steps

Gasoline Data			
	Miles traveled	Gallons used	Gallons per mile
Regular gasoline	762	45.34	0.059
Premium gasoline	661	42.30	0.064

Separating and Controlling Variables

In any experiment, it is important to keep everything the same except for the item you are testing. The one factor that you change is called the *independent variable.* The factor that changes as a result of the independent variable is called the *dependent variable.* Always make sure that there is only one independent variable. If you allow more than one, you will not know what causes the changes you observe in the independent variable. Many experiments have *controls*—a treatment or an experiment that you can compare with the results of your test groups.

Example In the experiment with the gasoline, you made everything the same except the type of gasoline being used. The driver, the type of automobile, and the weather conditions should remain the same throughout. The gasoline should also be purchased from the same service station. By doing so, you made sure that at the end of the experiment, any differences were the result of the type of fuel being used—regular or premium. The type of gasoline was the *independent factor* and the gas mileage achieved was the *dependent factor.* The use of regular gasoline was the *control.*

Interpreting Data

The word *interpret* means "to explain the meaning of something." Look at the problem originally being explored in the gasoline experiment and find out what the data show. Identify the control group and the test group so you can see whether or not the variable has had an effect. Then, you need to check differences between the control and test groups.

Figure 20 Which gasoline type is most efficient?

Science Skill Handbook

These differences may be qualitative or quantitative. A qualitative difference would be a difference that you could observe and describe, while a quantitative difference would be a difference you can measure using numbers. If there are differences, the variable being tested may have had an effect. If there is no difference between the control and the test groups, the variable being tested apparently has had no effect.

Example Perhaps you are looking at a table from an experiment designed to test the hypothesis: If premium gas is more efficient, then it should increase the fuel mileage of our family car. Look back at **Figure 19** showing the results of this experiment. In this example, the use of regular gasoline in the family car was the control, while the car being fueled by premium gasoline was the test group.

Data showed a quantitative difference in efficiency for gasoline consumption. It took 0.059 gallons of regular gasoline to travel one mile, while it took 0.064 gallons of the premium gasoline to travel the same distance. The regular gasoline was more efficient; it increased the fuel mileage of the family car.

What are data? In the experiment described on these pages, measurements were taken so that at the end of the experiment, you had something concrete to interpret. You had numbers to work with. Not every experiment that you do will give you data in the form of numbers. Sometimes, data will be in the form of a description. At the end of a chemistry experiment, you might have noted that

Figure 21

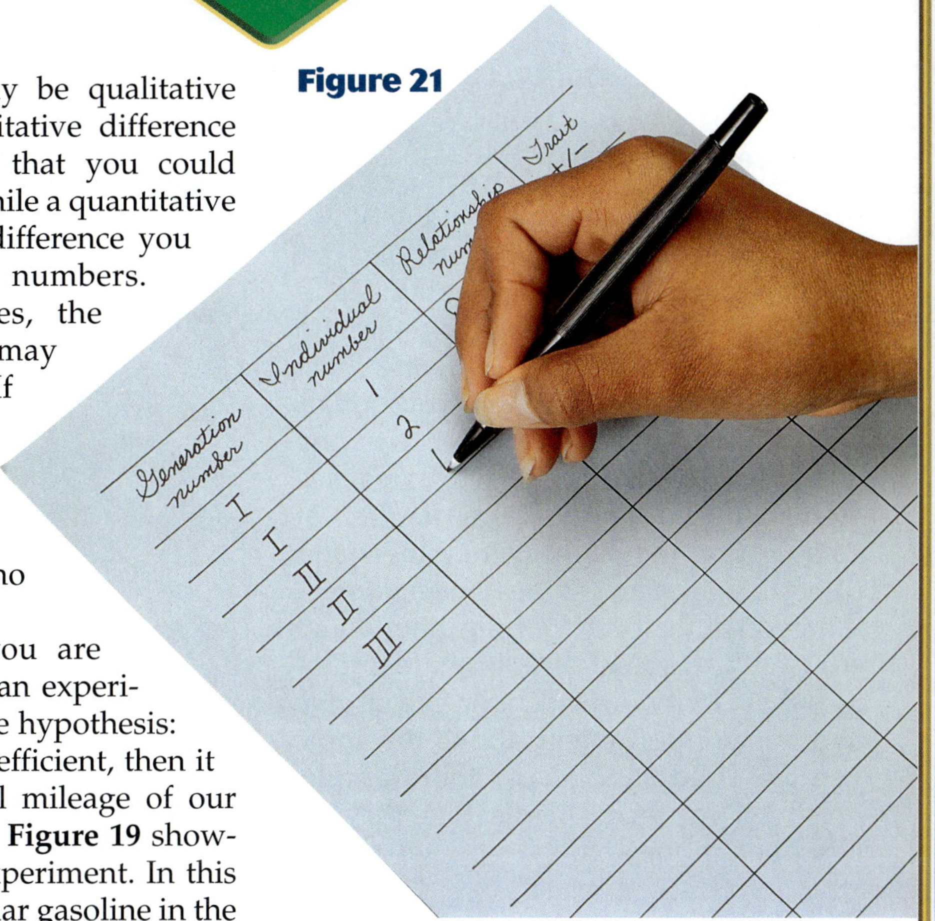

one solution turned yellow when treated with a particular chemical, and another remained colorless, as water, when treated with the same chemical. Data, therefore, are stated in different forms for different types of scientific experiments.

Are all experiments alike? Keep in mind as you perform experiments in science that not every experiment makes use of all of the parts that have been described on these pages. For some, it may be difficult to design an experiment that will always have a control. Other experiments are complex enough that it may be hard to have only one dependent variable. Real scientists encounter many variations in the methods that they use when they perform experiments. The skills in this handbook are here for you to use and practice. In real situations, their uses will vary.

Science Skill Handbook

Representing and Applying Data

Interpreting Scientific Illustrations

As you read a science textbook, you will see many drawings, diagrams, and photographs. Illustrations help you to understand what you read. Some illustrations are included to help you understand an idea that you can't see easily by yourself. For instance, we can't see atoms, but we can look at a diagram of an atom and that helps us to understand some things about atoms. Seeing something often helps you remember more easily. Illustrations also provide examples that clarify difficult concepts or give additional information about the topic you are studying. Maps, for example, help you to locate places that may be described in the text.

Examples

Captions and Labels Most illustrations have captions. A caption is a comment that identifies or explains the illustration. Diagrams, such as **Figure 22,** often have

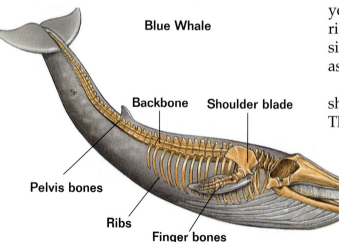

Figure 22 A labeled diagram of a blue whale

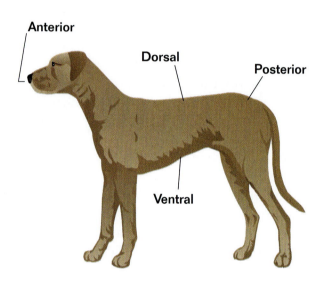

Figure 23 The orientation of a dog is shown here.

labels that identify parts of the organism or the order of steps in a process.

Learning with Illustrations An illustration of an organism shows that organism from a particular view or orientation. In order to understand the illustration, you may need to identify the front (anterior) end, tail (posterior) end, the underside (ventral), and the back (dorsal) side, as shown in **Figure 23.**

You might also check for symmetry. A shark in **Figure 24** has bilateral symmetry. This means that drawing an imaginary line through the center of the animal from the anterior to posterior end forms two mirror images.

Radial symmetry is the arrangement of similar parts around a central point. An object or organism, such as a hydra, can be divided anywhere through the center into similar parts.

Some organisms and objects cannot be divided into two similar parts. If an

Figure 24 A shark (A) illustrating bilateral symmetry and a pear (B) illustrating a longitudinal section and a cross section

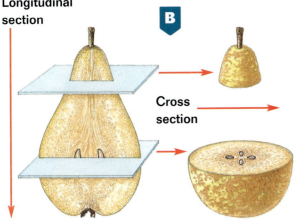

A

Bilateral symmetry

Two sides exactly alike

Longitudinal section

B

Cross section

organism or object cannot be divided, it is asymmetrical. Regardless of how you try to divide a natural sponge, you cannot divide it into two parts that look alike.

Some illustrations enable you to see the inside of an organism or object. These illustrations are called sections. **Figure 24** also illustrates some common sections.

Look at all illustrations carefully. Read captions and labels so that you understand exactly what the illustration is showing you.

Making Models

Have you ever worked on a model car, plane, or rocket? These models look, and sometimes work, much like the real thing, but they are often on a different scale than the real thing. In science, models are used to help simplify large or small processes or structures that otherwise would be dif-

ficult to see and understand. Your understanding of a structure or process is enhanced when you work with materials to make a model that shows the basic features of the structure or process.

Example In order to make a model, you first have to get a basic idea about the structure or process involved. You decide to make a model to show the differences in size of arteries, veins, and capillaries. First, read about these structures. All three are hollow tubes. Arteries are round and thick. Veins are flat and have thinner walls than arteries. Capillaries are small.

Now, decide what you can use for your model. Common materials are often most useful and cheapest to work with when making models. As illustrated in **Figure 25** on the next page, different kinds and sizes of pasta might work for these models. Different sizes of rubber tubing might do just as well. Cut and glue the different noodles or tubing onto thick paper so the openings can be seen. Then label each. Now you have a simple, easy-to-understand model showing the differences in size of arteries, veins, and capillaries.

What other scientific ideas might a model help you to understand? A model of a molecule can be made from balls of modeling clay (using different colors for the different elements present) and toothpicks (to show different chemical bonds).

from larger units to smaller, multiply by 10. For example, to convert millimeters to centimeters, divide the millimeters by 10. To convert 30 millimeters to centimeters, divide 30 by 10 (30 millimeters equal 3 centimeters).

Prefixes are used to name units. Look at **Figure 26** for some common metric prefixes and their meanings. Do you see how the prefix *kilo-* attached to the unit *gram* is *kilogram*, or 1000 grams? The prefix *deci-* attached to the unit *meter* is *decimeter*, or one-tenth (0.1) of a meter.

Examples

Length   You have probably measured lengths or distances many times. The meter is the SI unit used to measure length. A baseball bat is about one meter long. When measuring smaller lengths, the meter is divided into smaller units called centimeters and millimeters. A centimeter is one-hundredth (0.01) of a meter, which is about the size of the width of the fingernail on your ring finger. A millimeter is one-thousandth of a meter (0.001), about the thickness of a dime.

Most metric rulers have lines indicating centimeters and millimeters, as shown in

Figure 25 Different types of pasta may be used to model blood vessels

A working model of a volcano can be made from clay, a small amount of baking soda, vinegar, and a bottle cap. Other models can be devised on a computer. Some models are mathematical and are represented by equations.

Measuring in SI

The metric system is a system of measurement developed by a group of scientists in 1795. It helps scientists avoid problems by providing standard measurements that all scientists around the world can understand. A modern form of the metric system, called the International System, or SI, was adopted for worldwide use in 1960.

The metric system is convenient because unit sizes vary by multiples of 10. When changing from smaller units to larger units, divide by 10. When changing

Figure 26 Common metric prefixes

Metric Prefixes			
Prefix	**Symbol**	**Meaning**	
kilo-	k	1000	thousand
hecto-	h	200	hundred
deca-	da	10	ten
deci-	d	0.1	tenth
centi-	c	0.01	hundredth
milli-	m	0.001	thousandth

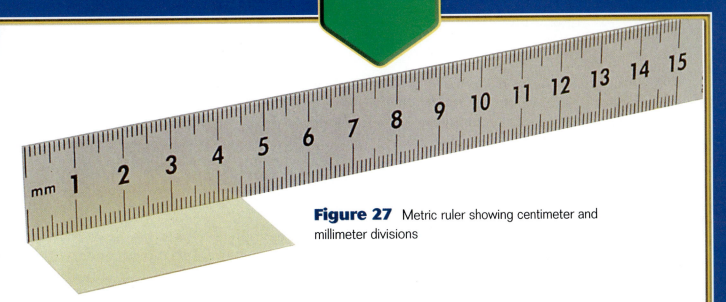

Figure 27 Metric ruler showing centimeter and millimeter divisions

Figure 27. The centimeter lines are the longer, numbered lines; the shorter lines are millimeter lines. When using a metric ruler, line up the 0-centimeter mark with the end of the object being measured, and read the number of the unit where the object ends, in this instance 4.5 cm.

Surface Area Units of length are also used to measure surface area. The standard unit of area is the square meter (m^2). A square that's one meter long on each side has a surface area of one square meter. Similarly, a square centimeter, (cm^2), shown in **Figure 28,** is one centimeter long on each side. The surface area of an object is determined by multiplying the length times the width.

Volume The volume of a rectangular solid is also calculated using units of length. The cubic meter (m^3) is the standard SI unit of volume. A cubic meter is a cube one meter on each side. You can determine the volume of rectangular solids by multiplying length times width times height.

Liquid Volume During science activities, you will measure liquids using beakers and graduated cylinders marked in milliliters, as illustrated in **Figure 29.** A graduated cylinder is a cylindrical container marked with lines from bottom to top.

Liquid volume is measured using a unit called a liter. A liter has the volume of 1000 cubic centimeters. Because the prefix *milli-* means thousandth (0.001), a milliliter equals one cubic centimeter. One milliliter of liquid would completely fill a cube measuring one centimeter on each side.

Figure 29 A volume of 79 mL is measured by reading at the lowest point of the curve.

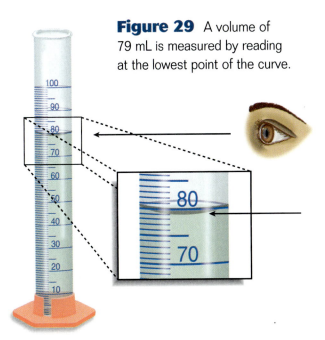

Figure 28 A square centimeter

1 cm
1 cm

Mass Scientists use balances to find the mass of objects in grams. You might use a beam balance similar to **Figure 30**. Notice that on one side of the balance is a pan and on the other side is a set of beams. Each beam has an object of a known mass called a *rider* that slides on the beam.

Before you find the mass of an object, set the balance to zero by sliding all the riders back to the zero point. Check the pointer on the right to make sure it swings an equal distance above and below the zero point on the scale. If the swing is unequal, find and turn the adjusting screw until you have an equal swing.

Place an object on the pan. Slide the rider with the largest mass along its beam until the pointer drops below zero. Then move it back one notch. Repeat the process on each beam until the pointer swings an equal distance above and below the zero point. Add the masses on each beam to find the mass of the object.

You should never place a hot object or pour chemicals directly onto the pan. Instead, find the mass of a clean beaker or a glass jar. Place the dry or liquid chemicals in the container. Then find the combined mass of the container and the chemicals. Calculate the mass of the chemicals by subtracting the mass of the empty container from the combined mass.

Predicting

When you apply a hypothesis, or general explanation, to a specific situation, you predict something about that situation. First, you must identify which hypothesis fits the situation you are considering.

Examples People use prediction to make everyday decisions. Based on previous observations and experiences, you may form a hypothesis that if it is wintertime, then temperatures will be lower. From past experience in your area, temperatures are lowest in February. You may then use this hypothesis to predict specific temperatures and weather for the month of February in advance. Someone could use these predictions to plan to set aside more money for heating bills during that month.

Figure 30 A beam balance is used to measure mass.

Using Numbers

When working with large populations of organisms, scientists usually cannot observe or study every organism in the population. Instead, they use a sample or a portion of the population. To sample is to take a small representative portion of organisms of a population for research. By making careful observations or manipulating variables within a portion of a group, information is discovered and conclusions are drawn that might then be applied to the whole population.

Scientific work also involves estimating. To estimate is to make a judgment about the size of something or the number of something without actually measuring or counting every member of a population.

Examples Suppose you are trying to determine the effect of a specific nutrient on the growth of black-eyed Susans. It would be impossible to test the entire population of black-eyed Susans, so you would select part of the population for your experiment. Through careful experimentation and observation on a sample of the population, you could generalize the effect of the chemical on the entire population.

Here is a more familiar example. Have you ever tried to guess how many beans were in a sealed jar? If you did, you were estimating. What if you knew the jar of beans held one liter (1000 mL)? If you knew that 30 beans would fit in a 100-milliliter jar, how many beans would you estimate to be in the one-liter jar? If you said about 300 beans, your estimate would be close to the actual number of beans. Can you estimate how many jelly beans are on the cookie sheet in **Figure 31?**

Scientists use a similar process to estimate populations of organisms from bacteria to buffalo. Scientists count the actual number of organisms in a small sample and then estimate the number of organisms in a larger area. For example, if a scientist wanted to count the number of bacterial colonies in a petri dish, a microscope could be used to count the number of organisms in a one-square-centimeter sample. To determine the total population of the culture, the number of organisms in the square-centimeter sample is multiplied by the total number of square centimeters in the culture.

Figure 31

Sampling a group of jelly beans allows for an estimation of the total number of jelly beans in the group.

Technology Skill Handbook

Using a Word Processor

Suppose your teacher has assigned you to write a report. After you've done your research and decided how you want to write the information, you need to put all that information on paper. The easiest way to do this is with a word processor.

A word processor is a computer program in which you can write your information, change it as many times as you need to, and then print it out so that it looks neat and clean. You can also use a word processor to create tables and columns, add bullets or cartoon art, include page numbers, and even check your spelling.

Example Last week in Science class, your teacher assigned a report on the history of the atom. It has to be double spaced and include at least one table. You've collected all the facts, and you're ready to write your report. Sitting down at your computer, you decide you want to begin by explaining early scientific ideas about the atom and then talk about what scientists think about the atom now.

After you've written the two parts of your report, you decide to put a heading or subtitle above each part and add a title to the paper. To make each of these look different from the rest of your report, you can use a word processor to make the words bigger and bolder. The word processor also can double space your entire report, so that you don't have to add an extra space between each line.

You decide to include a table that lists each scientist that contributed to the theory of the atom along with his or her contribution. Using your word processor, you can create a table with as many rows and columns as you need. And, if you forget to include a scientist in the middle, you can go back and insert a row in the middle of your table without redoing the entire table.

When you've finished with your report, you can tell the word processor to check your spelling. If it finds misspelled words, it often will suggest a word you can use to replace the misspelled word. But, remember that the word processor may not know how to spell all the words in your report. Scan your report and double check your spelling with a dictionary if you're not sure if a word is spelled correctly.

After you've made sure that your report looks just the way you want it on the screen, the word processor will print your report on a printer. With a word processor, your report can look like it was written by a real scientist.

Helpful Hints

- If you aren't sure how to do something using your word processor, look under the help menu. You can look up how to do something, and the word processor will tell you how to do it. Just follow the instructions that the word processor puts on your screen.

- Just because you've spelled checked your report doesn't mean that the spelling is perfect. The spell check can't catch misspelled words that look like other words. So, if you've accidentally typed *mind* instead of *mine*, the spell checker won't know the difference. Always reread your report to make sure you didn't miss any mistakes.

Technology Skill Handbook

Using a Database

Imagine you're in the middle of research project. You are busily gathering facts and information. But, soon you realize that its becoming harder and harder to organize and keep track of all the information. The tool to solve "information overload" is a database. A database is exactly what it sounds like—a base on which to organize data. Similar to how a file cabinet organizes records, a database also organizes records. However, a database is more powerful than a simple file cabinet because at the click of a mouse, the entire contents can be reshuffled and reorganized. At computer-quick speeds, databases can sort information by any characteristic and filter data into multiple categories. Once you use a database, you will be amazed at how quickly all those facts and bits of information become manageable.

Example For the past few weeks, you have been gathering information on living and extinct primates. A database would be ideal to organize your information. An entry for gorillas might contain fields (categories) for fossil locations, brain size, average height, earliest fossil, and so on. Later on, if you wanted to know which primates have been found in Asia, you could quickly filter all entries using Asia in the field that listed locations. The database will scan all the entries and select the entries containing Asia. If you wanted to rank all the primates by arm length, you would sort all the entries by arm length. By using different combinations of sorting and filtering, you can discover relationships between the data that otherwise might remain hidden.

Helpful Hints

- Before setting up your own database, it's easier to learn the features of your database software by practicing with an established database.

- Entering the data into a database can be time consuming. Learn shortcuts such as tabbing between entry fields and automatic formatting of data that your software may provide.

- Get in the habit of periodically saving your database as you are entering data. That way, if something happens and your computer locks up or the power goes out, you won't lose all of your work.

Most databases have specific words you can use to narrow your search.

- AND: If you place an AND between two words in your search, the database will look for any entries that have both the words. For example, "blood AND cell" would give you information about both blood and cells.

- OR: If you place an OR between two words, the database will show entries that have at least one of the words. For example, "bird OR fish" would show you information on either birds or fish.

- NOT: If you place a NOT between two words, the database will look for entries that have the first word but do not have the second word. For example, "reproduction NOT plant" would show you information about reproduction but not about plant reproduction.

Technology Skill Handbook

Using Graphics Software

Having trouble finding that exact piece of art you're looking for? Do you have a picture in your mind of what you want but can't seem to find the right graphic to represent your ideas? To solve these problems, you can use graphics software. Graphics software allows you to change and create images and diagrams in almost unlimited ways. Typical uses for graphics software include arranging clip-art, changing scanned images, and constructing pictures from scratch. Most graphics-software applications work in similar ways. They use the same basic tools and functions. Once you master one graphics application, you can use any other graphics application relatively easily.

Example For your report on bird adaptations, you want to make a poster displaying a variety of beak and foot types. You have acquired many photos of birds, scanned from magazines and downloaded off the Internet. Using graphics software, you separate the beaks and feet from the birds and enlarge them. Then, you use arrows and text to diagram the particular features that you want to highlight. You also highlight the key features in color, keeping the rest of the graphic in black and white. With graphics software, the possibilities are endless. For the final layout, you place the picture of the bird next to enlarged graphics of the feet and beak. Graphics software allows you to integrate text into your diagrams, which makes your bird poster look clean and professional.

Helpful Hints

- As with any method of drawing, the more you practice using the graphic software, the better your results.
- Start by using the software to manipulate existing drawings. Once you master this, making your own illustrations will be easier.
- Clip art is available on CD-ROMs, and on the Internet. With these resources, finding a piece of clip art to suit your purposes is simple.
- As you work on a drawing, save it often.
- Often you can learn a lot from studying other people's art. Look at other computer illustrations and try to figure out how the artist created it.

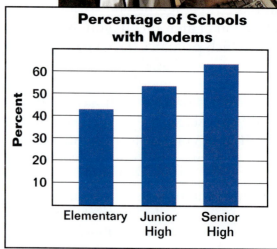

Percentage of Schools with Modems

Using a Computerized Card Catalog

When you have a report or paper to research, you go to the library. To find the information, skill is needed in using a computerized card catalog. You use the computerized card catalog by typing in a subject, the title of a book, or an author's name. The computer will list on the screen all the holdings the library has on the subject, title, or author requested.

A library's holdings include books, magazines, databases, videos, and audio materials. When you have chosen something from this list, the computer will show whether an item is available and where in the library to find it.

Example You have a report due on dinosaurs, and you need to find three books on the subject. In the library, follow the instructions on the computer screen to select the "Subject" heading. You could start by typing in the word *dinosaurs*. This will give you a list of books on that subject. Now you need to narrow your search to the kind of dinosaur you are interested in, for example, *Tyrannosaurus rex*. You can type in *Tyrannosaurus rex* or just look through the list to find titles that you think would have information you need. Once you have selected a short list of books, click on each selection to find out if the library has the books. Then, check on where they are located in the library.

Helpful Hints

- Remember that you can use the computer to search by subject, author, or title. If you know a book's author, but not the title, you can search for all the books the library has by that author.

- When searching by subject, it's often most helpful to narrow your search by using specific search terms. If you don't find enough, you can then broaden your search.

- Pay attention to the type of materials found in your search. If you need a book, you can eliminate any videos or other resources that come up in your search.

- Knowing how your library is arranged can save a lot of time. The librarian will show you where certain types of material are kept and how to find something.

Developing Multimedia Presentations

It's your turn—you have to present your science report to the entire class. How do you do it? You can use many different sources of information to get the class excited about your presentation. Posters, videos, photographs, sound, computers, and the Internet can help show our ideas. First, decide the most important points you want your presentation to make. Then, sketch out what materials and types of media would be best to illustrate those points. Maybe you could start with an outline on an overhead projector, then show a video, followed by something from the Internet or a slide show accompanied by music or recorded voices. Make sure you don't make the presentation too complicated, or you will confuse yourself and the class. Practice your presentation a few times for your parents or brothers and sisters before you present it to the class.

Example Your assignment is to give a presentation on bird-watching. You could have a poster that shows what features you use to identify birds, with a sketch of your favorite bird. A tape of the calls of your favorite bird or a video of birds in your area would work well with the poster. If possible, include an Internet site with illustrations of birds that the class can look at.

Helpful Hints

- Carefully consider what media will best communicate the point you are trying to make.
- Keep your topic and your presentation simple.
- Make sure you learn how to use any equipment you will be using in your presentation.
- Practice the presentation several times.
- If possible, set up all of the equipment ahead of time. Make sure everything is working correctly.

Technology Skill Handbook

Using E-Mail

It's science fair time and you want to ask a scientist a question about your project, but he or she lives far away. You could write a letter or make a phone call. But you can also use the computer to communicate. You can do this using electronic mail (E-mail). You will need a computer that is connected to an E-mail network. The computer is usually hooked up to the network by a device called a *modem*. A modem works through the telephone lines. Finally, you need an address for the person you want to talk with. The E-mail address works just like a street address to send mail to that person.

Example There are just a few steps needed to send a message to a friend on an E-mail network. First, select Message from the E-mail software menu. Then, enter the E-mail address of your friend. Next, type your message. Make sure you check it for spelling and other errors. Finally, click the Send button to mail your message and off it goes! You will get a reply back in your electronic mailbox. To read your reply, just click on the message and the reply will appear on the screen.

Helpful Hints

- Make sure that you have entered the correct address of the person you're sending the message to.
- Reread your message to make sure it says what you want to say, and check for spelling and grammar.
- If you receive an E-mail message, respond to it as soon as possible.
- If you receive frequent email messages, keep them organized by either deleting them, or saving them in folders according to the subject or sender.

Technology Skill Handbook

Using an Electronic Spreadsheet

Your science fair experiment has produced lots of numbers. How do you keep track of all the data, and how can you easily work out all the calculations needed? You can use a computer program called a *spreadsheet* to keep track of data that involve numbers. A spreadsheet is an electronic worksheet. Type in your data in rows and columns, just as in a data table on a sheet of paper. A spreadsheet uses some simple math to do calculations on the data. For example, you could add, subtract, divide, or multiply any of the values in the spreadsheet by another number. Or you can set up a series of math steps you want to apply to the data. If you want to add 12 to all the numbers and then multiply all the numbers by 10, the computer does all the calculations for you in the spreadsheet. Below is an example of a spreadsheet that is a schedule.

Example Let's say that to complete your project, you need to calculate the speed of the model cars in your experiment. Enter the distance traveled by each car in the rows of the spreadsheet. Then enter the time you recorded for each car to travel the measured distance in the column across from each car. To make the formula, just type in the equation you want the computer to calculate; in this case, *speed = distance ÷ time*. You must make sure the computer knows what data are in the rows and what data are in the

Test Runs	Time	Distance	Speed
Car 1	5 mins.	5 miles	60 mph
Car 2	10 mins.	4 miles	24 mph
Car 3	6 mins.	3 miles	30 mph

columns so the calculation will be correct. Once all the distance and time data and the formula have been entered into the spreadsheet program, the computer will calculate the speed for all the trials you ran. You can even make graphs of the results.

Helpful Hints

- Before you set up the spreadsheet, sketch out how you want to organize the data. Include any formulas you will need to use.
- Make sure you have entered the correct data into the correct rows and columns.
- As you experiment with your particular spreadsheet program you will learn more of its features.
- You can also display your results in a graph. Pick the style of graph that best represents the data you are working with.

Technology Skill Handbook

Using a CD-ROM

What's your favorite music? You probably listen to your favorite music on compact discs (CDs). But, there is another use for compact discs, called CD-ROM. CD-ROM means Compact Disc-Read Only Memory. CD-ROMs hold information. Whole encyclopedias and dictionaries can be stored on CD-ROM discs. This kind of CD-ROM and others are used to research information for reports and papers. The information is accessed by putting the disc in your computer's CD-ROM drive and following the computer's installation instructions. The CD-ROM will have words, pictures, photographs, and maybe even sound and video on a range of topics.

Example Load the CD-ROM into the computer. Find the topic you are interested in by clicking on the Search button. If there is no Search button, try the Help button. Most CD-ROMs are easy to use, but refer to the Help instructions if you have problems. Use the arrow keys to move down through the list of titles on your topic. When you double-click on a title, the article will appear on the screen. You can print the article by clicking on the Print button. Each CD-ROM is different. Click the Help menu to see how to find what you want.

Helpful Hints

- Always open and close the CD-ROM drive on your computer by pushing the button next to the drive. Pushing on the tray to close it will stress the opening mechanism over time.
- Place the disc in the tray so the side with no printing is facing down.
- Read through the installation instructions that come with the CD-ROM.
- Remember to remove the CD-ROM before you shut your computer down.

Using Probeware

Data collecting in an experiment sometimes requires that you take the same measurement over and over again. With probeware, you can hook a probe directly to a computer and have the computer collect the data about temperature, pressure, motion, or pH. Probeware is a combination sensor and software that makes the process of collecting data easier. With probes hooked to computers, you can make many measurements quickly, and you can collect data over a long period of time without needing to be present. Not only will the software record the data, most software will graph the data.

Example Suppose you want to monitor the health of an enclosed ecosystem. You might use an oxygen and a carbon dioxide sensor to monitor the gas concentrations or humidity or temperature. If the gas concentrations remain stable, you could predict that the ecosystem is healthy. After all the data is collected, you can use the software to graph the data and analyze it. With probeware, experimenting is made efficient and precise.

Helpful Hints

- Find out how to properly use each probe before using it.
- Make sure all cables are solidly connected. A loose cable can interrupt the data collection and give you inaccurate results.
- Because probeware makes data collection so easy, do as many trials as possible to strengthen your data.

Technology Skill Handbook

Using a Graphing Calculator

Science can be thought of as a means to predict the future and explain the past. In other language, if x happens, can we predict y? Can we explain the reason y happened? Simply, is there a relationship between x and y? In nature, a relationship between two events or two quantities, x and y, often occurs. However, the relationship is often complicated and can only be readily seen by making a graph. To analyze a graph, there is no quicker tool than a graphing calculator. The graphing calculator shows the mathematical relationship between two quantities.

Example If you have collected data on the position and time for a migrating whale, you can use the calculator to graph the data. Using the linear regression function on the calculator, you can determine the average migration speed of the whale. The more you use the graphing calculator to solve problems, the more you will discover its power and efficiency.

Graphing calculators have some keys that other calculators do not have. The keys on the bottom half of the calculator are those found on all scientific calculators. The keys located just below the screen are the graphing keys. You will also notice the up, down, left, and right arrow keys. These allow you to move the cursor around on the screen, to "trace" graphs that have been plotted, and to choose items from the menus. The other keys located on the top of the calculator access the special features such as statistical computations and programming features.

A few of the keystrokes that can save you time when using the graphing calculator are listed below.

- The commands above the calculator keys are accessed with the [2nd] or [ALPHA] key. The [2nd] key and its commands are yellow and the [ALPHA] and its commands are green.
- [2nd] [ENTRY] copies the previous calculation so you can edit and use it again.
- Pressing [ON] while the calculator is graphing stops the calculator from completing the graph.
- [2nd] [QUIT] will return you to the home (or text) screen.
- [2nd] [A-LOCK] locks the [ALPHA] key, which is like pressing "shift lock" or "caps lock" on a typewriter or computer. The result is that all letters will be typed and you do not have to repeatedly press the [ALPHA] key. (This is handy for programming.) Stop typing letters by pressing [ALPHA] again.
- [2nd] [OFF] turns the calculator off.

Helpful Hints

- Mastering the graphing calculator takes practice. Don't expect to learn it all in an afternoon.
- Programming a graphing calculator takes a plan. Write out all of the steps before entering them.
- It's easiest to learn how to program the calculator by first using programs that have already been written. As you enter them, figure out what each step is telling the calculator to do.

Skill Activities

Table of Contents

Observing and Inferring

Background

Scientists classify organisms because they are related in some way or several ways. One group of related animals is the Phylum Arthropoda. It has one of the largest groups of animals, the Class Insecta.

How can insects be classified?

The Class Insecta is divided into orders that are smaller groups with similar features. Below are the Latin names and wing descriptions for five orders of insects.

- *Hymenoptera* means "membrane wing" and both pair of wings are thin and transparent.

- *Coleoptera* means "sheath wing," and the front wings are hard coverings that protect a pair of membranous wings and the insect's abdomen.

- *Hemiptera* means "half wing." One half of the front wing is thick and leathery, and the other half is membranous.

- *Lepidoptera* means "scale wing," which describes the powdery scales on the wings.

- *Orthoptera* means "straight wing," and some members of this group have long straight wings.

Procedure

1. Copy the Insect Observations table in your Science Journal.

2. Examine the eight insects shown on this page.

3. From their appearance, decide which insects belong in which order and write their names in your Insect Observations table.

Insect Observations	
Order	Insects
Hymenoptera	
Coleoptera	
Hemiptera	
Lepidoptera	
Orthoptera	

Weevil

Butterfly

Wasp

Harlequin bug

Ladybug

Grasshopper

Moth

Bee

Practicing the SKILL

1. How might this sort of classification be useful to people who study insects?

2. Using the same eight insects, make another classification of them.

For more skill practice, do the Chapter 21 Interactive Exploration on the **Science Voyages Level Red CD-ROM.**

Recognizing Cause and Effect

Background

Have you ever wondered why something happened? Scientists often wonder "why." They carefully observe an event and then try to determine why it occurred. This relationship between an event and why it occurred is the *effect*. The reason it happened is the *cause*. One effect often may have more than one possible cause. It is often difficult to identify the specific cause, or causes, of a given event. For example, your grade on a test is an effect. The reasons you got that grade are the causes. These could include your study habits, attendance, attention in class, and your physical condition. Analyzing the causes of events can help change an effect if it was undesirable, or re-create it if it was good.

Procedure

Make a copy of the Cause-and-Effect Data table in your Science Journal, and fill in the appropriate cause or effect.

Cause-and-Effect Data	
Cause	**Effect**
1.	1. Desert animals rest during the day.
2. A population is separated from individuals of its own group and no longer can mate with them.	2.
3.	3. Ducks are able to migrate over long distances.
4. A sudden change occurs in the climate and environment.	4.

Practicing the SKILL

Look for possible cause-and-effect relationships in the figure at the left.

For more skill practice, do the Chapter 22 Interactive Exploration on the **Science Voyages Level Red CD-ROM.**

GLENCOE TECHNOLOGY

Predicting

Background

Large populations of organisms need to be counted to determine the overall health of the species. However, counting each individual in a population can be time consuming and confusing. Therefore, scientists have developed methods of estimating the number of individuals in a population in order to save time. In this activity, you will predict the number of beetles by estimating the total number.

Ladybird Numbers		
Predicted number _____ Time _____		
Number in top left square	× Total number of squares	= Estimated total number
_____	_____	_____
Actual number _____ Time _____		

Procedure

1 Estimate the number of ladybird beetles in the figure to the right and record the number in a table like the one shown.

2 Place tracing paper over the diagram. Make a population count by placing a checkmark next to each ladybird beetle. Record the actual number of beetles in the table. Next to this number, record the amount of time it took to make the count.

3 Count the ladybird beetle population a second time by sampling. A sample is made by selecting and counting only a portion of the population. Count the number of ladybird beetles in the top left square and record this number in the table.

4 Enter the total number of squares in the table. Multiply the number of ladybird beetles in the top left square by the total number of squares. Record this estimated total number in the table.

5 At the top of the table, record the amount of time it took to make the sample count.

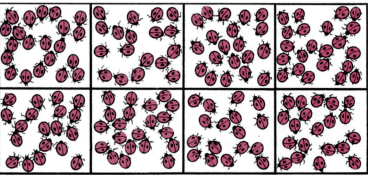

Practicing the SKILL

1 How many ladybird beetles did you estimate were shown?

2 Which way was faster—making an actual count or sampling?

3 Were the results exactly the same?

For more skill practice, do the Chapter 23 Interactive Exploration on the **Science Voyages Level Red CD-ROM.**

Observing and Inferring

Background

Living things survive in their environments because they have behavioral and physical adaptations that allow them to live. For example, a jackrabbit will run when it sees a coyote. This is a behavioral adaptation. The jackrabbit also has strong legs. This is a physical adaptation. Both adaptations, working together, give the jackrabbit an advantage in escaping predators. In this activity, you will observe adaptations that help living things near your classroom survive.

Procedure

1. Read Section 2, Land Environments. Pay special attention to the Adaptations of Desert Plants and Animals.

2. In a table like the one shown below, record the names of five living things you find near your classroom.

3. Briefly describe two behavioral adaptations and two physical adaptations for each. Record these in your table.

4. Write how you think each of the adaptations might give each organism an advantage that allows it to survive in the wild.

Practicing the SKILL

1. Many birds, insects, and bats are able to fly. What are the advantages of this adaptation?

2. Many mammals in both hot and cold climates have thick fur. What might the advantages of this adaptation be?

For more skill practice, do the Chapter 24 Interactive Exploration on the **Science Voyages Level Red CD-ROM.**

Organism Behavior			
Organism	**Physical adaptations**	**Behavioral adaptations**	**Advantages in the wild**

Observing and Inferring

Background

Suppose you smell a cinnamon-like scent. You might suspect someone nearby is baking cinnamon rolls. However, you might be wrong. The scent might be from candy or a kind of air freshener. You cannot be sure unless you actually see the source of the scent. Whenever you use your senses, you are making *observations* about the world around you. When you make a conclusion based on what you observe, you are making an *inference*. When you smell a scent and conclude that the scent is from a cinnamon roll, you are *inferring*.

Scientists use their senses to make observations. Based on what they observe, they make inferences. The inferences help them solve problems and predict future events. You can make observations and inferences about almost anything. Try improving your observing skills by looking carefully at an object. A visual observation should be made in an orderly way. First, look at the entire object. Then, look at its parts.

Procedure

1. Observe **Figure A** carefully. Write down your observations on a separate paper.

2. Did you notice (1) the color of the candle, (2) the blackened wick, (3) the melted wax on the candle and in the holder, and (4) the color of the holder?

3. Now, try making inferences based on what you observed in **Figure A.** You can base your observations on your own experience with candles. You might infer (1) how long the candle was lit (based on the amount of melted wax), (2) how much of the candle has melted, or

(3) why the candle is not burning now. Inferences are based on incomplete information. Therefore, they may be incorrect. The flame may have been lit for only a short time, for example.

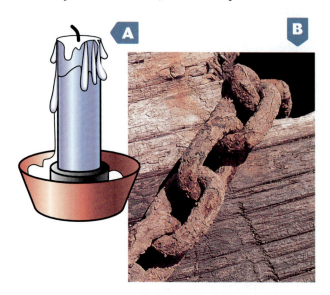

Practicing the SKILL

1. Look carefully at **Figure B.** On a separate sheet of paper, write down (1) what you observe and (2) what you can infer from the figure.

2. Identify any changes you see as physical or chemical. Are your identifications of chemical or physical changes observations or inferences? Explain.

For more skill practice, do the Chapter 25 Interactive Exploration on the **Science Voyages Level Red CD-ROM.**

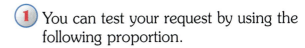

Using Numbers

Background

Consumers who are energy conscious and who live in sunny climates look to solar-energy technicians to help them utilize energy from the sun.

One type of solar-energy system that a solar-heating technician can suggest collects the sun's energy, transforms that energy into thermal energy, stores thermal energy in bins of rocks, and then distributes heated air to various parts of the house by means of duct work.

The diagram below shows the solar-collector component of a solar-energy system on the roof of a house.

A solar-heating technician calculates the area of a home and the area of the solar collectors in square feet (ft^2), instead of using a metric unit, such as the square meter (m^2). In the United States, the use of English units, such as feet and yards, is still a common practice in many industries. For example, fabric stores sell material by the yard, and gas companies calculate how much natural gas homes use by the cubic foot (ft^3).

The technician can use the fact that a home owner will need 1 ft^2 of solar-collector area for every 2.5 to 4 ft^2 of living space.

Suppose you are a home owner who wants to heat 1200 ft^2 of living space by using a solar-heating system. You contact a solar-heating technician and ask to have 400 ft^2 of solar collector installed. Is your request reasonable?

Procedure

1. You can test your request by using the following proportion.

$$\frac{\text{collector area}}{\text{living space}}$$

2. Solve the proportion.

$$\frac{\text{collector area}}{\text{living space}} = \frac{400 \text{ ft}^2}{1200 \text{ ft}^2} = \frac{1}{3}$$

3. Compare the calculated proportion you requested against the technician's given guidelines about area of solar collector per area of living space. Because 1 ft^2 of solar collector per 3 ft^2 of living space is between 1 ft^2 of collector per 2.5 ft^2 and 1 ft^2 of collector per 4 ft^2 of living space, the request is reasonable.

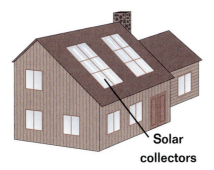

Solar collectors

Practicing the SKILL

Determine whether each estimate of collector space is reasonable. Explain each answer.

1. 300 ft^2 of collector per 1200 ft^2 of living space

2. 300 ft^2 of collector per 1500 ft^2 of living space

For more skill practice, do the Chapter 26 Interactive Exploration on the **Science Voyages Level Red CD-ROM.**

Interpreting Scientific Illustrations

Background

You may have heard the saying "A picture is worth a thousand words." A good scientific diagram often can explain an idea better than several paragraphs of words. In order to get the most from diagrams, do the following.

- Study the entire diagram. Review the part of the text that the diagram illustrates.

- If there is a caption, read it carefully.

- Read all the labels and identify the parts.

- Visualize the dimensions. Arrows often indicate distances and direction. Distances often are indicated between arrows. The heads of the arrows show where the measurements start and end.

Use these guidelines to interpret the diagram at right.

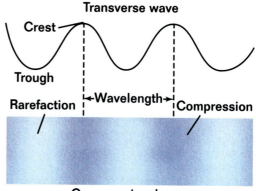

Procedure

1. What is the purpose of this diagram?

2. Identify the text in Chapter 5 to which the diagram relates. Locate the discussions about types of waves.

3. What does the crest of a transverse wave correspond to on a compressional wave?

4. What does the trough of a transverse wave correspond to on a compressional wave?

5. What is another way you can diagram the wavelength of a transverse wave?

Practicing the SKILL

1. What do the darker areas of the compressional wave represent?

2. What are the white areas?

3. How would you measure one wavelength of a compressional wave?

For more skill practice, do the Chapter 27 Interactive Exploration on the **Science Voyages Level Red CD-ROM.**

GLENCOE TECHNOLOGY

English Glossary

This glossary defines each key term that appears in **bold type** in the text. It also shows the page number where you can find the word used.

A

abiotic factors: all the nonliving, physical features of the environment, including light, soil, water, and temperature, and that help determine which species can survive in an area. (ch. 23, p. 823)

adaptation: any structure or behavior that helps an organism survive in its environment; develops in a population over a long period of time. (ch. 22, p. 794)

amplitude: measure of the energy a wave carries; one-half the distance between a crest and a trough of a transverse wave. (ch. 27, p. 949)

atom: small particle that makes up most types of matter and is made up of smaller parts called protons, neutrons, and electrons. (ch. 25, p. 885)

atomic mass: number that tells how heavy an element's atoms are compared with atoms of other elements. (ch. 25, p. 894)

atomic number: whole number that tells how many protons are in the nucleus of each atom of an element. (ch. 25, p. 894)

B

binomial nomenclature (bi NOH mee ul NOH mun klay chur): Linnaeus's system of classification, which gives a two-word name to every organism—the first word of the name is the genus and the second word is the specific name. (ch. 21, p. 768)

biodiversity (bi oh duh VUR suh tee): measure of the number of different species in an area. (ch. 22, p. 793)

biomes (BI ohmz): large geographic areas with similar climates and ecosystems; the six most common are tundra, taiga, temperate forest, tropical rain forest, grassland, and desert. (ch. 27, p. 859)

biosphere (BI uh sfihr): part of Earth that supports organisms, is the highest level of biological organization, and is made up of all Earth's ecosystems. (ch. 23, p. 822)

biotic factors: living or once-living organisms in the environment. (ch. 23, p. 825)

C

carrying capacity: largest number of individuals an environment can support and maintain over a long period of time. (ch. 23, p. 830)

chemical energy: energy stored within chemical bonds. (ch. 26, p. 933)

class: taxonomic group that is larger than an order but smaller than a phylum or division. (ch. 21, p. 772)

classify: to group information, objects, or ideas based on their similarities. (ch. 21, p. 766)

climax community: community that has reached the final stage of ecological succession. (ch. 24, p. 853)

common ancestor (AN ses tur): shared ancestor of different species that all arose from one population. (ch. 22, p. 803)

community: consists of groups of populations that interact with each other in a given area and depend on each other for food, shelter, and for other needs. (ch. 23, p. 826)

compound: pure substance produced when elements combine and whose properties are different from those of the elements from which it is formed. (ch. 25, p. 899)

compressional wave: wave in which matter in the medium moves forward and backward in the same direction the wave travels. (ch. 27, p. 947)

conduction: transfer of thermal energy from particle to particle through a material when there is a temperature difference (ch. 26, p. 926)

convection: transfer of thermal energy that happens when particles move from one place to another where there is a temperature difference (ch. 26, p. 928)

D

desert: driest biome on Earth that receives less than 25 cm of rain each year and supports little plant life. (ch.24, p. 864)

dichotomous (di KAH toh mus) **key:** detailed list of characteristics used to identify organisms and that includes scientific names. (ch. 21, p. 779)

diffraction: bending of waves around a barrier. (ch. 27, p. 956)

division: in the taxonomy of plants, the group smaller than a kingdom but larger than a class. (ch. 21, p. 772)

E

ecological pyramid: model used to describe the transfer of energy from the producers of an ecosystem through successive levels of organisms in the food chain. (ch. 23, p. 838)

ecological succession: process of gradual change from one community of organisms to another. (ch. 24, p. 850)

ecology: study of the interactions that take place among organisms and between organisms and the physical features of the environment. (ch. 23, p. 823)

ecosystem: consists of a biotic community and the abiotic factors that affect it. (ch. 23, p. 826)

electromagnetic waves: waves that do not need matter to carry energy; can travel through air, through solid walls, and through space and have wavelengths and frequencies that vary greatly. (ch. 27, p. 946)

electron: negatively charged particle found in a cloudlike formation surrounding an atom's nucleus. (ch. 25, p. 888)

element: naturally occurring or synthetic material that cannot be broken down to simpler materials by ordinary means, has a unique set of properties, and that is generally classified as a metal, a metalloid, or a nonmetal. (ch. 25, p. 892)

energy: ability to cause change; can affect the temperature, speed, shape, or direction of an object. (ch. 26, p. 912)

estuary: area where a river meets the ocean that contains a mixture of freshwater and salt water and serves as nursery for many species of ocean fish. (ch. 24, p. 870)

F

family: taxonomic group that is smaller than an order but larger than a genus. (ch. 21, p. 772)

food chain: model that describes the feeding relationships in a community, usually has three or four links, and shows how energy in the form of food passes from one organism to another. (ch. 23, p. 837)

food web: model used to describe a series of overlapping food chains and that shows the many organisms that feed on more than one level in an ecosystem. (ch. 23, p. 838)

fossil: traces or remains of ancient life. (ch. 22, p. 804)

fossil record: all the fossils that scientists have recovered from the ground; gives scientists strong evidence that life has changed over time. (ch. 22, p. 810)

frequency: number of waves that pass a given point in one second; measured in waves per second, or hertz (Hz). (ch. 27, p. 951)

G

genus (JEE nus): taxonomic group of different organisms with similar characteristics; can have one or more species. (ch. 21, p. 768)

geologic time scale: record of life on Earth put together by scientists that is divided into eras and periods and lists major evolutionary events. (ch. 22, p. 811)

grasslands: temperate and tropical regions that receive between 25 cm and 75 cm of precipitation each year and are dominated by climax communities of grasses. (ch. 24, p. 864)

H

habitat: physical location where an organism lives. (ch. 23, p. 833)

heat: energy transfer that causes a change in temperature. (ch. 26, p. 923)

I

interference: ability of two or more waves to combine and form a new wave when they overlap; can be constructive, forming a larger wave, or destructive, forming a smaller wave. (ch. 27, p. 958)

intertidal zone: portion of the shoreline that is covered with water at high tide and exposed to the air at low tide. (ch. 24, p. 870)

isotopes (I suh tohps): two or more atoms of the same element that have different numbers of neutrons. (ch. 25, p. 894)

K

kinetic (kuh NET ihk) **energy:** energy of motion; is influenced by an object's mass and speed and can be transferred from one object to another when objects collide. (ch. 26, p. 914)

kingdom: the first taxonomic category and the group that has the most members. (ch. 21, p. 767)

L

law of conservation of energy: states that energy cannot be created or destroyed but only transformed from one form to another. (ch. 26, p. 918)

law of conservation of matter: states that matter is neither created nor destroyed, only changed in form. (ch. 25, p. 886)

law of definite proportions: states that a given compound is always made of the same elements in the same proportion by mass. (ch. 25, p. 900)

limiting factor: any biotic or abiotic factor that restricts the number of individuals in a population. (ch. 23, p. 829)

M

mass extinction: large-scale disappearance of many species within a short time. (ch. 22, p. 813)

mass number: sum of an atom's protons and neutrons. (ch. 25, p. 894)

matter: anything that has mass and occupies space. (ch. 25, p. 884)

mechanical waves: waves that can travel only through matter; can be either transverse or compressional waves. (ch. 27, p. 945)

metalloids: elements that have characteristics of both metals and nonmetals, generally are brittle and dull, and are poor conductors of heat and electricity. (ch. 25, p. 896)

metals: elements that are malleable, ductile, generally have a shiny or metallic luster, and are not as good conductors of heat and electricity. (ch. 25, p. 895)

mixtures: combinations of two or more substances that have not combined to form new, pure substances; can be uniform, where the individual parts cannot be seen, or nonuniform, where you can see individual parts. (ch. 25, p. 901)

natural selection: process in which organisms with characteristics best suited for the environment survive, reproduce, and pass these traits to their offspring. (ch. 22, p. 800)

neutron: uncharged particle in an atom's nucleus. (ch. 25, p. 890)

niche: role of an organism in the ecosystem, including what it eats, how it interacts with other organisms, and how it gets its food. (ch. 23, p. 833)

nitrogen cycle: transfer of nitrogen from the atmosphere to plants and back to the atmosphere or directly into plants again. (ch. 23, p. 842)

nonmetals: elements that are usually dull and are poor conductors of heat and electricity. (ch. 25, p. 896)

nucleus (NEW klee us): positively charged, central part of an atom. (ch. 25, p. 890)

order: taxonomic group that is larger than a family but smaller than a class. (ch. 21, p. 772)

P

phylogeny (fi LAH jon nee): evolutionary history of an organism. (ch. 21, p. 771)

phylum (FI lum): taxonomic group that is smaller than a kingdom but larger than a class. (ch. 21, p. 772)

pioneer community: first community of organisms to move into a new environment. (ch. 24, p. 819)

plankton: microscopic algae, plants, and other organisms that float in warm, sunlit waters near the surface of freshwater lakes and ponds. (ch. 24, p. 869)

population: all the individuals of one species that live in the same area at the same time and compete with each other for food, water, mates, and space. (ch. 23, p. 826)

population density: size of a population that occupies an area of limited size. (ch. 23, p. 829)

potential (puh TEN chul) **energy:** energy that is stored and that comes from an object's position or condition. (ch.26, p. 916)

primary succession: ecological succession that begins in a place that does not have soil. (ch. 24, p. 851)

proton: particle in the nucleus of an atom that carries a positive charge. (ch. 25, p. 890)

R

radiation: energy that travels by waves in all directions from its source (ch. 4, p. 103); transfer of energy by electromagnetic waves. (ch. 26, p. 925)

reflection: occurs when a wave strikes an object or surface and bounces off. (ch. 27, p. 954)

refraction: bending of a wave as it moves from one medium into another. (ch. 27, p. 955)

S

secondary succession: ecological succession that begins in a place that already has soil and was once the home of living organisms. (ch. 24, p. 852)

species (SPEE sheez): smallest, most precise taxonomic classification. (ch. 21, p. 768)

substance: sample of matter that has the same composition and properties throughout. (ch. 25, p. 899)

symbiosis (sihm bee OH sus): any close relationship between two or more different species. (ch. 23, p. 831)

T

taiga (TI guh): cold region of cone-bearing evergreen trees that lies just below the tundra and is the world's largest terrestrial biome. (ch. 24, p. 860)

taxonomy (tak SAHN uh mee): the science of classification. (ch. 21, p. 766)

temperate deciduous forest: biome that lies at latitudes below about 50° in both the northern and southern hemispheres, usually has four distinct seasons, and supports a wide variety of plants and animals. (ch. 24, p. 861)

temperature: measure of the average kinetic energy of the particles in any object; the greater the average kinetic energy, the higher an object's temperature. (ch. 26, p. 922)

thermal energy: total amount of kinetic energy of the particles in a material. (ch. 26, p. 923)

transverse wave: wave in which matter moves back and forth at right angles to the direction the wave travels. (ch. 27, p. 946)

tropical rain forest: hot, wet, equatorial biome that contains the largest number of species. (ch. 24, p. 863)

tundra (TUN dra): cold, dry, treeless biome located at latitudes surrounding the north pole and that has winters six to nine months long. (ch. 24, p. 859)

W

water cycle: constant journey of water molecules on Earth as they rise into the atmosphere, fall to land or the ocean as rain or snow, and flow into rivers and oceans through the processes of evaporation, condensation, and precipitation. (ch. 23, p. 840)

wavelength: distance between a point on one wave and an identical point on the next wave, measured from crest to crest or trough to trough; in compressional waves, is measured from one compression or rarefaction to the next. (ch. 27, p. 950)

waves: regular disturbances that carry energy through matter or space without carrying matter; can have different amplitudes, frequencies, wavelengths, and speeds (ch. 27, p. 944)

Glossary/Glosario

Este glossario define cada término clave que aparece en **negrillas** en el texto. También muestra el número de página donde se usa dicho término.

A

abiotic factors / factores abióticos: Características físicas inanimadas que a menudo determinan los organismos que pueden sobrevivir en cierto ambiente. (Cap. 23, pág. 823)

adaptation / adaptación: Cualquier estructura o comportamiento que le ayuda a un organismo a sobrevivir en su ambiente y a llevar a cabo sus procesos vitales. (Cap. 22, pág. 794)

amplitude / amplitud: La mitad de la distancia entre una cresta y un valle de una onda transversal; una medida de la energía que transporta una onda. (Cap. 27, pág. 949)

atom / átomo: La partícula más pequeña que compone la mayoría de los tipos de materia. (Cap. 25, pág. 885)

atomic mass / masa atómica: Indica el peso de los átomos de un elemento en comparación con los átomos de otros elementos. (Cap. 25, pág. 894)

atomic number / número atómico: Indica el número de protones en el núcleo de cada átomo de un elemento. (Cap. 25, pág. 894)

B

binomial nomenclature / nomenclatura binaria: Sistema de clasificación de Linneo que usa dos términos, o nombre científico, para nombrar cada organismo. (Cap. 21, pág. 768)

biodiversity / biodiversidad: Medida del número de diferentes especies en un área. (Cap. 22, pág. 793)

biomes / biomas: Áreas geográficas extensas que poseen climas y ecosistemas similares. (Cap. 24, pág. 859)

biosphere / biosfera: La parte de la Tierra que sostiene organismos vivos. (Cap. 23, pág. 822)

biotic factors / factores bióticos: Cualquier organismo vivo o que alguna vez estuvo vivo, en un ambiente. (Cap. 23, pág. 825)

C

carrying capacity / capacidad de carga: El mayor número de individuos que un ambiente puede soportar y mantener durante un largo período de tiempo. (Cap. 23, pág. 830)

chemical energy / energía química: Energía almacenada (potencial) en los enlaces químicos de las partículas de una sustancia. (Cap. 26, pág. 933)

class / clase: Grupo taxonómico en el cual se divide el filo o división. (Cap. 21, pág. 772)

classify / clasificar: Significa agrupar ideas, información u objetos basándose en sus semejanzas. (Cap. 21, pág. 766)

climax community / comunidad clímax: Comunidad que ha alcanzado la etapa final de sucesión ecológica. (Cap. 24, pág. 853)

common ancestor / antepasado común: Antepasado que comparten especies diferentes, las cuales todas se originaron de una población. (Cap. 22, pág. 803)

community / comunidad: Grupo de poblaciones que interactúan entre sí en un área determinada. (Cap. 23, pág. 826)

compound / compuesto: Sustancia pura cuya unidad constitutiva está compuesta por átomos de más de un elemento. (Cap. 25, pág. 899)

compressional wave / onda de compresión: Onda en la cual la materia en el medio se mueve de un lado a otro en la misma dirección en que viaja la onda. (Cap. 27, pág. 947)

conduction /conducción: Transferencia de energía térmica de una partícula a otra a través de un material, cuando existe una deferencia de temperaturas. (Cap. 26, pág. 926)

D

desert / desierto: El bioma más seco de la Tierra. Recibe menos de 25 cm de lluvia al año y sostiene poca vegetación. (Cap. 24, pág. 864)

dichotomous key / clave dicotómica: Lista detallada de características que se usan para identificar organismos y la cual incluye el nombre científico. (Cap. 21, pág. 779)

diffraction / difracción: Doblamiento de una onda alrededor de una barrera. (Cap. 27, pág. 936)

division / división: Reemplaza el filo en los reinos de las plantas; es el grupo taxonómico más pequeño que el reino, pero más grande que una clase. (Cap. 21, pág. 772)

E

ecological pyramid / pirámide ecológica: Modelo que representa la transferencia de energía en la biosfera. (Cap. 23, pág. 838)

ecological succession / sucesión ecológica: Proceso de cambio gradual de una comunidad de organismos a otra. (Cap. 24, pág. 850)

ecology / ecología: Ciencia que estudia las interacciones entre los organismos y entre los organismos y los rasgos físicos del ambiente. (Cap. 23, pág. 823)

ecosystem / ecosistema: Consiste en una comunidad biótica y de los factores abióticos que la afectan. (Cap. 23, pág. 826)

electromagnetic waves / ondas electromagnéticas: Ondas que no requieren materia para transportar energía y que pueden viajar a través del aire. (Cap. 27, pág. 946)

electron / electrón: Partícula con carga negativa. (Cap. 25, pág. 888)

element / elemento: Material que no se puede descomponer en materiales más simples por medios comunes. (Cap. 25, pág. 892)

energy / energía: Capacidad de causar cambio. (Cap. 26, pág. 912)

estuary / estuario: Área en donde un río desemboca en el océano y la cual contiene una mezcla de agua dulce y salada. Sirve de vivero para muchas especies de peces oceánicos. (Cap. 24, pág. 870)

F

family / familia: Grupo taxonómico más pequeño que el orden, pero más grande que el género. (Cap. 21, pág. 772)

food chain / cadena alimenticia: Manera simple de mostrar cómo la energía de los alimentos pasa de un organismo a otro. (Cap. 23, pág. 837)

food web / red alimenticia: Serie de cadenas alimenticias sobrepuestas. (Cap. 23, pág. 838)

fossil / fósil: Restos o huellas de vida antigua. (Cap. 22, pág. 804)

fossil record / récord fósil: Todos los fósiles que los científicos han recobrado del suelo. Los fósiles de casi cada grupo principal de plantas o animales forman parte del récord fósil. (Cap. 22, pág. 810)

frequency / frecuencia: Número de ondas que pasan por un punto fijo en un segundo. Se mide en ondas por segundo o hertz (Hz). (Cap. 27, pág. 951)

G

genus / género: Grupo de diferentes organismos que poseen características parecidas. (Cap. 21, pág. 768)

geologic time scale / escala del tiempo geológico: Especie de diario del récord fósil de la vida sobre la Tierra que han recopilado los científicos. (Cap. 22, pág. 811)

grasslands / praderas: Regiones tropicales y templadas que reciben de 25 a 75 cm de precipitación anual y en la cual dominan la comunidad clímax de hierbas. (Cap. 24, pág. 864)

H

habitat / hábitat: Ubicación física en donde vive un organismo (Cap. 23, pág. 833)

heat / calor: Transferencia de energía que ocasiona un cambio de temperatura. (Cap. 26, pág. 923)

I

interference / interferencia: La capacidad de dos o más ondas de combinarse y formar una nueva onda cuando se sobreponen una sobre la otra. (Cap. 27, pág. 958)

intertidal zone / zona entre la marea baja y la alta: Porción de la costa cubierta de agua durante la marea alta y expuesta al aire durante la marea baja. (Cap. 24, pág. 870)

isotopes / isótopos: Átomos del mismo elemento que poseen diferentes números de neutrones. (Cap. 25, pág. 894)

K

kinetic energy / energía cinética: Energía que poseen los objetos en movimiento. (Cap. 26, pág. 914)

kingdom / reino: La primera categoría taxonómica y la más grande. (Cap. 21, pág. 767)

L

law of conservation of energy / ley de conservación de la energía: Ley que enuncia que la energía no puede ser creada ni destruida, solo puede ser transformada de una forma a otra. (Cap. 26, pág. 918)

law of conservation of matter / ley de conservación de la materia: Enuncia que la materia no puede ser creada ni destruida, pero que solo cambia de forma. (Cap. 25, pág. 886)

law of definite proportions / ley de proporciones definidas: Ley que enuncia que un compuesto dado siempre está formado por los mismos elementos en la misma proporción por masa. (Cap. 25, pág. 900)

limiting factor / factor limitante: Cualquier factor biótico o abiótico que limita el número de individuos en una población. (Cap. 23, pág. 829)

M

mass extinction / extinción en masa: La desaparición en gran escala de muchas especies en un lapso corto de tiempo. (Cap. 22, pág. 813)

mass number / número de masa: Equivale a la suma de los protones y neutrones de un átomo. (Cap. 25, pág. 894)

matter / materia: Cualquier cosa que posee masa y que ocupa espacio. (Cap. 25, pág. 884)

mechanical waves / ondas mecánicas: Ondas que solo pueden viajar a través de un medio: la materia. (Cap. 27, pág. 945)

metalloids / metaloides: Elementos que poseen características tanto de los metales como de los no metales y que son por lo general quebradizos y opacos; no son buenos conductores de calor y de electricidad como los metales. (Cap. 25, pág. 896)

metals / metales: Elementos que generalmente tienen lustre metálico o brillante, son buenos conductores de calor y electricidad, son maleables y dúctiles. Todos los metales, excepto el mercurio, son sólidos a temperatura ambiente. (Cap. 25, pág. 895)

mixtures / mezclas: Combinaciones de dos o más sustancias que no se han combinado para formar nuevas sustancias puras; pueden ser uniformes: en las que no se pueden ver las partes individuales, o no uniformes: en las que se pueden ver las partes individuales. (Cap. 25, pág. 901)

N

natural selection / selección natural: Proceso en que los organismos cuyas características los hacen más aptos para sus ambientes sobreviven, se reproducen y pasan esas características a su progenie. (Cap. 22, pág. 800)

neutron / neutrón: Partícula que no posee ninguna carga eléctrica. (Cap. 25, pág. 890)

niche / nicho: Papel de un organismo en el ecosistema. (Cap. 23, pág. 833)

nitrogen cycle / ciclo del nitrógeno: Transferencia de nitrógeno de la atmósfera a las plantas y de regreso a la atmósfera o directamente a las plantas nuevamente. (Cap. 23, pág. 833)

nonmetals / no metales: Elementos que por lo general son opacos y malos conductores de calor y electricidad. (Cap. 25, pág. 896)

nucleus / núcleo: Centro con carga positiva del átomo. (Cap. 25, pág. 890)

O

order / orden: Grupo taxonómico más grande que la familia, pero más pequeño que la clase. (Cap. 21, pág. 772)

P

phylogeny / filogenia: Historia de la evolución de un organismo. (Cap. 21, pág. 771)

phylum / filo: El grupo taxonómico más pequeño después del reino. (Cap. 21, pág. 772)

pioneer community / comunidad pionera: Primera comunidad de organismos que se mudan a un nuevo ambiente. (Cap. 24, pág. 851)

plankton / plancton: Algas, plantas y otros organismos microscópicos que flotan cerca de la superficie en las aguas cálidas y soleadas de lagos y lagunas de agua dulce. (Cap. 24, pág. 869)

population / población: Organismos individuales de la misma especie que viven en el mismo lugar y que pueden producir crías. (Cap. 23, pág. 826)

population density / densidad demográfica: El tamaño de una población que ocupa un área de tamaño limitado. (Cap. 23, pág. 829)

potential energy / energía potencial: Energía almacenada que no proviene del movimiento, sino de la posición o condición de un objeto. (Cap. 26, pág. 916)

primary succession / sucesión primaria: Sucesión ecológica que comienza en un lugar que no tiene suelo. (Cap. 24, pág. 851)

proton / protón: Partícula que posee una carga eléctrica positiva en el núcleo. (Cap. 25, pág. 890)

R

radiation / radiación: Energía que viaja en forma de ondas, desde su fuente, en todas direcciones. (Cap. 26, pág. 925)

reflection / reflexión: Ocurre cuando una onda choca contra un objeto o superficie y luego rebota. (Cap. 27, pág. 954)

refraction / refracción: Doblamiento de una onda a medida que se mueve de un medio a otro. (Cap. 27, pág. 955)

S

secondary succession / sucesión secundaria: Sucesión que comienza en un lugar que ya tiene suelo y el cual fue la morada de organismos vivos. (Cap. 24, pág. 852)

species / especie: La categoría de clasificación más pequeña y la más precisa. Los organismos pertenecientes a la misma especie pueden aparearse y producir progenie fértil. (Cap. 21, pág. 768)

substance / sustancia: Muestra de materia que tiene la misma composición y propiedades en toda su extensión. (Cap. 25, pág. 899)

symbiosis / simbiosis: Cualquier relación estrecha entre dos o más especies diferentes. (Cap. 23, pág. 831)

T

taiga / taiga: Región fría de árboles coníferos siempre verdes. (Cap. 24, pág. 860)

taxonomy / taxonomía: La ciencia que se encarga de clasificar. (Cap. 21, pág. 766)

temperate deciduous forest / bosque deciduo de zonas templadas: Comunidad clímax de árboles deciduos, los cuales pierden sus hojas en el otoño. (Cap. 24, pág. 861)

temperature / temperatura: Es una medida de la energía cinética promedio de las partículas de cualquier objeto. Entre más alta sea la energía cinética promedio de un objeto, mayor será su temperatura. (Cap. 26, pág. 922)

thermal energy / energía térmica: Es la energía cinética total de las partículas de un material. (Cap. 26, pág. 923)

transverse wave / onda transversal: Tipo de onda mecánica en la cual la materia se mueve de un lado a otro formando ángulos rectos con la dirección en que viaja la onda. (Cap. 27, pág. 946)

tropical rain forest / bosque pluvial tropical: La comunidad clímax más importante en las regiones ecuatoriales del mundo y que posee una vegetación frondosa. (Cap. 24, pág. 863)

tundra / tundra: Región fría, seca y sin árboles, que a veces se denomina desierto gélido porque tiene inviernos que duran de seis a nueve meses. (Cap. 24, pág. 859)

water cycle / ciclo del agua: Viaje continuo del agua entre la atmósfera y la Tierra; involucra los procesos de evaporación, condensación y precipitación. (Cap. 23, pág. 840)

wavelength / longitud de onda: Distancia entre un punto de una onda y otro punto idéntico en la siguiente onda, como por ejemplo, de una cresta a la siguiente o de un valle al siguiente. (Cap. 27, pág. 950)

Index

The index for *Science Voyages* will help you locate major topics in the book quickly and easily. Each entry in the index is followed by the numbers of the pages on which the entry is discussed. A page number given in **boldface type** indicates the page on which that entry is defined. A page number given in *italic type* indicates a page on which the entry is used in an illustration or photograph. The abbreviation *act.* indicates a page on which the entry is used in an activity.

Art Credits

Photo Credits